Stan Brakhage

IN THE SERIES

Wide Angle Books

Edited by Erik Barnouw, Ruth Bradley,
Scott MacDonald, and Patricia Zimmermann

Stan Brakhage

FILMMAKER

Edited by David E. James

Temple University Press   📖   Philadelphia

Temple University Press
1601 North Broad Street
Philadelphia PA 19122
www.temple.edu/tempress

Compilation and individual articles copyright © 2005 by Temple University, except

"Amateurs in the Industry Town: Stan Brakhage and Andy Warhol in Los Angeles,"
and "Stan Brakhage: The Activity of His Nature," copyright © 2005 by David E. James.

"Brakhage's Faustian Psychodrama," copyright © 2004 by P. Adams Sitney.
Reprinted by permission of Georges Borchardt, Inc., for the author.

"Camera Lucida / Camera Obscura," by Annette Michelson, copyright ©
Artforum (January 1973).

"Becoming Dark With Excess of Light," copyright © 2005 by Paul Arthur.

Text design by Kate Nichols

∞ The paper used in this publication meets the requirements of
the American National Standard for Information Sciences—Permanence of Paper for
Printed Library Materials, ANSI Z39.49-1992

Library of Congress Cataloging-in-Publication Data
Stan Brakhage : filmmaker / edited by David E. James.
p. cm. – (Wide angle books)
Includes bibliographical references and index.
ISBN 1-59213-271-5 (alk. paper)
ISBN 1-59213-272-3 (pbk. : alk. paper)
1. Brakhage, Stan—Criticism and interpretation. I. James, David E., 1945– II. Series.
PN1998.3.B74S72 2005
791.4302'33'092—dc22
2004062556

2 4 6 8 9 7 5 3 1

Contents

Acknowledgments

We gratefully acknowledge the following for permission to reprint noted material: Jonas Mekas and Anthology Film Archives for the photograph of Stan Brakhage by Briggs Dyer on the cover of the paperback edition, the photographs of Sergei Eisenstein, and the essays "Stan Brakhage" by Parker Tyler, "Notes on the New American Cinema" (extract) by Jonas Mekas, "Brakhage and Rilke" by Jerome Hill, and "On *The Art of Vision*" by Robert Kelly; Jennifer Dorn for Edward Dorn's "The First Time I Heard the Word 'Brakhage'"; Annette Michelson for "Camera Lucida/Camera Obscura," © *Artforum*, January 1973; the Literary Estate of Ronald Johnson for the extracts from the poem *ARK*, © 1996; Carolee Schneemann for the photo of her painting *Jane Brakhage*, her photo "Mary Jane Collom Brakhage. South Shaftsbury, Vermont, 1957(?)," her self-timed photo "Stan, baby Myrenna, Jane, C.S., Jim Tenney. Sidney, Illinois, 1960," and Jim Tenny's photos, "Jane, Stan & C.S. South Shaftsbury, Vermont, 1958" and "Jane, Stan, C.S. South Shaftsbury, Vermont, 1958"; and Willie Varela for two photographs of Stan Brakhage.

DAVID E. JAMES

Introduction

Stan Brakhage

The Activity of His Nature

Milton produced Paradise Lost *for the same reason that a silk worm produces silk. It was an activity of* his *nature.*—KARL MARX

Work on this collection of texts began some three years ago, when we hoped to publish it in 2003 to celebrate Stan Brakhage's seventieth birthday. Instead, belatedly, it mourns his death.

The baby who would become James Stanley Brakhage was born on 14 January 1933 in an orphanage in Kansas City, Missouri.[1] He was adopted and named by a young couple, Ludwig, a college teacher of business, and his wife, Clara, who had herself been raised by a stepmother. The family moved from town to town in the Middle West and, sensitive to the stresses of his parents' unhappy marriage, Stanley was a sickly child, asthmatic and over-weight. His mother took a lover, eventually leaving her husband, who subsequently came to terms with his homosexuality and also himself took a lover. In 1941, mother and son found themselves alone in Denver. Put in a boys' home, the child picked up the habits of a petty criminal, but before his delinquency became serious, he was placed with a stable, middle-class family in which he began to discover his gifts. He excelled in writing and dramatics and in singing, becoming one of the leading voices in the choir of the Cathedral of St. John's in Denver. Retrieving her now-teenaged son, his mother tried to make a musician of him, but Stanley resisted his tutors, even attempting to strangle his voice teacher.

In high school, he devoted himself to writing, winning many prizes and deciding that he wanted to become a dramatist or a poet. With a group of school friends, including Larry Jordan, who later became an important film-maker, and the musicians Morton Subotnick and James Tenney, he formed a dramatic group, the Gadflies. For Stan's sixteenth birthday, the Gadflies gave him a copy of Ezra Pound's *Cantos* as a joke, but he treasured the work all his life. After graduation, he was awarded a fine arts scholarship to Dartmouth College, but his difficulties with the academic program and especially with what he felt to be an overall hostility to the arts among his fellow students precipitated a breakdown, and he quit. Visiting his father in Chicago on the way home, he returned to Denver to work as a press operator. He attempted to write a novel and renewed his friendship with the Gadflies, attending movies with them and beginning to read some of the classics of film theory. Especially taken with Cocteau's *Orpheus* and *Beauty and the Beast*, he and two other Gadflies decided to make a film themselves. Directed by Brakhage, *Interim* (1951), a short depicting a brief romantic encounter, was his first work; he found making it so rewarding that he decided to study filmmaking at the California School of Fine Arts (renamed the San Francisco School of the Arts in 1961).

This college proved less traumatic but hardly more satisfying than the previous one, and he left without completing a degree. But Brakhage did make contact with the San Francisco poets, first Kenneth Rexroth, then Robert Duncan. He re-visited Colorado in 1952 to shoot his second film, *Unglassed Windows Cast a Terrible Reflection*, also an erotic melodrama, but then returned to San Francisco, living in a room in Duncan's basement formerly occupied by the poet and filmmaker James Broughton. In Duncan's circle, Brakhage found the community of artists he had long sought, and during his two years there, he met the most important poets, painters, and musicians of the time and young filmmakers, including Kenneth Anger and Bruce Conner. As his own filmmaking matured, he decided to in-vestigate Hollywood. While working as a projectionist for Raymond Rohauer at the Coronet Theater in Los Angeles in 1955, he renewed his acquaintance with Kenneth Anger, who encouraged him to send his films to Amos Vogel, an independent programmer and distributor in New York.

Moving to New York, Brakhage found a warm welcome among the grow-ing community of experimental filmmakers there, especially Marie Menken and Willard Maas, but also Maya Deren, Ian Hugo, Hillary Harris, Jonas and Adolfas Mekas, and Joseph Cornell. Deren, Menken, and Cornell were especially influential, and Brakhage lived in Deren's apartment for a time. Though he continued to make films, the eight months he spent in the city were also a period of crisis for him; attempting to survive on the proceeds of screenings of his work, he lived in great poverty and was seriously malnourished. He left and returned to Los Angeles, but decided not to accept the offer of an apprenticeship at MCA and instead worked at occasional film jobs. After again spending the winter in New York, where he visited Tenney and his wife, Carolee Schneemann, he returned to Denver, meeting a young woman, whom he intended to marry. The wedding was called off, and distraught with the apparent failure of both his artistic and romantic endeavors, he planned to commit suicide and to use his death as the termination of the long film he was then working on, *Anticipation of the Night*. But around that time, he met Mary Jane Collom, and the two were married on 28 December 1957. Brakhage shot the film without killing himself and completed the editing soon after.

By this time, Brakhage's reputation was growing, and a selection of his films was shown at the Second International Film Competition held in conjunction with the Brussels World's Fair, though *Anticipation* was greeted with derision. Still impoverished, the couple attempted to live in the East while he worked for a professional film company in New Jersey, but in 1959 they moved to the mountains in Colorado, finally settling in 1964 in a log cabin in Lump Gulch, a largely abandoned mining area above Boulder. There they raised five children, and Brakhage's films became largely preoccupied with the dailiness of his family life in the wilderness and the more general human concerns they reflected, "Birth, death, sex and the search for God," as he summarized in his first long statement of his aesthetics, the monograph, *Metaphors on Vision*, that he had begun writing around the time of *Anticipation of the Night* and his marriage.[2]

Living with his family very simply and often in financial privation, Brakhage nevertheless developed rapidly as a filmmaker, consolidating the principles and practice that together constituted the most radical intervention by a single individual in the medium's history. His vision of an uncompromised *art* of film understood art in a Romantic idealized form. It was supposed to proceed from a source that was simultaneously somatic and divine that he named, "the muse"; it entailed the complete primacy and autonomy of the visual sense and the re-creation in film of seeing in all its physiological and psychological forms, from the impulses of the brain cells to the sightings of cosmic events. It equally entailed the rejection of the narrative forms of the industrial feature film and indeed of all visualizations apart from the most assertively first person and instead proposed the sufficiency of a fundamentally domestic cinema, an art version of home movies in which family life and the filmmaking it engendered were lived as an aesthetic process. His concomitant rejection of the capitalist film industry and his commitment to the institutions of an alternative to it crystallized as the strongest and most coherent instance of the great countercultural cinematic initiatives of the 1960s.

The significance of Brakhage's work was quickly recognized, and in 1962 *Film Culture* awarded him its Fourth Independent Film Award for *The Dead* and *Prelude*. In the award statement, Jonas Mekas noted not only his innovation of "a style and a filmic language which is able to express with utmost subtlety the unpredictable movements of his inner eye," but also the social significance of his work: He has given "to cinema an intelligence and subtlety that is usually the province of the older arts. And he has done this with a fanatical consistency, upholding—and setting an example for others—the absolute independence of the film artist."[3] During this period, he also contributed, often loudly and angrily, to the debates of the vital film culture of the period, corresponding voluminously and making and losing many friends. He assisted with the formation of the Film-Makers' Cooperative in New York in 1963 and sat on its board for many years and for a time was a member of the selection committee of Anthology Film Archives before it opened in 1970. He also regularly returned to New York and other cities to screen his new films.

It was on the occasion of such a visit to New York in 1964 that his 16 mm editing equipment was stolen. Unable to afford to replace it, he instead purchased an 8 mm camera and with that began to make a series of short films he called *Songs*; as well as reducing expenses, the move to the essentially amateur medium also held the promise of his films being domestically screened and indeed collected in the manner of books or records. One of the songs, the hour-and-a-half *23rd Psalm Branch* (1966), dealt with his feelings about the U.S. invasion of Viet Nam, which the introduction of a television into his home made inescapable for him. With *Dog Star Man* and then the *Songs*, the fundamental terms of his aesthetic were in place, though he continued to pioneer further innovations for the remainder of the century.

Though he continued to shoot in 8 mm, a Rockefeller Grant in 1967 allowed him to return to 16 mm for his third extended cycle, the four-part *Scenes From Under Childhood*, in which he confronted the possibility of simulating the vision of infants. By the end of the 1960s, Brakhage's reputation was international. Retrospectives of his work and invitations to lecture became frequent, and he received many awards (including a Guggenheim Fellowship in 1978), and in 1969 he began teaching one semester a year at the Art Institute of Chicago, commuting there from his home. He continued to publish his ideas in the early 1970s, initially small chapbooks to guide young filmmakers (*A Moving Picture Giving and Taking Book* and *The Seen*) and then essays on the classic filmmakers derived from his lectures: *The Brakhage Lectures: Georges Méliès, David Wark Griffith, Carl Theodore Dreyer, Sergei Eisenstein*, and a *Scrapbook* collecting his most important theoretical writing, much of it culled from letters.[4]

In 1981, he resigned from the Art Institute to take up a position at the University of Colorado at Boulder, only twenty-five miles from his home. At his own request, he taught film history not filmmaking, offering both the university's silent and sound cinema surveys and courses of his own design, including one on the relation of painting and film, a comparison of the films and plays of Tennessee Williams and Eugene O'Neill, and one called "Sex, Death and Cinema." He did however begin to work informally with young filmmakers, collaborating with some them, and with a teacher of filmmaking at the university, Phil Solomon.

This new stability in his life was interrupted by an unexpected trauma, the collapse of the marriage he had shared with Jane for more than thirty years. They separated, and divorced in 1987, both of them leaving their cabin. Jane moved higher into the mountains and began to write, publishing among other works an account of the early settlers in Lump Gulch.[5] Brakhage moved to an apartment near the university, where he continued to work, beginning a series of Sunday evening salons at which he would present and discuss his own and others' films in a public forum. He became close to Marilyn Jull, a young Canadian woman who had studied visual arts at York University in Toronto, and two years later they were married. She, however, refused to allow him to photograph her or the two sons they eventually had; the prohibition, which Brakhage often described as a great relief, nevertheless terminated the domestic home movies that had been the most significant component of his oeuvre. Though he continued to work photographically and in the 1990s completed two major photographed film series, *Visions in Meditation* and the four "Vancouver Island" films, for the next decade he created mostly by painting and scratching on the film strip, returning to a process he had begun with *Dog Star Man*, and working much of the time in cafes in Boulder.[6] More of his writings were published: *Film at Wit's End*, a collection of essays on his fellow filmmakers, and eventually two more collections of critical writings.[7]

Brakhage was diagnosed with cancer in 1996, his doctors telling him that it might well have been caused by the coal tar dyes he had been using to paint on film. But, with treatment the cancer went into remission, and Brakhage worked as prolifically as ever. He continued to be extremely supportive of young filmmakers and of the community of avant-garde film, and new generations of young women filmmakers found his work especially revelatory. In 1994, he was made a Distinguished Professor by the university, and in May of the same year, he received an honorary doctorate from California Institute of the Arts.

A grant from the Donner Foundation assisted the library of the University of Colorado at Boulder in purchasing new prints of all his films, the collection of films by other people he had amassed over his life, and all his collected papers, including his correspondence and financial records—some eighty boxes, each containing approximately 2,000 items. The university is presently processing these materials, with a view to making them publicly available in the Stan Brakhage Experimental Film Center. As his seventieth birthday approached, the unique accomplishment of his work was recognized by retrospectives at the Venice, London, and Rotterdam film festivals and similarly by retrospectives in the next years as far away as Brazil, Korea, and Japan, as well as by equivalent programs at the National Gallery of Art in Washington and other sites in the United States.

In December 2002, he retired from his university post as a Distinguished Professor of Film Studies and left Colorado for his wife's native land, moving to Victoria, British Columbia. But, cancer had again been diagnosed that February, and most of his last months were spent in great pain. On 9 March 2003, after fifty years of filmmaking and almost 400 films, he died.

His funeral was small, mostly family, but including some representatives from the world of film. One of them, Phil Solomon, his friend, colleague at the university, and a fellow filmmaker, wrote a very moving account of it, e-mailing it around the world to those who loved him. It concluded:

All convened at the Brakhages' house, to talk and be with him and each other. You should know that he loved this house, and the bedroom that he was eventually confined to, with its beautiful window (Stan's Window) and peaceful street outside (Milton Street), with his books of Victor Hugo's poetry and Tom Thompson's paintings nearby his bed. He had no regrets about leaving Boulder at the time he did. I think he sensed an urgency. He came down from the mountains, to an island, in another country, at sea level. He wanted to make sure that his family was rooted, and would be safe and secure, so he returned Marilyn and the boys back to the island of her source, where her Garden is . . . he made it, across the Serious Sea, and did have, I believe, some peace of mind that he had taken care of business, that his films and legacy were in safe hands, that his family would be . . . alright . . . in due time, and that he had, finally, as he used to say, "done his bit."[8]

As indicated, this collection of essays was originally planned to mark Brakhage's seventieth birthday; had it been successful in doing so, it would have also marked the anniversary of an earlier and partially analogous critical project, a special "Eisenstein/Brakhage" issue of the journal *Artforum*, edited by Annette Michelson, simultaneously to celebrate Brakhage's fortieth birthday and the seventy-fifth anniversary of his predecessor's birth.[9] Containing several essays on each filmmaker separately, the journal was introduced by Michelson's own essay on both of them, "Camera Lucida/Camera Obscura," that proposed a dialectical reading of their joint significance. Noting the several parallels between the main terms of their achievements—their invention of essentially new forms of filmic expression, their eminence as both filmmakers and theorists, their common wariness of sound, and so on—Michelson attributed to the two "masters" a supremacy in the culture of their respective times so singular that it became perforce the measure of their contemporaries and commandeered the particular attention of all responsible film criticism: "I am saying, then, that filmmaking and the theory and criticism of film must, in their most intensive and significant instances, ultimately situate themselves in relation to the work and thinking of these two artists."[10]

Michelson's claim was hyperbolic, perhaps deliberately so, but not without justification in the film culture of the time. Since the late 1940s, the U.S. avant-garde had constructed its own formal alterity to the commercial narrative feature on Eisensteinian montage, as well as regularly invoking

Vertov and other early Soviet directors; in this, it anticipated the return to the revolutionary Soviet cinemas upon which French film theory staged the ideological critique of the entertainment film industry in the wake of the 1968 political insurrections. Indeed, though it was never acknowledged in that theory or in the translations of it that inaugurated British and American academic film theory, Brakhage's own work had anticipated "apparatus theory" and other aspects of this critical revolution, albeit from different principles. A decade before the English translations of Jean-Louis Baudry's critiques of the ideological effects of the standard cinematic apparatus, for example, Brakhage had addressed the relationship between bourgeois ideology and "the camera eye, its lenses ground to achieve 19th century compositional perspective," and even the "phallic nature" of bourgeois culture, as well as practically developing an unprecedented repertoire of techniques to subvert both the internal structure of the framed film image and the repression of difference between frames during projection.[11] And when French theory declared that such modernist subversion of rationalized vision was a prerequisite for radical political change, the U. S. avant-garde cinema had long been fired by a variety of conceptions of the imbrication of filmic experimentation in the social and cultural upheavals of the period, imagining cinema "as an emblem, harbinger, and social vehicle of the transfiguration of time."[12] But, though some seven years earlier, Michelson had envisioned such a revolutionary component in Brakhage and the avant-garde,[13] by this point she had re-assessed his social significance.

Instead of facilitating, or participating in, or even analogizing a political transformation in the manner of Eisenstein, Brakhage was now seen to ex-emplify the impossibility of a role for a filmmaker in such collective under-takings in the United States: Rather, he represented his culture by virtue of "his social function as defensive in the Self's last-ditch stand against the mass, against the claims of any possible class, political process, or structure, as-suming its inevitable assault on the sovereignty of the Self, positing the imaginative consciousness as inherently apolitical."[14] In her emphasis on the individual imagination, as well as the assertion of other cognate axioms, especially the correspondences between his formal innovations and the pro-cesses of vision and even consciousness itself, Michelson was both drawing on and attempting in some degree to reframe the understanding of Brakhage's significance that had developed during the previous decade, most author-itatively in the work of P. Adams Sitney, Brakhage's principal exegete.

Sitney's interest in Brakhage was long-standing, his commentary on him having begun at least as early as 1962 when *Filmwise*, the journal of the New Haven Film Society that he edited, devoted its inaugural issue to him. As well as an extended selection from Brakhage's *Metaphors on Vision* (which would be published complete in *Film Culture* a year later) and other texts by the filmmaker himself, this issue contained an overview of the press criticism Brakhage had received up to that point,[15] and statements by several other writers and filmmakers, including Charles Boultenhouse, George Landow, Gregory Markopoulos, Willard Maas, Jonas Mekas, Parker Tyler, and Sitney himself. Most of the brief essays were celebratory, affirming that the abstraction of Brakhage's recent work, especially the rapid editing and moving camera of *Anticipation of the Night*, instanced a remarkable and unprecedented assertion of an individual sensibility in film. The only dissenter was Parker Tyler, then the senior critic associated with the avant-garde, who had written the first substantial biographical and critical account of Brakhage's work.[16] Departing from his earlier approval of Brakhage's first films, Tyler criticized the phenomena that the others lauded, finding what he called Brakhage's "mobility-mania—the rapid transit of images too fleeting for even their most public associations to get across properly" to be "bad and perilous," "sacrificing style and form itself to the novelty invited by extreme mobility of vision."[17] Sitney's own "An Introduction to Stan Brakhage" was the summary evaluation of Brakhage's career to date, emphasizing the categorical division between his work and the commercial cinema, its greater resemblance to poetry (especially Gertrude Stein) and music (especially Bach) than to the industrial cinema, the break in his work from the "psychological-sexual dramas of adolescent frustrations" derived from the work of Maya Deren and her immediate followers, and the concomitant emergence of first-person lyric vision that had become fully articulate in *Anticipation of the Night*.

As Brakhage's work developed through the epic undertaking of *Prelude*, then *Dog Star Man* and other films of the 1960s, Sitney refined, elaborated, and extended the parameters of his reading of Brakhage's aesthetic and his knowledge of his peers and his significant predecessors in cinema, as well as himself making immense contributions to the critical and other institutions through which the American avant-garde realized itself as a significant social phenomenon. His complete account of what had by then established itself as one of the most innovative epochs in the history of cinema appeared in 1974: *Visionary Film: The American Avant-Garde.*[18] With this work, he fulfilled Michelson's mandate, presenting an account of the most radical cinema of the postwar period in which even the greatest of its other avatars were situated in relation to Brakhage.

Explicitly invoking the heritage of the English Romantic poets and the then-current Yale school of literary criticism about them, *Visionary Film* contained close readings and extended accounts of many other artists in the canon (which it simultaneously and definitively established), including especially persuasive and influential accounts of the work of Sidney Peterson, Kenneth Anger, Harry Smith, Peter Kubelka, and Jonas Mekas. The book's backbone was an analytic narrative of "the visionary strain within the complex manifold of the American avant-garde film,"[19] constructed on a historical morphology of its major structural modes, primarily the sequence, trance film, lyric film, film mythopoeia, and structural film; its heart was two long chapters devoted primarily to Brakhage.

The first of Sitney's modes, the trance film, he argued, was created by Maya Deren out of the heritage of the classic French avant-garde of the 1920s, particularly Surrealism. This provided the model for Brakhage's early works, the acted melodramas, and from it he made the break into the lyrical, first-person vision, first fully mobilized in *Anticipation of the Night*: "The lyrical film postulates the film-maker behind the camera as the first-person protagonist of the film. The images of the film are what he sees, filmed in such a way that we never forget his presence and we know how he is reacting to his vision."[20] Sitney recognized the influence of Marie Menken on the rhythm of the moving camera, the dynamics of its relation to the edge of the screen, the rapid montage, and other formal tropes of lyric film vision. Nevertheless, even though a decade later it had become all but ubiquitous in underground film, Brakhage's forging of the lyrical film was seen as fundamentally an individual achievement, unlike previous developments in the avant-garde, which had been collective.

In the chapter on the lyrical film, Sitney gave detailed formal descriptions of *Anticipation of the Night* and the series of short films that followed through the mid-1960s, many of them concerned with the dynamics of his relation with his young wife and their growing family, ending with a discussion of the similar work of Bruce Baillie. The next chapter, "Major Mythopoeia," approached the long, some of them serial, films that Brakhage had been working on during the same period, but that instanced a categorical formal development into the next mode, mythopoeia. Thus, the first of them, *Dog Star Man*, "elaborates in mythic, almost systematic terms, the world-view of the lyrical films.... it stations itself within the rhetoric of Romanticism, describing the birth of consciousness, the cycles of the seasons, man's struggle with nature, and sexual balance in the visual evocation of a fallen titan."[21] Again, the critical methodology for the reading of *Dog Star Man* and the *Songs*, the cycle that followed it, entailed detailed description of the films' formal and structural qualities. Informed by Brakhage's own account of his work (though also sometimes disputing it), Sitney framed Brakhage's achievement in both the dialectics of British and American Romantic poetry and contemporary developments in painting, specifically Abstract Expressionism, whose directives Brakhage had synthesized more comprehensively than any of his peers.

In Sitney's account, with the *Art of Vision* and the *Songs* Brakhage had achieved the epic film, the equivalent of the Romantic epic poem and resembling it in being centered on the reflexive investigation of the artist's own consciousness and its relation to nature. In this sense, the *Songs* constituted "an ultimate work,"[22] even though when he finished them in 1969, Brakhage was only in his mid-thirties and showing no signs of having exhausted his energies or completed his oeuvre. But the avant-garde's next phase, structural film, radically diverged from Brakhage's direction, and the new filmmakers of the late 1960s reflected, Sitney proposed, not Abstract Expressionism, but rather the reactions of pop, minimal and conceptual art against it.

In his last chapter Sitney attempted to theorize the formal appearance of the new films ("the shape of the whole film is predetermined and simplified") jointly with the teleology derived from his understanding of the history of the avant-garde thus far within the dialectics of Romanticism. Its dominant aspiration was "the cinematic reproduction of the human mind," and in this respect "the structural film approaches the condition of meditation and evokes states of consciousness without mediation; that is, with the sole mediation of the camera."[23] Though the self-conscious materiality of much of Brakhage's work allowed other commentators to propose some degree of continuity between it and the new mode, in Sitney's reading, structural film's fundamental project as well as its characteristic techniques involved rejection of the defining mode of Brakhage's lyricism and its mythopoeic extrapolations in an attempt to divorce metaphors for consciousness from the eyes and the camera somatically attuned to them; and so, the "major precursor of structural film" was not Brakhage, but Andy Warhol.[24]

Sitney's historical morphology was challenged for being procrustean and leading to the omission of significant artists, but his history of the American avant-garde until the early 1970s and of Brakhage's centrality in it was instantly definitive and displaced previous writing. Snipings, caveats, attempted reframings of course followed, but there has not since been a work of equivalent analytic force or with as detailed and sensitive knowledge of the canon or overall erudition.[25] But, though *Visionary Film* remains preeminent, not so the reputation of its privileged agonist, for Sitney's and Michelson's canonization of Brakhage was hardly in place before a tectonic shift in the ground of noncommodity cinema caused the filmmaker's reputation and the sense of his historical significance they had asserted to begin a drastic decline. The films, both those he had already made and the many more he was to make in the next quarter century, continued to be appreciated by groups of people worldwide, but instead of preoccupying the vanguard of progressive cinema as they had in the previous decade, they sank below the common culture's radar screen.

The exile of Brakhage and the aesthetic values he embodied reflected the diametric reversal of cultural priorities that we can now summarize, at least partially, as the shift from modernism to postmodernism in U.S. culture. Political developments were fundamental, especially the New Right offensive against the utopian cultural and social movements of the 1960s and the latter's resultant decline and eventual extirpation. Even as the inevitability of the failure of the U. S. invasion of Viet Nam was becoming plain, the corporate state rapidly proved victorious in its domestic war against the Black Panther Party, the student movement, and other forms of domestic social resistance, allowing the Reagan presidency to begin an attack on the working class and working-class organization of a ferocity not seen since the early Depression.

The cultural reverberations of these developments produced a more complex amalgam of resistance to the right-wing offensives and of assimilation to them. Though by the late 1970s the project of a universal emancipation that had fueled the global coalitions against American imperialism retained little domestic credibility, the New Social Movements that had emerged in the late 1960s were flourishing, if primarily in their bourgeois components. On the one hand, as what soon became known as "identity politics," the women's and the gay and lesbian movements and the parallel struggles for civil rights by ethnic groups were reconstructing the integrated cultural and political offensives that had been pioneered in the previous decade, and in doing so they generated new vanguardist cinemas, some of great power and theoretical sophistication. The most successful of them, the feminist cinemas, transformed avant-garde film and academic film theory alike.

On the other hand, as these identity cinemas developed, their initially artisinal, low-budget forms of filmmaking gradually were assimilated to larger, better-funded projects, eventually to industrial feature films designed for commercial distribution. As they did so, during the 1980s they met equivalent initiatives from the industry itself, which had recognized the various identities as potentially lucrative niche markets and so had recruited minorities to work on projects designed for specific minority constituencies. The rapprochement between corporate culture and movements originally opposed to it itself reflected the escalation of the culture industry's colonization of the public sphere and the corresponding precariousness of any substantial and socially viable alternative to it.

In all these developments, the specific constituents of Brakhage's aesthetics that had made him prototypical of the great flowering of non-commodity filmmaking in the 1960s made him apparently irrelevant for the 1980s. The values and aesthetics he stood for continued to command the allegiance of a small phylum of filmmakers and critics, and his films, both the classics of the 1960s and the late, purely abstract work, maintained very strong rentals from the two main distribution agencies of independent film— Film Makers' Cooperative in New York and Canyon Cinema in San Francisco. At least some recognition of him became unavoidable in college textbooks and anthologies of film theory,[26] and wherever the idea of an alternative film culture still had credibility, his achievement had to be acknowledged. But, overall Brakhage was negatively positioned in respect to developments in the moving-image culture of the last quarter of the twentieth century.

The first cracks in his reputation have been noted in Sitney's account of the emergence of structural film and its rejection of the immanentist principles of Brakhage's romantic personal expressivity. Always a vociferous defendant of his own reputation, Brakhage himself recognized the challenge and spoke out against the movement, even against some filmmakers he had previously espoused and befriended. That battle quickly ended, for by the end of the 1970s, structural film had hardly more credibility than Brakhage himself. But, as a middle-aged white patriarch he remained the spoken or unspoken other to the cinematic initiatives that displaced it: those based on identity politics and then the affirmative cultural studies that followed them. Indeed, major components of his aesthetic had been previously created in specific opposition to the positions they mobilized.

The intellectual and social environment in which Brakhage had worked was all but entirely white. In the late 1950s and early days when beat aesthetics had exerted considerable leverage on underground film, African Americans had held a privileged, sometimes fetishized, imaginary position, and African American music was the referential art form par excellence. Though some ethnic filmmakers later found inspiration in his work,[27] Brakhage himself had been less than enthusiastic about beat culture and had largely skirted it in the formulation of his aesthetic; he nowhere credits jazz among his musical influences, and nowhere in his work does a person of color prominently appear.[28] But, if Brakhage's disinterest in the black component of American culture may be charitably construed as the reflection of the relative ethnic homogeneity of the region where he spent most of his life and of the suffi-cient, indeed all-embracing, power of cultural traditions that were more immediate to him, his position in postmodern sexual politics is inescapably contentious.

An assertive and unqualified heterosexuality lay at the core of Brakhage's cinema. The first community of successful artists to welcome him, the group around Robert Duncan, was largely gay, the homosexual component of under-ground film was enormous, and Brakhage was personally close to James Broughton, Willard Maas, Kenneth Anger, and other gay filmmakers and artists. But, by his own testimony, he constructed his life and his aesthetic enterprise in a deliberate rejection of homosexuality: "Many of my friends who had been waiting for me to transform into a homosexual were bitterly disappointed, frustrated," he recalled, "A married artist was an incom-prehensible thing to many friends, artists working in film and other med-iums."[29] The influence of his adoptive father's homosexuality on the formation of Brakhage's sexual identity can only be conjectural, but at all events, once made, Brakhage's decision to be a heterosexual was lived un-ambiguously. He eventually fathered seven children in two successive nuclear families and of course made his first marriage the single most important topic of his films of the 1960s and 1970s, even attributing their origin to the family unit.[30] At exactly the time when the search for nonpatriarchal sex and family roles had greatest cultural urgency, Brakhage, interchangeably "bring[ing] forth films and children"[31] in the Colorado wilderness, appeared to embody not the solution, but the problem itself. Particularly contentious were the films in which his domestic aesthetic had been crucially pivoted, those of the birth of his children; in these his camera work, often understood as invasive and aggressive, appeared to feminist film theorists to epitomize the phallocentric gaze and the cultural order constructed on it. And, as feminist theory entered its next phase and sought to understand the production of filmic meaning and pleasure via Lacanian psychoanalysis, Brakhage's axiomatic and absolutely fundamental commitment to the investigation of pre- or nonlinguistic vision was again categorically counter to the times. But, worse was still to come.

When the moment of high Lacanian theory vaporized out of film studies, it was replaced, not by a return to a concept of art such as Brakhage espoused his whole life, but to its exact opposite: U.S. cultural studies' affirmation of corporate industrial cinema and television. Brakhage always enjoyed going to the movies, sometimes explaining the recreation as a means of staying in touch with the culture at large, but he never thought of the commercial cinema as in any way related to his own enterprise. Passionately devoted to the totality of the Western aesthetic tradition and especially to poetry and serious music—the very forms of the "dead white males" that cultural studies abominated as "high art"—and the embodiment of the most resolutely uncompromising alternative to the film industry, he epitomized a film style and a social location that were alike anathematized. His rejection of the form of the industrial feature, of narrative as a principle of composition, and of Hollywood as a manufacturing system (with the break from all of them summarily located in *Anticipation of the Night*, the film he was editing on his wedding night!) ensured his virtual disappearance from academic film studies.

Even Brakhage's shift of the main focus of his work from the photography of the family drama to the abstract, hand-painted films of the late 1980s and 1990s brought no relief. On the one hand, resistance to verbal language in the films reappears as resistance to verbal language about them, for Brakhage's interest in prelinguistic vision produced works that defy verbal summary and make critical commentary extremely difficult. On the other, these abstract films perforce came to being in the midst of a corporate-controlled culture that, centered in television and with advertisements and music video its essential products, was putatively a visual culture but one that had no use for sensuous seeing. If in the early 1970s Brakhage's oeuvre could be celebrated as the last (or perhaps the first) full flowering of modernism in film, by the late 1970s the "Warholization" of postmodern culture relegated him to irrelevance, his preeminence preempted by his similarly totalized other.

For whether or not Warhol had been the "major precursor of structural film," he was indisputably the major precursor of almost everything that came after it. Queer, fascinated with publicity and the psychic, material and social apparatuses of the mass-media, and especially with advertising, he epitomized the convergence of identity politics and the priorities of affirmative cultural studies in a cultural front administered jointly by the academy and entertainment industry cartels. Where Brakhage had fought to liberate film from Hollywood, Warhol's desire to find his own place in it provided the measure of the new times, and over the last quarter of the twentieth century, his rise matched Brakhage's decline in a cultural zero-sum game. The two main features of Brakhage's work that the period thrust into high relief—his negative positioning in identity politics and the categorical incompatibility of his work with the aesthetics, mode of production, and the industrial insertion of corporate capitalist culture—excluded him from virtually all the developments in public taste and in academic film theory between the early 1970s and the end of the century, in the thirty years between Annette Michelson's *Artforum* essay and the present project.

This collection of texts has been organized with an eye to the historical trajectory of Brakhage's standing in American culture sketched above. It begins with some of the early commentary that marked the emergence and establishment of his reputation and that now, as historical documents in their own right, indicate the terms by which his achievement was initially measured. Thereafter, it presents recent scholarly essays, mostly on films made after the mid-1970s, that is, after the publication of the first edition of *Visionary Film*, and so produced in the period when his work, new and old, received little critical attention. Alternating with these are more personal estimations of the general significance of Brakhage's contribution to the art of film made by other artists who came to know him and his works at various points throughout his life.

Los Angeles, 25 September 2003

NOTES

1. In the absence of a reliable biography of Brakhage, information about his life has been drawn from Gerald R. Barrett and Wendy Brabner, *Stan Brakhage: A Guide to References and Resources* (Boston, MA: G. K. Hall, 1983), Fred Camper's "A Short Biography" and the obituaries and other texts collected by him on his Web site, www.fredcamper.com, as well as from conversations and correspondence with P. Adams Sitney, Paul Arthur, Don Yannacito, and others. The Camper Web site is presently the most comprehensive guide to Brakhage material of all kinds. *Stan Brakhage* largely repeats Brakhage's own accounts of his parents, childhood, and adolescence, which reproduced the mythopoeic inventiveness of his biographies of other filmmakers. The need for independent biographical research remains.

2. *Metaphors on Vision* was first published complete in 1963 as a special issue, number 30, of the journal *Film Culture*. The issue was not paginated.

3. "Fourth Independent Film Award," *Film Culture*, 24 (Spring 1962), 5. Brakhage's early work also met with a good deal of hostile and uncomprehending criticism from, among others, Ernest Callenbach ("The structure is that he throws in first one shot and then another and some others") and Pauline Kael ("the subtle manipulation of nothing"). For these and a review of early commentary on Brakhage, see Eric Arthur Gordon, "Stan Brakhage's Critics," *Filmwise*, 1 (1962), 16–18.

4. *A Moving Picture Giving and Taking Book* (West Newbury, MA: Frontier Press, 1971); *The Seen* (San Francisco: Zephyrus Image, 1975); *The Brakhage Lectures: Georges Méliès, David Wark Griffith, Carl Theodore Dreyer, Sergei Eisenstein* (Chicago: The Good Lion, 1972), expanded version, *Film Biographies* (Berkeley, CA: Turtle Island, 1977); *Brakhage Scrapbook: Collected Writings, 1964–1980*, ed. Robert A. Haller (New Paltz, NY: Documentext, 1982).

5. Jane Wodening, *The Lump Gulch Tales* (Nederland, CO: Grackle Books, 1993).

6. In early 1993, when he turned sixty, Brakhage was interviewed, "Brakhage at Sixty" (http://www.smoc.net/mymindseye/naples/brakhage.html). Containing his detailed account of the process of painting on film, the interview is one of the most summary and profound of the many he gave.

7. Respectively, *Film at Wit's End: Eight Avant-Garde Filmmakers* (Kingston, NY: Documentext, 1989), *Essential Brakhage: Selected Writings on Filmmaking* (New Paltz, NY: Documentext, 2001), *Telling Time: Essays of a Visionary Filmmaker* (Kingston, NY: Documentext, 2003).

8. The complete text together with Phil Solomon's eulogy may be found at http://www.fredcamper.com/Brakhage/Funeral.html.

9. *Artforum*, 11, 5 (January 1973). In fact another publishing undertaking, roughly cognate with the present one, more closely coincided with Brakhage's seventieth birthday, *Stan Brakhage: Correspondences*, a special edition of the *Chicago Review* edited by Eirik Steinhoff (47, 4/48, 1 [Winter 2001, Spring 2002]). As well as a selection of writings by Brakhage, it also contained essays by both scholars and poets.

10. "Camera Lucida/Camera Obscura," 31. The essay is reprinted below.

11. Brakhage quotes are from *Metaphors on Vision*, (unpaginated). Baudry's "Ideological Effects of the Basic Cinema Apparatus" appeared in French in *Cinéthique* in 1970, and in English in *Film Quarterly* 28 (2) (Winter 1974–75), 39–47. Usually thought to manifest a putatively reactionary Romanticism, Brakhage's films and theory were anathema in the period when apparatus theory and then Lacanian psychoanalysis dominated U.S. and

British academic film studies; even as comprehensive a retrospective anthology as Philip Rosen's *Narrative, Apparatus, Ideology: A Film Theory Reader* (New York: Columbia University Press, 1986) made no reference to him.

12. Paul Arthur, "Routines of Emancipation: Alternative Cinema in the Ideology and Politics of the Sixties," in *A Line of Sight* (Minneapolis: Minnesota University Press, 2005), 1.

13. See her "Film and the Radical Aspiration," *Film Culture*, 42 (Fall 1966), 34–43.

14. Ibid., 31.

15. Gordon, "Stan Brakhage's Critics."

16. "Stan Brakhage," *Film Culture*, 18 (April 1958), 23–25, reprinted below.

17. "An Open Letter to Stan Brakhage From Parker Tyler," *Filmwise*, 1 (1962), 18–19. Tyler continued to express reservations about this aspect of Brakhage's style; as late as 1969, for example, he complained that Brakhage's "breathtaking (and breakneck)" method of composition "simply pushes to the extreme and beyond the viewer's tolerance for repetition of quality and extension of effect"; *Underground Film: A Critical History* (New York: Grove Press, 1969), 170.

18. New York: Oxford University Press, with subsequent enlarged editions in 1979 and 2002.

19. *Visionary Film*, x (all references to *Visionary Film* are to the first, 1974, edition).

20. Ibid., 180.

21. Ibid., 211.

22. Ibid., 258.

23. Ibid., 407–8.

24. Ibid., 409.

25. *Visionary Film* was not unchallenged. Amos Vogel, for example, denounced what he saw as "the enforced revelation of non-existing patterns based on preconceived ideas" as an act of "supreme desperate, ludicrous audacity" ("A Reader's Digest of the Avant-Garde," *Film Comment* [July–August 1976], 36); William Moritz found "its primary value . . . lies in the degree to which its false assumptions are challenged" ("Beyond 'Abstract' Criticism," *Film Quarterly* 31, 3 [Spring 1978], 29); and Constance Penley and Janet Bergstrom harped on Sitney's putative "phenomenological approach" that eliminated "consideration of the spectator's unconscious relation to the film, the screen, the entire viewing situation, an aspect that has received much attention in French and English film theory" ("The Avant-Garde: Histories and Theories," *Screen*, 19, 3 [Autumn 1978], 118); Sitney replied in "Letters from . . . P. Adams Sitney," *Screen*, 20, 3–4 (Winter 1979–80), 151–6. But, none of these offered an alternative historiographical model of comparable extensiveness and persuasiveness, and the dialectics of Romanticism established by Sitney framed subsequent commentary. In *The Untutored Eye: Childhood in the Films of Cocteau, Cornell, and Brakhage* (Cranbury, NJ: Associated University Presses, 1986), Marjorie Keller explored Brakhage's use of children, especially his own, as the vehicle of his investigation of filmic vision. In *Allegories of Cinema: American Film in the Sixties* (Princeton, NJ: Princeton University Press, 1989), David E. James again situated Brakhage in relation to the British Romantic poets, but proposed a counterreading emphasizing the position of the avant-garde cinemas of the 1960s in respect to contemporaneous political and social movements and to industrial culture. Somewhat later, William Wees approached the specifically visual aspects of Brakhage and one phylum of independent filmmaking in *Light Moving in Time: Studies in the Visual Aesthetics of Avant-Garde Film* (Berkeley: University of California

Press, 1992), and James Peterson explored the institutional situation of the avant-garde and the implicit viewing procedures it supplied in *Dreams of Chaos, Visions of Order: Understanding the American Avant-garde Cinema* (Detroit: Wayne State University Press, 1994). Still later, R. Bruce Elder in *The Films of Stan Brakhage in the American Tradition of Ezra Pound, Gertrude Stein and Charles Olson* (Waterloo, Ontario, Canada: Wilfrid Laurier University Press, 1998) comprehensively situated Brakhage's films and theoretical writing in the context of American poetics, not only of the poets listed in the book's title, but also of Michael McClure and others of the Beat generation, and in the traditions of Western philosophy from Schopenhauer to Merleau-Ponty.

26. Brakhage received appreciative consideration in the two standard American college film histories, Gerald Mast and Bruce F. Kawin, *A Short History of the Movies,* 7th ed. (Boston: Allyn and Bacon, 2000) and Kristin Thompson and David Bordwell, *Film History: An Introduction,* 2d ed. (Boston: McGraw-Hill, 2003); excerpts from *Metaphors on Vision* appeared in Leo Braudy and Marshall Cohen, eds., *Film Theory and Criticism: Introductory Readings,* 5th ed. (New York: Oxford University Press, 1999).

27. See, for example, the essay by Willie Varela in this book.

28. The only attempt I know of to suggest a jazz influence on Brakhage is Michael McClure's observation that "[Robert] Creely has followed jazz, and through Creely, Stan is inheriting a sense of jazz improvisation which neatly accompanies his sense of Pollock-like in-spiration"; "Realm Buster: Stan Brakhage," *Chicago Review,* 47.4 and 48.1 (Winter 2001, Spring 2002), 173. I find this unpersuasive.

29. P. Adams Sitney, "Interview With Stan Brakhage," *Metaphors on Vision,* unpaginated.

30. Thus, in 1963: " 'By Brakhage' [the signature on the films of the 1960s] should be understood to mean 'by way of Stan and Jane Brakhage,' as it does in all my films since marriage. It is coming to mean: 'by way of Stan and Jane and all the children Brakhage' "; *Metaphors on Vision,* unpaginated.

31. *Metaphors on Vision,* unpaginated.

PARKER TYLER

Stan Brakhage

S
tan Brakhage's career as a Film Experimentalist is already well launched although he is, being only twenty-five, one of the very youngest of the accredited group of American Experimentalists. That he was adopted exactly when fourteen days old saved him from what is sometimes a baby-orphan's traumatic fate: growing up in an orphanage. He was reared in the Midwest and has lived in Arizona, New Mexico, Colorado, and California, where he went to join the avant-garde film movement at the School of Fine Arts in San Francisco; however, finding its leading lights absent, he was discouraged in the first flush of his Experimentalist zeal, and having reached failure in the love affair which had been coincident with his first film, *Interim*, he switched capriciously to writing.

Interim had been made in Denver, his home, following a willful secession from Dartmouth, where for one semester he had been studying on a scholarship (with poor results) and where a psychological crisis had been the cause of his desertion. Brakhage is not reticent about his temperamentality, and yet his accounts of certain episodes in his life have been inconsistent. One may be sure of two things, however, and these are traits typical of the youthful

First published in *Film Culture*, 18 (1958), pp. 23–25.

artist: Love has been a major problem for him, while still, rather than permit it to interfere with his film work, he has always tended to instrumentalize it. One such attempt, and remarkably successful, was *Interim* itself, which he filmed as a simple erotic episode in pantomime: The only accompaniment to the young lovers' accidental meeting and ephemeral contact is the music score by James Tenney, which is excellent and paced well with the idyllic action.

There is nothing sensational, technical or otherwise, about *Interim*. It is specifically, deliberately, an "episode"—like life for one who was then (in 1951) only eighteen. Yet as a young Experimentalist's first endeavor, it is phenomenally free of awkwardness, showing a very rare quality: the taste that is "tact." True, tact itself is not among the most decisive Experimental factors, for it is also conspicuous in the best French commercial films and in a film such as Dreyer's *Day of Wrath*. Perhaps, in passing, a definition of the aesthetic content of the term *tact* may be given. Quite apart from imaginative daring, scope of vision, or novelty of technique, tact is that firm, rhythmic touch upon all elements (story, actor, camera, and psychology) which makes a work of art agreeable, neat, and in no way offensive. It never pays to underrate this faculty, in whatever domain of film, especially because an ambitious young Experimentalist may be a little wild or a little vulgar without realizing it. Such elder Experimentalists as Maya Deren and Sidney Peterson, at this date, top Brakhage in imagination, but considering the total output of all the Experimentalists I know about, Brakhage emerges with the highest score in tact among all his fellow craftsmen.

Continually broke in San Francisco, but writing and studying poetry while talking with elder poets Kenneth Rexroth and Kenneth Patchen, Brakhage felt, at last, stalemated. He therefore returned to Denver to start a theater in a surplus war tent, where he tackled Wedekind, Strindberg, and Chekhov. But his eye was still on filmmaking, and with specially raised funds he made his second film, *Unglassed Windows Cast a Terrible Reflection*, in an abandoned mine's surface buildings. It was a bit overambitiously planned (owing mainly to too large a demand on amateur actors), but it showed his smooth, tactful touch despite its reliance on what, in 1953, was an Experimentalist cliché: the contemporary ruin as a neo-Gothic background. There was, even here, further proof of Brakhage's control of camera rhythm, if nothing positively original in mood or technique.

Restive, without funds for creating, the young Experimentalist once more turned toward San Francisco, where he now became friends with the poet Robert Duncan and lived in a basement room below Duncan's apartment. Then Brakhage's father, when he went home for the next Christmas, agreed to finance a film for him. The result was *Desistfilm*, based on a cult of the local youth in which Brakhage was joined by a small circle of friends. The subject is simply a wild party in which young people of both sexes get high on wine and behave in provincial emulation of such international fashions as Existentialism and Dada, with the accent, however, on rejection rather than *engagement*. The film remains, at best, fragmentary. Now a plan to tour, and make films along the way, started with his collaboration with Larry Jordan, *The Extraordinary Child*, a self-consciously zany work that flowed out of *Desistfilm* but showed sloppiness and did not come off. Brakhage ended broke in a eucalyptus grove outside Nyles, California. Drawing courage from this briefly enforced term of meditation, he went back to San Francisco to establish a film workshop and by filming TV commercials for various civic organizations made enough to do his next two films: *In Between* and *The Way to Shadow Garden*.

Himself a writer of felicitous verse, Brakhage has always been eager to communicate with poets, and his works usually echo his current social relations in the shape of poetic "influences" as both consciously and unconsciously transmitted to him. *In Between*, done in the milieu of Duncan and his friends, is not a happy effort, being marred by amateurism to an embarrassing degree, not that Duncan and his friends were to blame: An artist is responsible to his influences as well as to himself. Brakhage, up to this point, was uneven. But *The Way to Shadow Garden*, which followed, marks a distinct advance in his imaginative development. Here, according to his own account, he investigated the "drama" of the protagonist's relationship with the objects in his room, the latter reversing the order of nature and acting upon him. As usual, though the idea was a very subjective one, Brakhage used one of his friends as his projected self. Some of the film's details are unconvincing, yet the whole is a sensitively executed, if slight, "epic" of modern psychological tension. Beginning with *The Way to Shadow Garden*, an upward arc is discernible in Brakhage's filmic oeuvre.

Probably his decision to come to New York, and present his talent on as wide a stage as possible, was a token of his victorious growth as well as of his self-confidence. Self-doubt, of course, has infallibly assailed Stan Brakhage as it does all artists, but his drive has never deserted him for long. He did not complete editing on the last two films till after he arrived in New York, where he not only proceeded to make two more films but also met other Experimentalists, including Maya Deren and Willard Maas, and other poets and critics, among them the present writer. Brakhage, I believe, has a genuinely passionate nature, by which, of course, I mean something fundamentally psychic, while excluding from it neither the heart nor the flesh. The combination of passion and inexperience inevitably leads to the confusion of interpersonal complications, and most certainly in New York, where Neurotica is the Tenth Muse. Moreover, there the sense of rivalry is keen no matter on what level or in what sphere of professionalism; hence, in New York, Brakhage's temperamentality was duly put through its paces and yet, happily, not to his or anyone's serious detriment. Economically and artistically, he repeated all his previous patterns: poverty, caprice, and desperation on one hand; the kindness of friends and institutions, the will and the capacity to work, on the other. A benefit performance of four of his films was held in the auditorium of the Living Theatre. From the Creative Film Foundation, which began operating about this time, he received a grant whose value in cash terms turned out to be less than he had expected; nevertheless, a brief film was inaugurated with its help.

Meanwhile, Brakhage's mind and heart were involved with the idea of turning love into marriage; For some while, he was engaged—or at least felt engaged—to a young woman from Denver who had come to New York to start a theatrical career. Frustration, professional and private, is usually an artist's natural, if transient, lot. Maybe Brakhage has had a bit more than his share of it; anyway, he never married the Denver girl, even though he came near it. Till his marriage at the beginning of 1958, his most serious romance was with her. Brakhage has found New York, admittedly, both fascinating and forbidding and spasmodically feels drawn there, when away, as he used to feel drawn to San Francisco.

Inner and outer crises tempted him away from New York following the summer of 1955 (when he had spent more than six months there and made *Reflections on Black* and *The Wonder Ring*) to Los Angeles. In this city, he formed a connection with Raymond Rohauer, who commissioned what turned out to be Brakhage's best film that, to date, has been exhibited: *Flesh of Morning*. It has his most personal signature by virtual necessity because, for the first time, he enacts his own protagonist. Because, moreover, he photographed it himself without help, it issued as a remarkable tour de force, and challenges for supremacy any other short lyric film I know.

Nightcats was begun in Los Angeles and completed along with two new, quite brief, films (*Daybreak* and *White Eye*) during his second sojourn in New York, which came in 1956. During this period he also worked transiently—but with loyal application—in the bookshop managed by his friend Charles Boultenhouse. Along with the beautifully poetic *Flesh of Morning* and the beautifully apt *Wonder Ring*, which technically form his high points, Brakhage is faced, in *Nightcats* and *White Eye*, by two works directly posing for him the artist's ineradicable problem of the threatening gap between intention and achievement, meaning and form. Both these films are visually tactful; the disturbing quality they share, about equally, is the implication of straining for a difficult statement in which they fall heroically short.

In *Nightcats* (his third color film) Brakhage has deliberately used real organisms, cats, as color and black-and-white abstractions; this dominantly abstract method automatically ignores the second-level tension produced by feline image and behavior in contrast with the first-level tension composed by pure color and value relationships. Some of the transitions created by camera movement between such abstractions and objects are artful, but the basic problem of the proper interrelation of levels has not been solved. The same is true of *Whiteye*: The interior/exterior tension between the snowy landscape, seen beyond windows, and a hand inside, attempting to write a love letter, has no lucid resolution. *Daybreak*, on the contrary, is an excellent vignette dealing with a highly critical passage in a young woman's psychic life even if, photographically speaking, it is a bit tame.

Verbal soundtracks might solve the artistic problems of the other two films; as a rule, Brakhage depends (for reasons of economy) on rather makeshift musical scores, and in his work, music has never been a major creative factor. No suspended formal problem of any kind handicaps either *Reflections on Black* or *The Wonder Ring*, the latter of which was made possible by the artist Joseph Cornell, who wished to see a film record made of the Third Avenue "El" in New York before it ceased operation prior to its demolition. *Reflections*, being purely a psychological fantasy involving a set of domestic scenes between lovers, offered a problem infinitely removed from that of the El film. Yet Brakhage had no trouble handling both films very competently. Entered in the first Creative Film Foundation annual competition, *Reflections on Black* won an award and, like other films of Brakhage's, is now distributed by Cinema 16.

Whatever difficult meaning inheres in the sequence of cryptic dumb shows furnished by the domestic partners in *Reflections* is contained entirely in the action itself, without such independent formal motivation as Brakhage imposed on *Nightcats*. Again, in *The Wonder Ring*, the color and chiaroscuro, the changing movement of the El train, and the varied rhythm and texture of images seen through the irregular window glass flow simply and naturally from the eyesight of the observer with his camera: a passenger enjoying the same views that had been available for so many years to countless El riders. This is a gemlike little film precisely because its maker's tact eliminated the possibility of any pretentiousness; it has no smallest trace of the artiness from which Brakhage's first color film, *In Between*, suffered.

Loving, his latest film to be released, was made—like the still-unreleased *Anticipation of the Night*—in Denver in 1957 and is a brief but interesting, and very probably unique, exercise in cinematic sensibility; we are, say the first few shots, in the woods on a sunshiny day. Then a quick succession of glimpses shows us a couple in the throes of unceremonious lovemaking. So close are the images that, while we never doubt what is going on, everything seems optically discursive, like things seen through half-shut eyes, things seen (as preoccupied lovers would see them) with half or less than half conscious recognition of the setting, and sometimes upside down; this is because the truer, dominant sensations are tactile, not optical, and in turn, it is as if the growing things see the lovers as a corresponding succession of details torn from context, as though the human beings, too, could become fluid, vanishing abstractions.

A very superior little "essay" in optical psychology, *Loving* is fragmentary when considered beside *Flesh of Morning*. Not only is it much shorter, but also, in terms of sexual experience, it is at the antipode from the earlier film, where the young male is alone in a state of temptation toward self, surrounded by fetishes of the loved girl—and with a camera handy; psychologically, the camera is identical with the protagonist, for as I said, here Brakhage performed the bravura feat of enacting the Narcissistic drama himself. The tension is simply composed but exquisite in duration: Shall he or shall he not satisfy himself in the usual way? The orgasm approaches like a tragic fate. . . . Though its nature somewhat restricts its exhibition, Brakhage had the courage to include it among the films he submitted to the Brussels international festival, whose prizes are yet to be awarded.

Already, Stan Brakhage has won his special admirers, and these wish him well in the career that, given even moderate good fortune, certainly lies ahead of him. I have not yet seen *Anticipation of the Night*. But the young Experimentalist's program note, accompanying his newest film on its flight to Belgium, is so poetically suggestive that perhaps this monograph can be ended no better than with its quotation entire:

> The daylight shadow of a man in its movement evokes lights in the night. A rose bowl, held in hand, reflects both sun and moon-like illumination. The opening of a doorway onto trees anticipates the twilight into the night. A child is born on a lawn, born of water, with its promissory rainbow, and the wild rose. It becomes the moon and the source of all night light. Lights of the night become young children playing a circular game. The moon moves over a pillared temple to which all lights return. There is seen the sleep of the innocents and their animal dreams, becoming their amusement, their circular game, becoming the morning. The trees change color and lose their leaves for the morn, becoming the complexity of branches on which the shadow man hangs himself.

JONAS MEKAS

Brakhage. Breer. Menken.
The Pure Poets of Cinema

R obert Breer, Stanley Brakhage, and Marie Menken thematically and formally represent, in the new American cinema, the best of the tradition of experimental and poetic cinema. Freely, beautifully, they sing the physical world, its textures, its colors, its movements, or they speak in little bursts of memories, reflections, meditations.

Unlike the early avant-garde films, these films are not burdened by Greek or Freudian mythology and symbolism; their meaning is more immediate, more visual and suggestive. Stylistically and formally, their work represents the highest and purest creation achieved in the poetic cinema.

It was a short film by Stanley Brakhage, *Desistfilm* (1954)—still one of the most influential of all modern American films—that started the stylistic revolution that has now reached the documentary and is beginning to be noticeable in the commercial dramatic film. (Truffaut kicks and shakes his camera in *Jules et Jim* to destroy static, "professional" smooth pans and tilts.) Very few other filmmakers have been as preoccupied with style and techniques as has been Brakhage. Ironically enough, it is Brakhage who is

From "Notes on the New American Cinema"; first published in *Film Culture*, 24 (1959), pp. 6–16.

usually picked up by the old school critics when they need an example of bad style and bad techniques. They couldn't have chosen a more fallacious example, for Brakhage is truly one of the virtuosos of modern cinema.

In his latest film, *Prelude* (1961), Brakhage achieves a synthesis of all his techniques. In this film of exquisite beauty, the images become like words; they come back, in little bursts, and disappear, and come back again, as though in sentences, creating visual and mental impressions, experiences. Within the abstract context, the flashes of memories of a more personal and temporal nature appear, always in a hinting, oblique, indirect manner—the images of foreboding clouds, memories of the atom bomb, endless cosmic spaces, dreams and fears that constitute the subconscious of modern man. If the contemporaneity of the other filmmakers discussed here is very real, emotional, raw, and still a part of our daily experience—in *Prelude* (as in the work of Robert Breer and Marie Menken), this contemporaneity is abstracted, filtered; it becomes a thought, a meditation occurring in a world of its own, in the world of a work of art.

Brakhage, from a letter to a friend (1958), before beginning his work on *Prelude*:

> I am now considering a second feature-length film, which will dwell cinematically upon the atomic bomb. But, as *Anticipation of the Night* is a work of art rather than an indictment of contemporary civilization in terms of the child, so too my prospective film will dream upon the bomb, create it out of, as I envision it, an almost Spinozian world of mathematical theory, visualize the flowering of its form in relation to the beautiful growths as well as to those more intellectually parasitic, and, in the wake of its smoke, deal with the devastation it leaves in the human mind, rather than material devastation, the nightmare and also the "devoutly to be wished" that it engenders, ergo, religion—the end, the resolve with death.

There are only one or two other filmmakers working today who can transform reality into art as successfully as Brakhage, Breer, and Menken. A landscape, a face, a blotch of light—everything changes under their eyes to become something else, an essence of itself, at the service of their personal vision. To watch, in Brakhage's *Whiteye*, a winter landscape transform itself, through the magic of motion, temperament, and light, into pure poetry of white, is an unforgettable experience.

JEROME HILL

Brakhage and Rilke

Brakhage may very well be planning an eleventh *Song*. I don't know. At this time there are ten, and the series is already an entity. The way they came to me—by mail, or handed me directly by Brakhage singly or in twos and threes—made my initiation a tantalizing and increasingly rewarding experience.

The great discipline that I had learned to admire in the work of Brakhage that I already knew is only slightly reflected in the ten *Songs* of which I am writing—his most recent work—a series of disarmingly spontaneous eight-millimeter films of conspicuous brevity.

The French have a word "egrener" that defies exact translation. The root of it is the syllable "gren" which is akin to "grain." The first meaning is "to pick grapes off a bunch, to take seeds out of their pods." A secondary definition, "to count" or "recount" has led to its most commonly used meaning: "to tell beads, as in a rosary." The *Songs* of Brakhage are strung together like a chaplet.

One follows another with a casual but nonetheless recognizable inevitability. The word "suite" (French again, from the verb "suivre", "to follow")

First published in *Film Culture*, 37 (1965), pp. 13–14.

has some of the same overtones. The individual parts of a Bach suite, for instance, have elements in common, comply with traditional conventions, are not fixed in number; they form, in other words, a sort of garland. They neither "relate" nor "build" in the same fashion that the movements of a symphony do.

In so many ways do Brakhage's ten *Songs* as a suite recall to me the ten *Duino Elegies* of Rilke that I feel it may clarify what I want to express to dwell for a moment on the resemblances. Without making the mistake of pushing too far the comparison between two such manifestly different works, let me first point out that they are both essentially lyric in character. Lyric, as opposed to epic or dramatic poetry, is to be read in intimacy, if possible aloud; to be read often; to be learned by heart. The *Songs*, to me who am used to viewing them in small rooms in the presence of limited gatherings, are not public statements. They address the viewer personally. Each one is over almost before it has begun. They bear many re-viewings.

The films are, of course, altogether in a lighter mood than the poems. They are, after all, songs and not elegies. But the ordered balance between foreboding and joy in the first series is as sensitive and crucial as the interplay of despair and hope in the second. Both Brakhage and Rilke, moreover, play on the equivocal emotions that partake at the same time of laughter and tears. Both men express big themes through intimate imagery. Both allude to extraneous subject matter that is not and need not be explained, so powerful is its poetic overtone.

Several leitmotifs run through the *Songs* like colored threads in a texture, and yet, as in the *Duino* series, each section has its own subject matter, its own mood, its own form, and even its own technique.

Like the *Elegies*, the *Songs* were conceived and partially realized in an order different from the one in which they are finally presented. They are made out of the simplest elements of Brakhage's daily life. From the very onset there is Jane Brakhage; and she is present either in image or in implication throughout. She stands in relation to this series as Rilke's "Angel" does to his. We see children at play, a wedding, a love making, a birth. We see a book, a toy, an eye, a moon, a sun, a station wagon, a light. There are rows of San Francisco houses, and people, not many, but people still, who pass in the streets. Doors and windows assume enormous importance. And there is pattern,—a flowered linoleum or carpet,—a rocky cliff seen from a moving car,—the dappled foam of the sea,—a spotted dressing gown. Only twice do the darkly felt archetypal animals appear,—the mythical beasts that preside over so many of Brakhage's films. At one time, it is turtles and crustaceans in *Song 8*—the aqueous Song. At another it is the powerful symbolic rhinoceros with his life-imparting horn in *Song 9*—the Epithalamion—and the rhino, as if by a superior order of destiny, has the shadow of a window on his flanks!

Objects, elements, images, gestures, rhythms, events.

The humanity of *Song 1* contrasts with the abstraction of *Song 2*. After the drama of *Song 5*, the serenity of *6*. *Songs 8*, *9*, and *10* make a three-part finale where themes stated earlier in fragment are brought to fruition.

Never does Brakhage allow one to forget the medium. The fabric of cinema shows constantly like the plaster under a Giotto fresco—light flashes, heavy grain, exposed leader, inscribed emulsion, even an occasional mid-frame splice. This apparent casualness has no implication of carelessness. It is vertiginous to contemplate what a small role the laboratory has played here. These dissolves and double exposures couldn't have been planned in the relaxed atmosphere of a cutting room, later to be executed by an optical technician. Each "effect" had to be made at the time of shooting. (Eight millimeter doesn't permit A and B roll printing.) Brakhage had to remember his motion and rhythm, note his footage, wind back and shoot the material he wanted superimposed directly over it.

One has the feeling that Brakhage lives with a camera in his hand, that his viewer is tantamount to his eyes, that the stuff of his films is the course of his life.

Let us hope that the voice of conventional criticism is never raised on the subject of these delicate poems. Reputed film reviewers these days are being very patronizing on the subject of the "cult," the "in-group," the "initiated." What would happen, one wonders, if musical criticism, for instance, were assigned to untrained, complacently tone-deaf journalists?

ROBERT KELLY

On *The Art of Vision*

A n *art of vision* possible in a medium that has dominated our century and that herewith frees itself from dependence on all other art forms. Film has tended, even in the most experimental contexts, to be a composite of literary and plastic arts, dance and music, the eye at the mercy of intention, culture, pretense, and imitations. Now Brakhage's *Art of Vision* exists utterly free of all that. It is a totality of making so intense it becomes a systematic exploration of the forms and terms of the medium itself. To explore the form without exhausting the form: A definitive making in any art is the health of the whole art, of the arts. Art in its oldest sense is skill, skill of making; *The Art of Vision* is the skill of making seeing. *The Art of Vision, The Art of The Fugue*, a presumptuous comparison only so long as we accord film only evidential value. This film makes immediate the integrity of the medium. Climax of the edited film, a new continent of the eye's sway. Mind at the mercy of the eye at last.

* * *

Is the word art lost to us? Skill in making is what it once meant, a way of making, so that art of vision = how to see.

First published in *Film Culture*, 37 (1965), pp. 14–15.

* * *

What difference does it make what the film has been? Who am I to speak of this question? Of it? What do I know? What is the film now? I speak of one film.

* * *

Brakhage's film is not free of story in the literary sense. Brakhage paraphrases his film too easily. If the film is not free of story, why do I say it is? *Dog Star Man* is deeply implicated with story—i.e., in this context, preexistent temporal intent. But *The Art of Vision* is not *Dog Star Man.*

* * *

The word art has lost its balls. This title may grow them again.

* * *

Art is not the pomposity of Bayreuth, the bathos of Lincoln Center, the pack rat trove of the Louvre. Art is making.

* * *

The motto of the city of New York is *So What?* Be aware that it is not a rhetorical question.

* * *

It is time we understood *art* as a function, not an attitude.

* * *

Film, through its newness and availability, generates attitude more frequently than it does response. The attitude of an audience is not the filmmaker's problem.

* * *

It is important to call things by their right names.

EDWARD DORN

The First Time I Heard the
Word "Brakhage"

The first time I heard the word "Brakhage" was in 1959, high in the
mountains of New Mexico. Shortly thereafter I had a taste of his
outlandishly accurate writing in a little magazine of the time called
Blue Grass. It was going to be a few years before I actually saw the films. By
the time I did have a chance to see the films at the Vancouver Arts Festival
in 1963 I had some notions about him and the art of his family. Word
formations flying through the mountain chains of the West. How Jane
Brakhage could get an audience of 75 beavers together in the aspen groves
just about any afternoon for a flute concert. There is a certain critical attention mountain dwellers must pay to the phenomena of their location, and I
always paid close attention to news of the Brakhages.

Brakhage is a definitional writer. He starts with more or less common
knowledge (or common controversy) and shows us where the language
(both verbal & visual) leads into the interior. Through the draws to the
hidden vale. Or up over the passes to the whole outside. The journey has to
be made, but The Way derives from nature. This is not a "psychological"

First published in Stan Brakhage, *Film Biographies* (Berkeley, CA: Turtle Island, 1977), pp.
112–113.

determination. It is both more serious and grander than that. The definitions track through the forest of puns, a vigorous prose on antrogenetic legs. Invested sometimes with the truly bewildering meanings of its subject.

The truly deep comic is animal. When the soundtrack comes on, the impression rises suddenly lighter even than air to the head. Of Jean Vigo's *Jean Taris, Champion of Swimming*, Brakhage writes: "Conquering water in every conceivable way, concluding with his camera-created Jesus-act of walking on it." That suggests something beyond and "above" something funny. Walking and chewing gum simultaneously is simply too entirely physical, though sprung from the same primeval gestural medium.

The Chaplin lecture is the greatest illumination of that difficult subject I've ever read. Was he just another insidious influence bubbling up from the lower classes or the heaviest prescription for a comedian yet writ? Brakhage avoids both those limitations. He is an artist—"The United States was his bridge, he danced upon it almost half a century, a marionette dangling from a string of vicious gags, with a cane in one hand and a woman's arm in the other—tightrope walking across a Niagara Fall of dollars." Charlie Chaplin left for the West at Kansas City, pretty near where everybody else entrained.

San Francisco, 1977

ANNETTE MICHELSON

Camera Lucida/
Camera Obscura

For Jay Leyda

I

We celebrate, as this year begins, the birthdays of two master film makers: Eisenstein, were he living at this hour, would be 75 years of age, and Stan Brakhage this month turns 40. Convergences and parallels of aspiration and achievement suggest themselves in such force and number as to strain the limits and categories, national and formal, which critical and historical discourse on cinema most generally employ. As one begins to think about the work of these two men, their kinds and intensities of energy, the trajectories which they describe through the culture of our

First published in *Artforum*, 11, 5(January 1973), pp. 30–37. © *Artforum*, January 1973. Author's note: This comparative and celebratory study was written in the conviction that the movement of independent production in post–World War II America revivified the intensive and rapid editing (montage) which the Soviet avant-garde of the post-revolutionary generation had introduced into the modern cinema. The fact that its deployment by Stan Brakhage, a prime force within independent production, was directed toward a very different end is indicated partly by the essay's title. It is further developed in the account of the manner in which Brakhage's enterprise was grounded in a radical revision of cinematic spatiality and temporality. Annette Michelson, 1 December 2003.

time and, more specifically, through its paradigmatic esthetic mode—the cinema—one has a fresh, keen sense of that mode's continuity.

I will take that sense as signaling that for cinema, too, it is coming to be true, as Eliot some 50 years ago claimed in the most celebrated of his critical texts, that,

> No poet, no artist of any art has his complete meaning alone. His significance, his appreciation is the appreciation of his relation to the dead poets and artists. You cannot value him alone; you must set him, for contrast and comparison, among the dead.[1]

One is impressed by the importance of this

> as a principle of aesthetic, not merely historical criticism. . . . The necessity that the artist shall conform, that he shall cohere is not one-sided; what happens when a new work of art is created is something that happens simultaneously to all the works of art which preceded it. The existing monuments form an ideal order among themselves which is modified by the introduction of the new (the really new) work of art among them.

And Eliot, suggesting that "this existing order must be if ever so slightly altered by the supervention of novelty," thereby proposes what one might term a dialectical view. He goes on to say that the artist will "in a peculiar sense" be aware, as well, that "he must inevitably be judged by the standards of the past. I say judged, not amputated by them. . . . It is a judgment, a comparison in which two things are measured by each other."

A sense of this also being true for cinema is produced by one's sense of this occasion as dynamic in its effect, as acting to sharpen focus, to disclose the contours of a tradition within a sensationally rapid succession of individual talents. One's view of history, of history's claims upon one are thereby altered. To think and write on cinema has largely been to propose hypotheses, protocols, and fictions to the world at large, and to propose them with a levity wholly unthinkable in any other area of inquiry—a levity that has guaranteed their incomparably rapid and steady supercession. It is, however, the speed and dynamism of cinema's development which has steadily confounded the noblest attempts to constitute, the most prudent efforts to reflect upon, its ontology. Occasions such as these invite us, then, to reconsider the reasons, and to think of ways in which to reinvent historical and critical tasks, review their relation to each other, redefining film form, remaking film sense. More immediately and most generally, what are the ways in which we can make sense of this particular conjunction, how explain the manner in which these anniversaries are felt as one occasion, fusing in a dialectical moment of a movement which comprehends them both, and so much more?

Here are some ways. One has first the sense of these two men as Masters, as artists who invent strategies, vocabularies, syntactical and grammatical forms for film, and as men whose innovative functions and special intensity of energy are radical, defining the possibilities of the medium itself for their contemporaries. One sees, as well, that they share a common function, through a conjunction of *praxis* and *theoria*, to define those possibilities and to determine the arenas of discourse and of action. In so doing, they force the very best of their contemporaries to define themselves, in work and discourse, in relation to them. You may, then, view Eisenstein and Brakhage negatively, postpone judgment, recommend rejection, but you cannot, I will claim, avoid situating yourself in relation to them. I am saying, then, that film-making and the theory and criticism of film must, in their most intensive and significant instances, ultimately situate themselves in relation to the work and thinking of these two artists, and I will infer correlatively, that failure to do so may be seen most indulgently as provincialism, must more exactly be termed unseriousness.

We have the sense, as well, of artists whose notions of their art are philosophically informed; they are shaped by the ideological structure in which they are formed—structures so greatly divergent as that of dialectical materialism and a romantic idealism—and they take film as inheriting a philosophical function. Thus each will hypostasize an esthetic principle into an epistemology and, ultimately, an ethics. For Eisenstein, "montage thinking is inseparable from thinking as a whole"; for Brakhage, filmic poesis is the visual instantiation of the imperial sovereignty of the Imagination. Both men propose forms and styles as embodiments of a filmic ontology, and both will posit the making and experiencing of such film as, ultimately, a privileged mode of ontological consciousness itself.

Here, then, are two artists generating in their work the formal stylistic modes, textual mythic themes central to the work of their time. Both support and greatly extend their work through writing which can be seen as inseparable, as I have suggested, not from the sense of their work alone, but from its development. To think about *October* is constantly to be referred back to the mind at work in *Film Form* and *Film Sense*; to reflect upon *The Art of Vision* is to touch at every point the proliferative meditation of *Metaphors on Vision*, to become aware of the way in which both artists sustain a characteristically modern dialectical relation between poetic and critical functions.

Both men are solidly rooted in and sharply responsive to the social structures and energies of their times. That is, they experience its forms of alienation as the special kind of frustration inhering in the artist's relation to his public. Eisenstein's sense of himself as actively, deeply involved—of that self subsumed, as it were, in the historical process of the Revolution—gives us the sense of his work as vectorial in the context of that transformational process. Brakhage is infinitely less privileged in his lonely commitment to revelation, his guerrilla stance in defiance of the culture of mid-century America. It is a tragedy of our time (that tragedy is not, by any means, exclusively, but rather, like so much else, *hyperbolically* American) that Brakhage should see his social function as defensive in the Self's last-ditch stand against the mass, against the claims of any possible class, political process, or structure, assuming its inevitable assault upon the sovereignty of the Self, positing the imaginative consciousness as inherently apolitical.

The forms of their cinemas will, then, respectively be epic and lyrical, engaged, respectively as well, in an encounter with, a reclamation and testing of, the dramatic and the mythical. Generated by antithetical postures, their forms diverge. But the fundamental seriousness and wholeness of concern and the will to define his function in the culture of his time, to speak as artists for the necessity to assume or overcome the condition of alienation, are common to both men. And the concern, the will, are, of course, reflected in the difficulties which attended the progress of their careers. If we may count as blessed the culture not in need of heroes, we may measure, as well, the problematic nature of both American and Soviet society by the manner in which both men figure, through an achievement contested but sustained in a lifelong battle with repressive authority, as "heroes" of a larger Western culture.

For both men are, more specifically and intimately, part of the culture of modernism and of the modernist art of their times. Eisenstein was formed, as we know, by the poetry, painting, and theater which developed in the complex itinerary of immediately pre- and post-Revolutionary Russia, from Futurism through Cubism and Constructivism. Similarly Brakhage must—in one way, among others—be understood in the movement from the space and conceptual frame-work of Cubism through Surrealism to Abstract Expressionism. We know Eisenstein more intimately for our knowledge of Rodchenko, Tatlin, and the way in which they comprehended the lessons of Cubism. We have, as well, a sharper view of the genesis of his editing style when we know how it grew from his decision as a young theater designer and director to adopt, as he puts it, "the principles of the cubists." In his staging of the Pletnev play *Precipice*, he decided

> to use not only running scenery . . . but also—possibly under the demands
> of shifting scenery—to connect these moving decorations with people.
> The actors on roller skates carried not only themselves about the stage,
> but also their piece of city . . . thereby solving the problem—the inter-
> section of man and milieu.[2]

But one has an even clearer view of that genesis and its consequences when we see the manner in which Eisenstein's move from theater into film is confirmed by and takes place in, a movement more general in the art of his time, when we attend to Tatlin, speaking of his own design for the stage production in 1923 of Khlebnikov's *Zangezi*.

> The *Zangezi* production is to be related to the principle that the word is
> a building unit, material, a unit of organized space. Khlebnikov himself
> characterized this supernarration as an architectural work built of nar-
> rations and each narration as an architectural work built of words. He
> regards the word as plastic material. The properties of this material make
> it plausible to operate with it to build up "the linguistic state."
>   This attitude on the part of Khlebnikov gave me an opportunity to
> do my work in staging it. Parallel with his word construction I decided
> to make a material construction. This method makes it possible to fuse
> the work of two people into a unity. . . . In one of the "planks of the
> play," the "planks of which *Zangezi* is built," we find a succession of
> thing-like sounds. . . . To emphasize the nature of these sounds I use
> surfaces of different materials, treated in different ways. *Zangezi* is in its

structure so many-faceted and difficult to produce that the stage, if it is spatially enclosed, will be unable to contain its action. To guide the attention of the spectator, the eye of the projector leaps from one place to another, creating order and consistency. The projector is also necessary to emphasize the properties of the material.[3]

In the year following this collaborative work by Tatlin and Khlebnikov, as I have on a previous occasion pointed out,[4] Eisenstein found himself propelled out of theater into the space of cinema, as a direct consequence of his staging Tretiakov's *Gas Masks* within a factory situation.

In *Gas Masks* we see all the elements of film tendencies meeting. The turbines, the factory background, negated the last remnants of make-up and theatrical costumes, and all elements appeared as independently fused. Theater accessories in the midst of real factory plastics appeared ridiculous. The element of "play" was incompatible with the acrid smell of gas. The pitiful platform kept getting lost among the real platforms of labor activity. In short the production was a failure. And we found ourselves in the cinema.[5]

And Eisenstein, with an exact and vivid sense of the practical consequences to be drawn from experience, makes his first film in and around a factory and its "real platforms of labor activity," initiating his cinema of montage with a sumptuous movement of the camera through that factory's space, inspired, no doubt, in a way characteristic of him, by the concrete structure of the space and its industrial cranes.

His propulsion into cinema had been, then, anticipated by Tatlin's realization, as he worked with Khlebnikov in a radically Constructivist theatrical enterprise, that the spatiality of the stage could no longer contain the complexity, nor render the desired immediacy, of the movement and materials of his construction. Something then had to be invented to confer "order, consistency," and a certain illusionistic intensity upon that spectacle; the invention is the leaping projector, that surrogate camera. This kind of interplay is accounted for in Victor Shklovsky's recent remark that:

At that time the individual arts developed and flowed in one common stream. It is impossible to understand Eisenstein . . . without Mayakovsky.

Neither can his [Mayakovsky's] poem *About This*—whose hero passes from one milieu to another, undergoing various transformations—be understood without a knowledge of the cinematography of the time, without an awareness of what it then meant for artists to be confronted with the collision of fragments endowed with a unity of meaning, revealed in a series of conflicts.[6]

Eisenstein moves through and with the developing art of his time, discovering through theater and the plastic arts, the space of cinema, inflecting, in turn, through his "montage of attractions," his systematization of conflict in the percussive rhythm of that montage, the forms of poetry. Brakhage develops in explicit concern with the major esthetic innovations of the '50s and '60s. For Brakhage, poetry undoubtedly plays the revelatory role that theater had for Eisenstein. He has an intensive interest in making new and vivid the poetics of Romanticism, sustained by a constant commerce with men such as Charles Olson, Robert Kelly, John Cage, Robert Duncan, and an intensive involvement with the work of Pound and Stein as presiding, more than any other artists of this century, over the direction of his own filmic enterprise. If Eisenstein cannot be understood without Mayakovsky (and, one must add, Meyerhold), Brakhage's mature work is hardly to be thought of without that of Pound and Stein. Both men are voracious in their reading as well as energetic in their responses to the efforts of contemporaries. Both are also (and this deserves a special stress) candid and uniquely generous in their judgments of the work of colleagues, as only men deeply secure in the knowledge of their own worth and the solidity of their culture can be.

And both film makers are, interestingly enough, extremely wary of sound and its uses in the making of film. Eisenstein's reticence, shared by many of his more innovative colleagues, is a matter of historical record. The collective "Statement on Sound of 1928," presumably written by Eisenstein and endorsed by Pudovkin and Alexandrov,[7] is understood fully only when one remembers that the montage style was, for Eisenstein, isomorphic with dialectical process, that he proposed through that style, the filmic possibility of access to a heightened consciousness. Endowed, then, with a filmically ontological status, montage is the instrument of filmic revolution, the agent of revolutionary consciousness in and through film. Eisenstein's sense of sound as a threat to cinema is directly grounded in the apprehension that sound meant talk and that talk meant the restoration, through synchronous dialogue, of theatrical structure. He sees that restoration as profoundly, inexorably retrogressive in its consequences: sound, thus misused, is an agent of "illusionism," destructive of "the culture of montage," subversive of revolutionary cinema. One must read this text as articulating the particular intensity of that sense of danger imminent in the worldwide adoption of sound. One must understand it as a call to militant action against a reinforced illusionism's subversion of the revolutionary achievement through a kind of filmic Allied Expeditionary Force, mobilized in the name of the Restoration around the new recording technology. Therefore the manifesto, the warning, the program for further extension of the montage style into sound; therefore the insistence on their contrapuntal asynchronous organization as yet another dialectical moment in the consolidation of the filmic revolution.

Brakhage's categorical rejection of sound has its undoubted origin in his vehement commitment to the primacy or "nobility"[8] of sight and to his expansion, literalization, and revivification of the Visionary claim, the sense of the Imagination as indeed primarily and concretely generative of images. He therefore eliminates sound from almost all of his mature work, going so far as to suppress a completed and extremely fine sound track composed for Part One of *Scenes From Under Childhood*, which functions as a refinement of superimposition effect, depositing its clear, acoustical articulation of an unseen space upon the space we are given on the screen. And two of Brakhage's most interesting works (*Fire of Waters* and *Blue Moses*) are by no means incidentally sound films, though they propose on every level, critical alternatives to the main options of his development.

To understand Brakhage's elimination of sound, why he feels it to be subversive of the primacy of the moving image, one should consider not only his own statements but also two major sources of influence. First the figure of William Blake. If we may see his talk of angelic visions, recorded elsewhere in this issue, as a possible culmination of an important influence, one must certainly locate it as another theme in a constantly renewed repertory of eidetic imagery. Refining upon a reading of Northrop Frye's, Harold Bloom points out that the poet shows us "two gates to that Garden of Beulah which itself, at its upper limits, becomes the Gates of Paradise, and that at that upper level, the sense of hearing drops out and is subsumed by a more intense sense of sight."[9] And Brakhage quotes Gertrude Stein, as he frequently does, in a recent letter:

It has always bothered me a good deal that and as in America hearing plays such a large part in everything and it is a thing that makes anyone really creating worry about everything . . . lots of voices make too much sound, any one voice sounds too much like that voice, and soon I do not worry, hearing human voices is not real enough to be a worry. When you have been digging in the garden or been anywhere when you close your eyes you see what you have been seeing, but it is a peaceful thing that and is not a worry to one. . . .[10]

Each film maker, then, derives a sense of the problematic nature of sound from the intensity and integrity with which his forms reflect a sense of, and his structures stand for philosophical commitment. That intensity and integrity are the source of a power which transcends the exactitude of arguments or invulnerability of positions.

There is finally one other way—and this brings us to the heart of things, to the formal ordering of the work and its consequences for the cinema at large. We can begin to think of Eisenstein and Brakhage as engaged in enterprises that are comparable; each man undertaking to reassess the past, reclaiming those impulses and strategies which seem to hold promise for the future and devoting the totality of his energies to their radicalization.

II

Eisenstein thought and wrote a great deal about American film and his involvement with it. When young, he loved the Pearl White serials, Fairbanks's *Mark of Zorro*, and speaks of them as having been "exciting for their possibilities"[11] in a manner which recalls Godard's taste for Monogram's Series B. In "Dickens, Griffith and The Film Today" he is at pains to make clear his debt to Griffith. Speaking, however, for "our cinema [as] neither a poor relative nor an insolvent debtor of his," he defines the task of Soviet film makers as a systematization, a conversion of the limited, empirical use of montage into something stronger, more complex, more cogent. Eisenstein's proposal of the dialectic in filmic form is the finest expression of a more general theorization of the medium, of a full acceptance of its synthetic nature, typical of the early Soviet period.

Sergei Eisenstein.

Eisenstein during the shooting of *October*, 1927.

Analyzing Griffith, Eisenstein discusses the manner in which parallel editing reflects the structure of bourgeois society itself, inferring that montage can be other, can be dialectical, an agent of dialectical consciousness. Eisenstein saw that a radicalization of the techniques and applications of parallel editing was required, and took it as his task, extending the dialectic of montage to every level of film, creating films conceived as moments in the development of historical consciousness as well as that of filmic consciousness. Generally, Eisenstein's films are seen as historical; somewhat loosely, they tend to be described as "epic" in style. This is a term I should like to consider.

Erich Auerbach, preparing to define the qualities of epic style in Homer, cites in the first chapter of *Mimesis* the celebrated excursus which interrupts the account of Ulysses' encounter, on his return home, with Euryclea, the housekeeper, and the circumstances surrounding the infliction of an ancient scar upon his neck, perceived by her with a start of recognition while washing his feet. The incidents are recalled in a leisurely manner; indeed, as we are told, more than 70 verses are given to the digression, preceded, then followed, by 40 on each side. The interruption comes just at the point when Euryclea recognizes the scar—that is, at the moment of crisis...and all is narrated again with such a complete externalization of all the elements of the story and of their interconnections as to leave nothing in obscurity. . . . Not until then does the narrator return to Penelope's chamber; not until then, the digression having run its course, *does Euryclea, who had recognized the scar before the digression began, let Odysseus' foot fall back into the basin.*[12]

Auerbach then goes on to say that "the first thought of a modern reader—that this is a device to increase suspense—is, if not wholly wrong, at least not the essential explanation of this Homeric procedure." He then makes clear that the effect is rather "to leave nothing which it mentions half in darkness and unexternalised, it conforms to a basic impulse of the Homeric style: to represent phenomena in a fully externalized form, visible and palpable in all their parts." He adds that one's sense of the presentness of what is happening eliminates everything else from the stage, filling the reader's mind entirely, conjuring away any intimation of that which is not there, then present.

I will suggest that Eisenstein developed through the radicalization of montage a style which we can indeed now see as grounded deeply and specifically in the Homeric form here described. And he came not unprepared for this task as the student of both Meyerhold and of Kuleshov.

Looking at the sets for the great Meyerhold productions of the biomechanical period—at the set for *The Magnificent Cuckold*, for example—one reads in it the utter impossibility of the hidden, internalized, discreet, subtly evocative, shaded action. It provides no place for casual or imprecisely articulated gestures. You cannot dawdle, hesitate, lounge, meditate, or reflect in it. You *can* stride, bounce, slide, jump, solicited by a set that is a machine for action. Nothing, neither action, attitude—nor even, of course, the stage machinery itself—is hidden. And to project, to externalize temporality itself, a colored wheel turns, its revolutions making visible the passage of time. This theater was Eisenstein's theater, its style his own, and it instructed him in the uses of complete and equal intensity of externalization, in the techniques of rendering visible and palpable.

The utter plasticity afforded by montage, the extension beyond the conventions of parallel editing as proposed by Griffith, he learned, as others did, through Kuleshov. He was aware that acceptance of the radically synthetic possibilities inherent in the editing process could not only synthesize disparate spaces, objects, but could also be used to contract and distend the temporality of film and in so doing create radically new spatiotemporal objects of apprehension. It remained for him to invent for those objects a form and style which could be felt as isomorphic with dialectical process.

It is at this point, which is to say, during the making of *October*, that he perfects the use of the excursus as a heightening of montage technique in the service of that epic style. Examples abound, but none more powerfully instructs us than the sequence, in the section entitled "The July Days," of the lifting of the bridge. Protesting crowds have been fired upon by the government forces during a demonstration, and the lifting of the bridge, ordered by the government, cuts off avenues of action and escape to the demonstrators. The sequence is composed of three discrete, related parts: Part I (comprising shots 1 through 62) is an attack on a demonstrator by an officer in the company of bourgeois women; Part II (shots 63 through 102) is the raising of the bridge; Part III (shots 103 through 139) gives us the triumph of bourgeois witnesses to the event, drowning copies of *Pravda* and banners in the river. The middle section, with which we are particularly concerned, represents one of the most radically interruptive sequences in Eisenstein's work. Uniquely powerful in its conjunction of metaphoric, dramatic, and formal functions, it expands in a great deccelerando between the explosive rhythms of Parts I and III, its distending excruciation intensified by the symmetrical contrast of their rapid and percussive violence.

Opening the bridge, Eisenstein opens, as well, a vast wedge of time within the flow or progress of action. A girl has died upon that bridge, and she lies, her long hair loosened, upon a junction of its splitting surface, as the angles of vision, the distances from which we perceive her corpse, are multiplied. In eight shots, their lengths averaging at 25 frames,[13] she appears in view. A horse and carriage dangle in counterweight at extravagant height from the center of the opening bridge, as it slowly, inexorably swings open. The bridge's rising and stationary sides are given as vantage points; the horse is seen from the rising side and from below in tilt at angles which progressively intensify its dizzying ride in air. We see the carriage dangling, from below, at the rising bridge's summit, then from the open side in still another position. The movement of horse and carriage, of the girl's loosened hair, dangling and gliding, are testimony to the absolute, unalterable authority presiding over this massacre.

A reordering of chronology begins to appear within the sequence. Shots are repeated; a shot will be followed by another unquestionably representing an earlier point in time of the recorded action. Thus the girl appears, with head and torso both visible after her head has been seen in a previously placed shot, to pass out of the frame. We infer a rising of the bridge beyond the point of our experience of it. Again and again she reappears, in a complex intercutting with shots of the bridge's rising, its girders. Her hair slips finally free into the growing gap; the slow progress of movement is reinforced *in* its slowness by the distension of slow motion.

Eisenstein renders, in the repetition and variation of this sequence, the gaze of fascination and analysis joined in the full disclosure of an action in its multiplicity of aspects and of moments. He reorders the action through a temporal staggering and a spatial dislocation which suspend that action, recomposing its progress into a distended present moment. The movement of the bridge is subjected to a disjunctive, analytic process; it opens, closes, and then opens back upon itself. The movement forward and then back in time suspends the action in an abeyance of time's passing, investing the sequence with the fullness of the present. Detailed views of the bridge's underpinnings, the slow motion of the girders are seen in characteristic compositional oppositions of movement within the shot, antithetical camera movements which slowly recompose not only the complex architecture of the bridge, but, as we very gradually perceive, the space of the far shore, effecting a dislocation of the horizon line, wresting the shore from its narrative location, its spatial function, proposing, as the horizon slips into diagonality, a space that flattens into inaccessibility.

What are the further effects of the particular strategies of the bridge sequence? As action is subjected to the extensive analytic reordering, when a multiplicity of angles and positions of movements and aspects alters the temporal flow of the event and of the surrounding narrative structure, the disjunctive relations of its constituents are proclaimed, soliciting a particular kind of attention, and the making of inferences as to spatial and temporal order, adjustments of perception. And the inferences, the adjustments thus solicited reinforce the visibility of things, make for a particular kind of clarity. The visibility afforded by this particular excursus is created by the refinement and complexity of the editing which creates it. Eisenstein gives us within this insertion another complex of insertions that intensify our sense of temporal flow in abeyance, conferring upon the sequence (and upon a film which makes other, ample use of the retarding technique) something we may call the *momentousness* of the epic style.

Eisenstein, then, is proposing in the unity of his filmic innovation a radical renewal of two specific traditional strategies of narrative form: the excursus or retard of epic style and the editing style of Griffith. We know, of course, that he was not alone among his contemporaries in so doing. Brecht's theater and theory are the most consequential parallel effort in this direction, and it is helpful to recall the major features of that effort as described by Walter Benjamin.[14] The epic theater, then, is primarily a "theater of gesture, sharply delineated, frequently interrupted." Its style is grounded "not in reproduction of events but rather in their disclosure." It seizes, then, upon the technique of interruption as the means of "making action clearer." Gesture is interrupted by action, but by placards, songs, and commentary as well. It is a theater primarily philosophical (analytic) rather than religious (empathic) in impulse. Its best subjects tend to be those familiar in advance to its audience, because they can be subjected to the dialectical exploration of the relation between object (or action) and its means of representation. Historical subjects are therefore privileged in epic theater.

It is essential to realize that Eisenstein's epic plasticity and clarity greatly depend upon the fostering of the spectator's sense of *disjunction* between shots, angles, movements, and, in some cases, light sources. The distended moment, the retarding sequence is experienced as unfolding, as a laying out before one, fold by fold, of a fabric that is the event. Or to put it differently, *momentousness* is the result of an additive, cumulative sequence, the unity of constituents sensed, however obscurely, as discrete.

Kerensky's climb to power, figured in the ascent of an almost never-ending staircase, is dependent for its effect upon our experience of a continuity of action which seems to exceed the limits of the actor's field of physical action, suggesting to us as we view it that the action *is* a trope, called into being by extension, repetition, a splicing which extends its time and space. Kerensky's moment of final access to power, figured in the reception by the lackeys of the Romanoffs and his crossing of the threshold into the Czar's apartments, offers another intensive use of the retard. Seen in medium shot from the back, gloves in hand, then in close-up of his booted feet, Kerensky's hesitation is extended by three shots of the lackeys' faces, a shot of official insignia, of officers standing at attention, two close-ups of them, the head of a bronze peacock, its feet. Then once again, Kerensky seen from the back, gloves in hand, the peacock's head, again, two shots of the bronze mechanical bird's tail in a movement of spread, its head, the spread of tail feathers. Once again we see Kerensky from the back, again with gloves in hand, then the spread of feathers, the officers, the peacock turning, in close-up, followed only now by the doors beginning to open before Kerensky. Once more the bird's tail is seen, the doors open, once more the bird, now seen to have a fettered claw. We see that fettered, padlocked claw again in close-up and Kerensky only now enters the doors which have opened—*without closing*—three separate times in the quick succession of visual stutter.

This sequence is followed by the creation of the people's army—that vast and complex undertaking— figured in the assemblage of a single rifle for use in military drill. The temporal distension and compression are subtended by one's awareness of the shots as discrete and of the manner in which they are articulated within a whole. Eisenstein speaks at one point of the percussive effect of montage as providing a kind of motor impulse that drives the film ahead, proceeding, as Benjamin remarks of Epic theater, through a series of jolts. Thus, in *The General Line*, the celebrated sequence of the cream separator derives its power from Eisenstein's violation of the conventions regulating degree of change in angle for the photographing of still objects, subverting the visual flow and continuity guaranteed by those conventions. In all cases, the disjunctiveness of the filmic event refers one back to its ordering process, so that when one turns from the experience of those events to the texts which serve to generate and explicate them, one discovers with a start of recognition the following statement:

> The juxtaposition of these partial details in a given montage construction calls to life and forces into the light that general quality in which each detail has participated and which binds together all the details into a whole, namely into that generalized image wherein the creator, followed by the spectator experiences the theme.
>
> The strength of montage resides in this, that it includes in the creative process the emotions and mind of the spectator. The spectator is compelled to proceed along the self-same creative road that the author traveled in creating the image. The spectator not only sees the represented elements of the finished work, but also experiences the dynamic process of the emergence and assembly of the image just as it was experienced by the author. And this is, obviously, the highest possible degree of approximation to

transmitting visually the author's perceptions and intention in all their fullness, transmitting them "with that strength of physical palpability" with which they arose before the author in his creative work and his creative vision.[15]

Eisenstein then goes on to suggest the relevance to this consideration of Marx's definition of "the course of genuine investigation":

Not only the result, but the road to it also, is a part of the truth. The investigation of truth must itself be true, true investigation is unfolded truth, the disjunct members of which unite in the result.

III

Eliot once remarked, in a phrase I can neither quote nor locate exactly, that we know more than the artists of the past and that they are precisely what we know. Eisenstein was part of the past Brakhage came to know as a young film maker beginning his work in the early 1950s. That knowledge was, however, mediated by the use of Eisenstein's work made by Brakhage's lonely predecessors, the American Independents of the postwar period, and most particularly by the work and theory of Maya Deren.

Deren worked and argued for a "lyrical" film, positing its "vertical" structure and ultimately its disjunctiveness, as against the "horizontality" or linearity of narrative development. She thereby claimed for film the stylistic polarities which Jakobson, formulating the basic structural attributes of speech through an analysis of its disorders in aphasia, has proposed in the metonymic and metaphoric modes. Deren's work extends the extraordinary intuition with which Cocteau had seized upon the primary Eisensteinian impulse. Inserting within the literally split (spliced) instant of a tower's crash, a poet's odyssey of self-discovery, he had pushed the strategy of disjunction to that point at which its analytic function dissolved. He had, moreover, in the most nakedly autobiographical of films, inverted the direction of Eisensteinian energy, reinstating the Self as subject, multiplying the modes of its appearance—in mask, signature, voice-over, tableaux, autobiographical incident and allusion—substituting that multiplicity of apparitional modes for the disjunction of the given event. He pays homage,

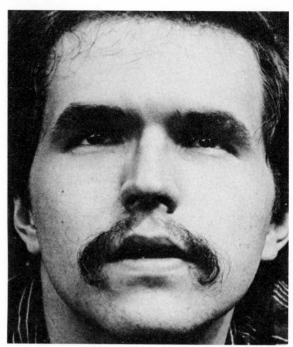

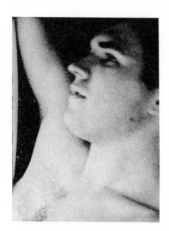

Stan Brakhage in *Window Water Baby Moving*, 1959.

Stan Brakhage.

in his opening address to the spectator, to Uccello, Piero della Francesca, Andre del Castagno, as painters of coats of arms and enigmas, implicitly enjoining us to decipher or read the film as a text. He is, of course, paying homage to the development of perspective in Renaissance painting, and one is therefore not surprised to read, in his Postscript to the published script of *Blood of a Poet*,[16] of his reluctance to "deform" space. Fearing, no doubt, the *Caligarisme* which was his film world's name for its form of a more general, French detestation of expressionism, he confines himself to manipulating the time of action while attempting to respect its spatial integrity. The result is an important film, an engaging hybrid, and a work of particular consequence for young Americans in the '40s and '50s to whom the major works in the Surrealist tradition were still largely unfamiliar.

Deren, arguing for her personal, "vertical," "lyric" film, was to work in a direction which reversed Cocteau's. Rather than splice a moment of time into which she could insert the integrality of a film, she attempted to work with the single moment, distending it into a filmic structure of exquisite ambiguity underwritten by the braver spatial strategies that came perhaps more easily to the developed kinetic sense of one who had been trained as a dancer.

It was left for Stan Brakhage to radicalize this revision of filmic temporality in positing the sense of a continuous present, of a filmic time which devours memory and expectation in the presentation of presentness. To do this one had, of course, to destroy the spatiotemporal coordinates in terms of which past and present events define themselves as *taking place in time*. The assault of Brakhage upon the space of representation then, brings the final dissolution of that spatial integrity which Cocteau, neoclassicist that he was, had been at pains to preserve. And it is, of course, at this point that Brakhage moves into the climate of expressionism, pushing the abstractive process, contracting the depth of the visual field, to the point where he dissolves the spatiality of narrative. In so doing he redefines time as purely that of sight, the time of appearance. He replaces the filmic scene of action by the screen of eidetic imagery, projecting the nature of sight itself as the subject of the cinema. His editing style, at once assertive and fluid, creates that "convergence of a hundred spaces" which Klee had called for and which only a radically redefined temporality could provide. It is in that strict sense Utopian.

Slow motion, the anamorphic lens, the superimposition which contracts space and arrests temporal flow, extreme close-up, change of focus, the out-of-focus shot, the use of leader, the inversion of images, the sensed rhythm of the body in the camera movement, the violent contrast of volumetric and flat areas, the rapid flash-pan, the painting and scratching of the surface, and the affirmation of the grain of film begin to compose an inventory of personal strategies. *Wonder Ring*, a film of the Third Avenue El shot in 1955 for Joseph Cornell, must have served a crucially educative purpose. For the movement of the train itself, the framing of its windows, the reflective surfaces of both windows and doors, the distortions produced by unevenness in those surfaces, all propose a composite inventory of the resources in the camera itself. Dispersed throughout the structure and the trajectory of the elevated railway, they are reassembled, as it were, and the sequence of formal strategies available is discovered as the course of a journey.

It is, however, in *Anticipation of the Night*—still tied, ever so tenuously, to the narrative theme of suicide contemplated—that Brakhage reaches the threshold of his major innovations. This film is, in a way, his *October*. In it his distinctive editing style will emerge. If Eisenstein's cinema of intellection depends upon the unity of the disjunct, sensed *as* disjunct, the cinema of sight will be, from this point on, incomparably fluid. It will be, as well, the cinema of the hypnagogic consciousness aspiring to a rendering of a totally unmediated vision, eluding analytic grasp.

It is suggested by Sartre that the hypnagogic consciousness is the consciousness of "fascination."

> This does not mean, in fact, that consciousness is not fully centered on its object; but not in the manner of attention. . . . What is lacking is precisely a contemplative power of consciousness, a certain way of keeping oneself at a distance from one's images, from one's own thoughts and so to permit them their own logical development, instead of depositing upon them all of one's own weight, of throwing oneself into the balance, of being judge and accused, of using one's own power to make a synthesis of whatever sort with no matter what. A coach appeared before me which was the categorical imperative. Here we see the fascinated consciousness: it produces an image of a carriage in the midst of thinking about Kantian morality.[17]

It is, of course, precisely this fascinated state of consciousness, the depositing upon them of all one's own weight, throwing one's self into the balance which Brakhage introduces as the pivotal principle of his cinema. In so doing he develops a theory of Vision and a cinematic style, both irreducibly, intransigently critical of all conventions—and most immediately those of Renaissance spatial logic, and of perspectival codes. The cinema of the hypnagogic consciousness, of the image, inaccessible to analysis, devours in its constant renewal both memory and expectation, projecting that "continuous present" which Brakhage had sensed as Gertrude Stein's great and particular lesson for him. The agents of its sustained instantaneity are camera movement, light, and the editing process itself. In *Anticipation*, then, Brakhage's shadow hovers over light emerging through door and window, the brilliance of car lights streaks through the black night, a garden is seen as light reflected from its green, a rainbow forms in the water of a garden hose. In the dark of night, the complex play of lights animating an amusement park move, spinning, circling, whirling, in a space of infinite depth and total ambiguity. The camera moves with and against light. An image is reversed, and that movement of reversal flattens, transforms the space of the garden in the image. Pans, shot away from the light, from within the park's ride, send light careening across the screen and into the obscurity of its surface. The camera gains from that obscurity the ability to reverse the reality of its own movement into the illusion of the object's motion, so that a moon and a templelike structure are seen in pans to streak across the screen.

In this film we see as well Brakhage's editing style reach maturity. Its fluidity almost belies its total sovereignty. The cuts are many and quick (Brakhage in his mature work also makes great use of the fade), but—and this is Brakhage's point of dialectical intensity—they are fused by a camera movement sustained over cuts. Disparate images (car lights and a boy in a garden, for example) are united by movement or direction either repeated or sustained through the cut. Disparate spaces are unified in a consistent flattening or obscuring of spatial coordinates and that unity is intensified by the synthetic effect of continuous movement produced in editing.

Brakhage has moved, then, through the climate and space of Abstract Expressionism, severing every tie to that space of action which Eisenstein's montage had transformed into the space of dialectical consciousness. Brakhage posits optical space as the "uncorrupted" dwelling of the Imagination which constitutes it. Dissolving the distance and resolving the disjunction Eisenstein had adopted as the necessary conditions for cinema's cognitive function, he proposes, as the paradigm of contemporary montage style, an alternative to Intellectual Cinema: the Cinema of Vision.

NOTES

1. T.S. Eliot, "Tradition and the Individual Talent," *Selected Essays* (New York: Harcourt Brace and Company, 1932), pp. 4–5.

2. Sergei Eisenstein, "Through Theatre to Cinema," *Film Form: Essays in Film Theory* (New York: Harcourt Brace, 1949), p. 14.

3. Vladimir Tatlin, "On Zangezi," *Catalogue of the Vladimir Tatlin Exhibition*, trans. Troels Anderson and Keith Bradfield (Stockholm: Moderna Museet, 1968), p. 69.

4. *Robert Morris: An Aesthetics of Transgression* (Washington, D.C.: The Corcoran Gallery of Art, 1969), p. 75.

5. Eisenstein, "Through Theatre to Cinema," p. 16.

6. Viktor Shklovsky, *Once Upon a Time, Memoirs and Notes* (Moscow, 1966), p. 447.

7. Reprinted with an editor's note by Jay Leyda in the first direct translation into English from the original Russian text, as Appendix A to his English edition of *Film Form*, pp. 257–260.

8. Hans Jonas, *The Phenomenon of Life, Toward a Philosophical Biology* (New York, 1966), pp. 135–156.

9. Harold Bloom, *The Visionary Company, a Reading of English Romantic Poetry* (Ithaca, New York: Cornell University Press, 1971), p. 30.

10. Quoted by Stan Brakhage in a letter of November 1972 to Hollis Frampton. Source is not given.

11. Eisenstein, *Film Form*, p. 204.

12. Erich Auerbach, *Mimesis, the Representation of Reality in Western Literature*, trans. Willard R. Trask (Princeton, N.J.: Princeton University Press, 1968), p. 4.

13. I am indebted to Phoebe Cohen for a frame count prepared as part of a research project undertaken for a seminar in Soviet Film at New York University's Department of Cinema Studies.

14. Walter Benjamin, *Essais Sur Bertolt Brecht*, trans. Paul Laveau (Paris, 1969), pp. 1–37.

15. Eisenstein, *Film Sense*, trans. and ed. Jay Leyda (New York: Harcourt Brace and Company, 1949), p. 82.

16. Jean Cocteau, *Blood of a Poet* in *Two Screenplays*, trans. Carol Martin-Spreey (New York: Orion Press, 1968).

17. Jean-Paul Sartre, *The Psychology of Imagination*, trans. Bernard Frechtman (New York, 1966), p. 57.

JAMES TENNEY

Brakhage Memoir

S tan was already something of a legend at South High in Denver, where I had arranged to spend my last year of high school, even though I did not live in that district. Because of its reputation as a good school for the performing arts, I had persuaded my mother to let me drive my old Buick halfway across town to get there, and I very quickly fell in with a group of students in the drama club who had known Stan before he graduated the preceding year. He had been the best actor in the club, playing Stage Manager in Thornton Wilder's *Our Town*, among other parts, and was a fine singer and poet. This year, he was away at Dartmouth on a scholarship, though that was not to last very long. A couple of months into the semester, he had what he would later describe as a "nervous breakdown" and returned to Denver and the circle of friends, which now included me. Others whose names I still remember were Bob Benson, Yvonne Fair, Bill Fisher, Larry Jordan, Windy Newcomb, and Stan Phillips.

I think it was at about this time—winter 1951–52 and not before—that Stan's interest in film began to grow. We had formed a kind of film club, once a week or so renting classic films (D. W. Griffith, Eisenstein, Cocteau, et al.), getting together at somebody's house to view and discuss them. And, while Stan's original interest in these films was probably more literary than visual, his desire to make a film developed in this environment. The result was *Interim*, shot during the summer of 1952 in the railroad yards under the viaducts of Denver. In then-typical filmmaking fashion, Stan wrote the screenplay and directed, but did not actually shoot the film; the cinematography was done by Stan Phillips. I was just a piano student, with hardly any experience yet in composition, but for some reason Stan believed that I was destined to become a composer and asked me to compose music for *Interim*. I wrote it for piano solo, and for several months after the film was made, I had to play it "live" whenever it was shown because none of us could afford the cost of recording it on a soundtrack. Incidentally, that belief of his was probably one of the main reasons I did become a composer.

During that last year in high school, I had been awarded a scholarship to the Engineering School of the University of Denver, and I enrolled there in the fall of 1952. I had no intention of becoming an engineer, though I had considered studying architecture, but I thought it was a way to get through some of the general education requirements common to all programs; in any case, I continued to take piano lessons and even private lessons in harmony. Our film club continued to get together frequently, if irregularly, but our activities were now more varied, including poetry readings, plays, museum and gallery exhibitions, and so on, and Stan made another film, *Desistfilm*, involving considerable improvisation by the "actors" (most of us) and in the making of the sound track.

It was around this time that we met Angelo DiBenedetto, an older and established painter living in the mountains in the former gold-mining town of Central City. The following summer (1953), several members of the group decided to form a theatrical troupe, giving plays (Chekhov, Shaw, etc.) in a tent on a lot next to Angelo's huge old stone house/studio, and they rented a house nearby to live in for the summer. Although I visited them frequently, I did not take part in their performances. It was here, during that summer, that Stan's next film, with the ungainly title *Unglassed Windows Cast a Terrible Reflection*, was made. In this case, Stan did the cinematography as well as the writing and directing, and although there is still a strong "literary" or "psychodramatic" aspect to the film, one can clearly see the beginnings of that more purely visual element that would later become the singular focus of his work. Again, he asked me to compose music for it, which I did, but I was more ambitious this time with respect to instrumentation, including flute and strings in addition to piano. My lack of experience and training in orchestration and score and part writing turned out to be fatal, however, because the time available for rehearsal and recording of the music was not enough to surmount all the practical problems in the parts. As a result, Stan finally had to use some other recorded music for the sound track of this film.

It must have been shortly after this that Stan went to San Francisco, where he met the poet, Robert Duncan and his partner, Jess Collins, and the filmmakers, Kenneth Anger and James Broughton and where he made at least two more films, *The Way to Shadow Garden* and *In Between*. By the time he returned to Denver, he was all fired up about being a filmmaker and began thinking about moving to New York City and meeting the great experimental filmmakers then living there: Marie Menken, Willard Maas, and Maya Deren, among others. I had also been planning a move to New York City, having auditioned for and been accepted as a student at the Juilliard School of Music. I do not remember how Stan traveled to New York, but I hitched a ride with some friends who were driving there.

In addition to wanting to meet other filmmakers, there was another project of his that ended up involving me. He had planned to use a recording of *Ionisation* by Edgard Varèse as sound track for *The Way to Shadow Garden* and a portion of John Cage's *Sonatas and Interludes* for *In Between*. Stan arranged a meeting with each composer to ask their permission to use their music and—knowing my interest in the work of both composers—invited me to come along. Interestingly, Varèse had to refuse Stan's request (probably because he did not own the copyright), but Cage said "I'm not interested in that music any more, so you can do what you want with it" (this was 1954, and Cage did not yet have a publisher for his music). Through Stan, I was also privileged to meet Marie Menken, Willard Maas, and Maya Deren, and somewhat later Jonas Mekas and his brother Adolfas, the film critic Parker Tyler, and others involved in the experimental film scene in New York. For a while later that year, Stan and I shared an apartment in Little Italy; it was a terrible single room with no heat. I had rented an upright piano, and sometimes I literally had to practice with gloves on. Later, I moved to a rented (and heated!) room uptown near the school, and soon after that Stan returned to Denver.

Near the end of that year, a lot of things changed in my life: I met Carolee Schneemann, decided to quit Juilliard and take private lessons in composition with Chou Wen-Chung, got a typing job to earn a living, and moved into an apartment with Carolee.

The following summer (1956), Carolee and I drove from New York to Denver and spent a good deal of time with Stan, including the time spent acting in another film of his, *Loving*. Then, we drove again across country to Bennington, Vermont, where I was to earn my tuition to the Bennington Composers' Conference by working as conference copyist. While there, I met a member of the faculty of Bennington College who was a great teacher: a pianist and composer named Lionel Nowak. This led to my becoming a student again, this time at Bennington College (when it was still a women's college).

There had been important changes in Stan's life, too, having met and fallen in love with Jane Collom. Carolee and I had found an apartment in South Shaftsbury, a few miles north of Bennington, and Stan and Jane visited us that year, during which time another film was made, *Cat's Cradle*, which Stan was to describe later as involving a huge amount of psychological and emotional tension, although I do not remember that aspect of it.

The foregoing is much of what I now remember of the early days of my relationship with Stan Brakhage; it stops short of telling the whole story, including, as it would have to if it was to be nearly complete, all the years from about 1957 up to Stan's death in March 2003. Our relationship was always positive, mutually respectful, and loving (in fact, I may be one of the few of Stan's friends who never had a falling out with him—even though we often disagreed on things like politics and religion—and I am proud of that). More important, his were the most powerful personality and most brilliant mind I have ever encountered, and I believe he was one of the greatest artists of the twentieth century, in any medium. In his mature works, and especially in his later painted films, what we see is a visual music the likes of which had never yet been heard.

October 14, 2003

DAVID E. JAMES

Amateurs in the Industry Town

Stan Brakhage and Andy Warhol in Los Angeles

The concept of the amateur has had both a long tradition and substantial theoretical leverage in defining a noncommodity practice of film distinct from the dominant capitalist industrial cinema. The seminal formulation for the postwar period was made by Maya Deren, a Trotskyite youth organizer in the mid-1930s and a student of symbolist poetry and dance in the late 1930s, who found her way to cinema in Hollywood in the early 1940s. There, just before the blacklist destroyed all progressive presence in the industry, she made *Meshes of the Afternoon* (1943), the film that became the inspiration for Kenneth Anger and Curtis Harrington and others in the group of young filmmakers in Los Angeles in the late 1940s and the foundational film for the next two decades of the avant-garde American cinema.

After returning to New York, where she made her other, equally seminal films, she published a brief essay "Amateur Versus Professional," which now appears as the manifesto for this movement. Together with an earlier, somewhat more extended piece, "Planning by Eye: Notes on 'Individual' and 'Industrial' Film," "Amateur Versus Professional" condensed the ideas she had developed in the fifteen years since *Meshes*, the amateur film she made in the center of the Hollywood industry. The two essays celebrate an entirely independent cinema, understanding its autonomy from the industry as the source, not of limitations, but of distinct advantages that facilitate the more complete practice of the art's essence: "The very classification 'amateur' has an apologetic ring. But that very word—from the Latin *amateur*—"lover" means one who does something for the love of the thing rather than for economic reasons or necessity. And this is the meaning from which the amateur filmmaker should take his clue."[1]

Deren's binary "Amateur Versus Professional" framed the vanguard film cultures of the late 1950s and 1960s, but it was hardly original. It had first emerged in the late 1920s, when fears that the technological difficulties attendant on sound, especially on lip sync, would cause formal experimentation to fall prey to the "standardization" of commercial cinema. A brief, but fully cogent, example from 1929, one that symptomatically appeared in a journal otherwise devoted to modernist painting, was C. Adolph Glassgold's essay "The Films: Amateur or Professional?"[2] Opening with the assertion that the "artistic future of the motion picture in America rests in the hands of the amateur," Glassgold proposed a rudimentary form of the correlation between medium specificity and political integrity that in the next decade both Theodor Adorno and Clement Greenberg would emphasize in their theories of the distinction between avant-garde and kitsch. The commercialization of the medium then under way, Glassgold argued, was inseparable from the industry's relinquishing of "all contact with intrinsically cinematic forms." Apart from one or two works from abroad, notably *Ballet mécanique* and *The Passion of Joan of Arc*, he argued, only films by amateurs, who for silent production could anyway be as well equipped as professionals, could be expected to "save the cinema from the standardization and falsification of the commercial product."[3]

In fact, amateur film practices in the 1930s were complex and various. As in Europe, sectors of the formalist avant-garde in the United States became politicized and, organized as the nationwide Workers Film and Photo Leagues, joined the struggles for unionization and against police brutality and fascism. But at the same time, 16 mm equipment marketed for domestic use spurred the growth of the amateur filmmaking clubs that sprang up across the country catering mainly to the wealthier classes. By the late 1930s, approximately 200,000 amateur filmmakers were amalgamated in a national network of some 250 such clubs; most were amalgamated in the Amateur Cinema League (ACL), and its monthly journal, *Movie Makers*, sustained the national network.[4]

While unsophisticated home movies continued to be made, these clubs in various ways were colonized by Hollywood, and amateurs in them typically aspired to reproduce the industry's styles and values. Many of them undertook ambitious documentary and narrative projects in which Hollywood's expressive conventions and its overall technical accomplishments were artisinally simulated. The close adjoinment at this time of amateur and professional practices is vividly illustrated by the circulation of ideas about the most signal instance of experimentalism in the industry, Gregg Toland's contributions to *Citizen Kane*.[5] Toland himself wrote two versions of essentially the same article, one, "Realism for *Citizen Kane*," in the professional journal *American Cinematographer* and the other, "How I Broke the Rules in *Citizen Kane*" for the amateur magazine *Popular Photography*. In both, he summarized the difference between the soft-focus, narrow depth of field, industry norm of the time and *Kane*'s pan focus and candidly recounted his photographic innovations, such as shooting directly into lights, and the devices he had used: wide-angle, stopped-down lenses; the Opticoating system that minimized loss of light through refraction; increased set illumination; ceilinged sets; and so on. But before the first of these articles appeared, and in fact three months before the film's release date, much of the same information had already appeared in the ACL's own journal, *Movie Makers*, in another essay (not by Toland), "*Citizen Kane*'s New Technique."

More than a dozen of these clubs flourished in Los Angeles in the 1930s, and there were perhaps several thousand nonprofessionals in the area who were seriously committed to filmmaking that approached professional standards in its technical and aesthetic accomplishment; this represents a more substantial noncommercial use of the medium than at any other time, including the 1960s, and the neglect and probable destruction of these films is a great cultural loss. This interface between amateur and industrial production was the context in which Deren began to work when she came to Los Angeles, and she continued to have close relations with this world. Her first film, *Meshes*, was an amateur essay in an experimental industrial tradition that had crested in *Citizen Kane*. She entered it in the 1945 ACL competition, and it won an Honorable Mention. Next year, *Movie Makers* made a point of noting their regret that she had not entered her *Ritual in Transfigured Time* in that year's Ten Best competition and carried a report on the "SRO night" at the February 1946 screening of her first three films in Greenwich Village.[6] In return, even though the concept of the amateur she developed was oriented away from rather than toward Hollywood, Deren published several essays in *Movie Makers* and one in *Popular Photography* that elaborated her own shooting style and especially editing methods that categorically contradicted industry principles.[7]

So, although amateur filmmaking had a number of well-established, fully self-conscious traditions by the 1950s, it was the nexus of conflicting impulses, in some ways opposed to the film industry but in others inhabited by or collusive with it. The American underground film flowered in the field of these contradictory possibilities, and the careers of Stan Brakhage and Andy Warhol are the prototypical instances of the two opposite routes taken by the avant-garde in the 1960s.

Following Deren's lead in his practice and often invoking her etymology in his lectures and writings, Brakhage rejected the languages of the Hollywood film and the capitalist mode of film production. He committed his life's work to the ideal of an amateur avant-garde cinema that in several respects resembled home movies, and in the late 1960s he wrote an essay, "In Defense of Amateur," arguing that "An amateur works according to his own necessity . . . and if he takes pictures, he photographs what he loves or needs in some-such sense—surely a more real, and thus more honorable, activity than work which is performed for some gain."[8] The fundamental dichotomy—"according to his own necessity" against "performed for some [surely, financial] gain"—reproduces Deren's priorities and summarizes the terms of his attempt to make a cinema responsive to the existential urgency and authenticity of an individual life.

Like much fine art of the 1960s, Warhol's also was imbricated in his own and his associates' attempts to erase the boundary between art and life, and many of his significant innovations in painting had their origins in occasional jeux d'esprit, often drawings made for immediate psychosexual pleasure rather than for money. But overall the concatenation of achievements that made him the exemplary artist of the last quarter of the twentieth century involved erasing a contrary set of boundaries, those between fine and commercial art, and the apogee of his accomplishment was to incorporate the practices of business pure and simple in and as his art. Not only did Warhol paint advertisements, but also he made and himself appeared in many ventures that have yet to be fully incorporated into critical accounts of his oeuvre.[9] His most audacious transgression, then, entailed his imitation of the prostitute in Walter Benjamin's figure; he became seller and commodity in one.[10] But before that consummation, when the potential and credibility of an amateur avant-garde countercinema were historically at their greatest, Warhol redirected it toward Hollywood, with which he was thoroughly preoccupied. He began as an amateur filmmaker but quickly rejected its implications and turned to the commodity cinema. After directing a series of remarkable films critically interrogating the mass media, he became a producer of feature films and eventually merchandised his celebrity as a brand name for productions conceived and directed by other people.

At the beginning of their filmmaking careers, both Brakhage and Warhol came to Los Angeles and made films there. Because Los Angeles is so uniquely identified with Hollywood, film representations of the city, especially amateur films made by visitors, are commonly inflected by the filmmaker's attitude to the industry. Hollywood's power over the Los Angeles avant-garde was especially great and in many ways productive during the 1960s, when the city also appeared to be an incarnation of the spirit of Pop Art itself. In the films they made in Los Angeles, both Brakhage and Warhol radically reconfigured the complex traditions of the amateur to define their own positions in relation to the industry. Though the films both made in the city are concerned with the difficulties of heterosexual romance—that is, with the staple of the Hollywood cinema—in all other respects they are very different and are so in ways that reflect their respective orientations to the industry and the different alternatives to it they planned. Their respective visions of Los Angeles followed suit: Hollywood supplied them different optics through which they saw the city, and so their works appear as spatial figurations of the specific forms of filmmaking they each developed.

In fall 1956, the twenty-three-year-old Brakhage returned to Los Angeles— he had lived briefly in the city in the summer of 1955—this time hoping to work with Charles Laughton, then slated to direct *The Naked and the Dead*.[11] By the time he arrived, Laughton had been replaced on that project, but Brakhage did obtain an interview with the president of MCA and was offered a salaried position to train under Hitchcock as a director for the *Alfred Hitchcock Presents* television series. Two incidents aborted this apprenticeship and conclusively turned Brakhage from the industry to the amateur cinema: First, he was asked to demonstrate his competence by making a short film with lip-sync sound; second, when the MCA executive casually averred that Hitchcock was the world's greatest director, Brakhage did not protest. Despite his commitment to silent film, he had been prepared to complete the lip-sync assignment, but his failure to disagree with the executive and to nominate Eisenstein in

Stan Brakhage, *Flesh of Morning.*

place of Hitchcock so distressed him that he did not follow up on the interview. Instead, he took odd jobs with commercial filmmaking houses, where he perfected his technical skills to satisfy himself that the idiosyncrasies of his personal films could not be attributed to incompetence.

In return for room and board, he worked as a projectionist and janitor for Raymond Rohauer at the Coronet, the city's leading art theatre, and as a sometime lecturer for programs of experimental films there, including one of his own. He met other avant-garde filmmakers who were exploring different forms of practical or imaginary engagements with the industry and its myths: Sidney Peterson, then working for Disney; Kenneth Anger, who was pre-occupied with the sexual implications of the mythology of Hollywood; and Curtis Harrington, who was himself about to make what he recognized as the "dangerous compromise" of moving from the avant-garde to the industry, in his case to a position as an executive assistant to Jerry Wald at 20th Century Fox.[12] Living in Watts, Brakhage made two films that fall. The first, *Flesh of Morning*, which filmmaker George Landow soon recognized as "a home movie in the pure sense,"[13] was the last of the black-and-white trance films in

Stan Brakhage, *Nightcats.*

which he dramatized his own sexual anxieties, and the second, *Nightcats*, a color study of neighborhood cats, explored the textures of their fur and the play of light over their bodies as they moved. He then left Los Angeles, returning to Denver, where the next summer he shot *Anticipation of the Night*, the film in which he abandoned the objective framing of the protagonist of his early psychodramas and committed himself to the intricate splendors of subjective vision and the rejection of Hollywood grammar that mark his mature and signal achievement.

Warhol's encounter with Hollywood also took place just as his film aesthetic was crystallizing, but the Los Angeles he found was very different from that of Brakhage. In 1963, at the height of his success as a Pop Art painter, he had bought a 16 mm camera and photographed Jack Smith in the process of shooting his *Normal Love* and several hours of the poet John Giorno sleeping. Before the latter footage was developed, he drove cross country to Los Angeles, where Irving Blum had promised him a second show for his "Jackie" and "Elvis" paintings. Accompanying him was Taylor Mead, who in 1960 had become involved in beat filmmaking in Venice[14] and who had already been featured in two important underground films directed by Ron Rice, *The Flower Thief* and *The Queen of Sheba Meets the Atom Man*, as well as in Adolfas Mekas's *Hallelujah the Hills*, works that were bringing the New American Cinema to public attention. Mead seemed more likely than any other actor to make the corresponding move from underground to mainstream stardom and so was a promising vehicle for Warhol's own bid to become an aboveground filmmaker.

When Warhol arrived in Los Angeles, Dennis Hopper's wife, actress Brooke Hayward, arranged a suite for him at the Beverly Hills Hotel, and on

Andy Warhol, *Tarzan and Jane, Regained Sort Of.*

their first night in Hollywood, the Hoppers threw a movie star party at their home in Topanga Canyon, with guests including Peter Fonda, Dean Stockwell, Russ Tamblyn, Troy Donahue, and Suzanne Pleshette. Warhol remembered it as the most exciting thing that had ever happened to him and regretted only that he had left his new Bolex at the hotel. It may well have been the last time in his life he made such a mistake, and a few days later he was resolutely filming from an improvised script. Naomi Levine, an habitué of the New York underground and herself a filmmaker and actress, was also in Los Angeles; she sought Warhol out and was recruited to play Jane to Mead's Tarzan in Warhol's first attempt at a narrative film, *Tarzan and Jane, Regained Sort Of.*

As the echoes in its title suggests, *Flesh of Morning* was one of the several essays in the mode of Deren's *Meshes of the Afternoon* that were made in Los Angeles in the period. Photographed by Brakhage himself as well as being the first film in which he played his own protagonist, it also resembled Kenneth Anger's *Fireworks* and Curtis Harrington's *Fragment of Seeking* in featuring a sexually traumatized youth who encounters the images of his desires in an environment onto which he projects his torment. Objective shots of Brakhage himself taken with a fixed camera so that he moves through its field alternate with subjective, mostly hand-held shots of this protagonist's perceptions that register his physical and mental disturbance. A crumpled note with an illegible message that magically flowers open begins the film, introducing him in the kitchen of a working-class apartment. Agitated by the letter, he restlessly scrutinizes the kitchen, encountering images of his distraught self in reflections in a toaster or furtively glimpsed in mirrors and similar surfaces in fugitive corners of the room. An abrasive sound track of snatches of music played backward parallels his anxiety, as do the progressively more abstract shots of kitchen fixtures that become correlatives of his psychic crisis: A kettle boils, and the kitchen sink overflows. Abstracted through high-contrast lighting, irregular exposure, loss of focus, or unnatural angles, the objects around him acquire an ominous charge. To escape them, he goes onto the apartment's veranda, but the blinding sun makes the shabby clapboard buildings and local stores almost invisible; all that can be clearly seen in the harsh light is his own shadow on the ground which, because of the angle of his arm, the shadow seems to be sporting a giant erection.

After he returns inside, the dominant overexposure of the first movement is replaced by darker, more saturated tones. He finds a woman's stockings and underclothes and then her picture, and then she herself appears, alternately mocking and enticing in the shadows. As she takes off her coat, gloves, and stockings, he also undresses and gets into bed. The close-up photography of the early scrutiny of the kitchen recurs but now its object is Brakhage himself. Made abstract by the lighting and camera angles, then switching into negative, and intercut with images of the woman, the film becomes a surreal geography of his body that he punishes as he masturbates, struggling "to identify her image with his own flesh."[15] After his orgasm, the film cuts to shots of children playing on the street outside, then returns to end on his exhausted face as he mouths incomprehensible words to the camera.

The second film, *Nightcats*, an eight-minute short, has no human protagonist but instead continues the exploration of first-person vision that Brakhage had begun the previous year in his first nondramatic film, *The Wonder Ring*, a study of the Third Avenue El in New York commissioned by Joseph Cornell. Though the organic forms of cats roaming among the shrubbery of a backyard garden partially illuminated by bright electric lights replaces the earlier film's investigation of manufactured objects, it, too, is concerned primarily with the play of light and motion. It begins with the gleaming eyes of a black cat staring directly into the camera out of the darkness. Short shots with a gestural, handheld camera reveal other parts of the animal's body, some of them in tight close-up, and then a second, tawny, cat is introduced. The film cuts irregularly back and forth between these two, emphasizing the texture and movement of their fur as the cats stalk each other and eventually come together in the same frame, striking out at each other with their claws. A third, gray, cat turns this hostile dance into a triple parallel montage that flares up into an extended fight between the gray and the tawny, when a sequence of very short shots brings the film to the edge of abstraction. As the tension dissipates, the entrance of a fourth cat provides a concluding coda.

Between the two films occurred the fundamental break in Brakhage's early work, the final rejection of more or less realistic dramatic narratives in favor of the expanded, often abstract, expressivity of first-person vision and montage structure. First fully articulated the next year in *Anticipation of the Night*, this break inaugurated his mature work, one of the most profoundly original personal oeuvres in the history of cinema that also stands as one of the most categorical critiques of the industrial cinema. Some forty years later, he recognized *Nightcats'* importance, referring to it as "certainly the 'turning-point' in my work, which makes the later seminal *Anticipation of the Night* possible."[16]

Warhol's film *Tarzan and Jane, Regained Sort Of* is an extremely rudimentary work, much of it technically incompetent and entirely lacking the sophisticated photography and editing of Brakhage's films. A hybrid home movie, it records Warhol's visit to the then-emerging Los Angeles art world (including attendance at Duchamp's important retrospective at the Pasadena museum and a gallery opening for Claes Oldenburg), a film portrait of Mead, and an amateur reenactment of a Hollywood film genre. This last mode was already common in the underground, associated especially with Jack Smith, whose *Flaming Creatures* Warhol had seen. Smith's transvestite re-creation of the Arabian fantasy world of Maria Montez was itself only a highly idiosyncratic version of the burlesques of Hollywood films that had been a staple of amateur filmmaking since the 1930s, and when living in Los Angeles in the early 1950s, Smith had in fact made his initial sketches in this mode in *Buzzards Over Bagdad*, a domestic remake of a scene from Universal's *Arabian Nights*.[17] Warhol had better celebrity access than Smith, and *Tarzan* takes place in Hollywood itself, with its supporting players including up-and-coming actors and artists. Their fabrication of engaging personae that secure screen presence inevitably modulates into their citation of roles from the commercial cinema, also introducing the themes of exhibitionism and the mass media construction of personal identity that are the concern of Warhol's mature cinema.

Mead, then, is a *sort-of* Tarzan, the Lord of the Apes who, according to a voice-over, has returned to the jungle "to save the heart of civilization from the forces of evil." Periodically beating his chest, he plays on workout equipment at Venice beach, swims in the pool at the Beverly Hills Hotel, and watches as Jane romps naked in the water in an ersatz Esther Williams interlude. A long intimate scene with Jane in the bath follows, reducing his costume to the tiniest bikini, which is all he wears for the rest of the film. Various junkets over the next few days take Tarzan and Jane to a wealthy heir living in a trailer in the Santa Monica Mountains, to the carousel on Santa Monica pier, and to the Watts Towers, where Jane has been captured and tied up by the natives. After a breakfast of fresh fruit in Wallace Berman's garden, Tarzan visits Dennis Hopper. When he refuses to follow the script that calls for him to climb a palm tree, the supermacho Hopper does it for him, while Warhol, making an unusual Hitchcockian cameo appearance as the film's director, lashes his recalcitrant star on his bare buttocks. Another visit, this one to Claes Oldenburg, leads to a series of mock-epic conflicts: first, a fight in which Tarzan vanquishes the acrimonious sculptor, then he struggles with a malevolent garden hose, a fierce tortoise, and finally a domestic poodle that chases him round the lawn. Scarcely has he triumphed over these than he spies a broken plastic doll in distress in the Venice canals, so he dives in to rescue her and saves her life with artificial respiration. The climax to his adventures comes when Jane is captured by Berman and another white headhunter in the jungles of Berman's home in Beverly Glenn. Again, Tarzan comes to the rescue and, after a fight, takes Jane off to the A&W for a victory feast.

Though Warhol adopted Jack Smith's basic premise, his antiaesthetic, and something of his temporal attenuation, he modified their overall tenor. Whereas Smith elaborated peripheral poses and gestures from prized films into concertos of bizarre lugubriousness, Warhol's irony is at once lighter and more sadistic. Both filmmakers were centrally concerned with sexual ambiguity, but whereas Smith was interested mainly in transvestitism, here Warhol cavorts with male effeminacy. If Brakhage's shadowy erection summarizes the assertive but traumatized heterosexuality of his masturbatory fantasy, Warhol whipping Mead's naughty ass is the equivalent image of sissified masculinity. Mead's musculature and his sexual response to Jane are equally undeveloped, and he becomes comic as his mincing puniness parodies Tarzanic virility. Jane's pleasure in making a spectacle of her breasts is exuberant, but Mead bares his buttocks like a furtive, yet compulsive, child. And so the movie's first—and overall very positive—review argued that his responses to her "demonstrate and somehow sanctify the essence of faggotry."[18] The hero's pathetic inadequacies also infect the narrative and the location: Instead of swinging through the jungle, Tarzan plays on a "jungle gym" on the beach; kittens and puppies replace lions and tigers; the hotel pool stands in for the jungle lagoon; the generic fight with the crocodile becomes the desultory encounter with the tortoise; the white slavers' menace is gestural at best; and so on. The editing and sound track, done back in New York by Mead, complete the generic deflation. The miscellaneous pop songs and unconnected fragments of a medical lecture on the biology of reproduction he added are interspersed with his own disparaging, distancing comments on the film's weaknesses; the bathtub scene is, he correctly observes on the sound track, endless; and midway through the final jungle scene, he remarks that the film should have ended there.

The disparity between the film and its genre and indeed all standards of professional accomplishment frames Warhol's meditation on the historical meaning of Hollywood. He shows no signs here of Jack Smith's belief that genuine expressivity and presence could be glimpsed in the spaces between bad actors and their roles (though this would be a concern in later films), and his nostalgia has no regret for lost aesthetic quality. Rather, Hollywood's vacuousness is celebrated as a liberation, a refuge from the demands of real personal relations. "The Hollywood we were driving to that fall of '63 was in limbo," he later recalled, "The Old Hollywood was finished and the New Hollywood hadn't started yet.... But this made Hollywood *more* exciting to me, the idea that it was so vacant. Vacant, vacuous Hollywood was everything I ever wanted to mold my life into. Plastic. White-on-white. I wanted to live my life at the level of the script of *The Carpetbaggers*."[19]

Los Angeles-as-Hollywood has a long history as the figure for this desire, with the vacuity of the film business that Warhol celebrated permeating the city itself, and in fact Warhol's personal disposition allowed him to live and articulate the generalized social alienation with real trenchancy. But at the same time, his representation of Los Angeles is original and distinctive. His hero's encounters may exploit the bathos of their disparity in comparison with the world depicted in Hollywood films, but their relation to the city itself is more oblique. Los Angeles is, it is true, experienced via the movies; its topography turns out to be a repository of generic motifs, and they are the legend by which it may be decoded and negotiated. But these are not essentially *urban*, as they would have been if Warhol had read the city in terms of film noir; rather they are *natural*, for his Los Angeles is cast as a literal, not a metaphoric, jungle.

The transition between geography and the movies is supplied by the city of Tarzana, renamed in 1927 in honor of Tarzan and his creator, Edgar Rice Burroughs. The film opens, as do so many films about Los Angeles, with shots of the freeway taken from inside a moving car, which in this case lead to the Tarzana exit in the San Fernando Valley, where Mead is found reclining under the freeway overpass. But after this, the freeways and other common motifs of urban Los Angeles give way to environments that, however deprecatingly, figure a natural wilderness—which is what the city must have seemed like to Warhol, who had previously known only Pittsburgh and New York.

Brakhage, on the other hand, found Los Angeles to be another of the urban sexual purgatories his alter ego would wander through until he married and moved to the actual wilderness in Colorado a couple of years later, where the subjective vision of the external world for the first time became central to his work. For him, space in Los Angeles is bifurcated into an interior domestic world of masturbatory torment and a harsh alienating world outside that offers no escape. To be sure, South Central is glimpsed, and *Flesh of Morning* is one of the few depictions of it until Charles Burnett's *Killer of Sheep* and other independent black films of the 1970s (in Warhol's visit to this part of the city, the Watts Towers are disconnected from their urban context, and the black children there are made over as denizens of Tarzan's jungle). But, the seedy apartment buildings and the blinding light drive the protagonist back inside to the waiting femme fatale—herself, like Maya Deren's alter egos and Curtis Harrington's temptress in *Fragment of Seeking*, inherited from film noir. Looked at differently, the most mundane elements of that outside world—cats on a backyard fence—also offered him an adventure in perceptual richness in which the psychosexual tensions of the observed could be manifested in purely sensual, nonnarrative terms.

As amateur filmmakers, then, both Brakhage and Warhol dramatized their personal narratives by assembling images of Los Angeles, and though quite different from each other, they were nevertheless both mediated by

Hollywood and by other cultural practices. The noir references that inform *Flesh of Morning*'s structure and iconography had previously been processed in Los Angeles avant-garde trance films. Though Warhol developed his structural motifs directly from mass culture genres, the touristic excitement provided by the detritus of Hollywood was intertwined with the parallel pleasures of the Los Angeles art world, which at that time intersected more thoroughly with the industry than ever before; Dennis Hopper, his friend and the only one of the new movie generation with anything like his cultural sophistication, was the denominator common to both milieus. Brakhage's use for noir vocabulary was almost spent, soon to be abandoned along with Hitchcockian menace and Hollywood's narrative modes. For him, the industry's threat was reciprocated in the city's threat, and the combination of the two drove him into a painful personal psychodrama that he expressed by making an avant-garde amateur version of a Hollywood film. But, it also drove him out of that mode to the entirely personal cinema that, in the next years in Colorado, like an Eisenstein in the wilderness, he developed into the most ecstatic alternative to industrial narrative film style.

Warhol's engagement with Hollywood, already consummated in the paintings of Elvis as a film star that brought him to Los Angeles, would continue throughout his career, and negotiations with the industry would occupy him for the remainder of the decade. For him, Hollywood was a fantasy that Los Angeles ubiquitously incarnated, and in his amateur film he found both place and industry the matrix from which he would construct his own career in cinema across the interface between art and capital. His attempt to make Hollywood films would always contain some edge of critical reservation of the kind indicted here in the parenthetic, "Regained Sort Of." After he noticed that, in films like *Midnight Cowboy*, "people with money were taking the subject matter of the underground, counterculture life and giving it a good, slick, commercial treatment,"[20] that reservation became narrow enough for him to return to Los Angeles six years later in the surrogate form of the producer's credit on *Flesh* (1969), Paul Morrissey's remake of *Sunset Boulevard*. *Flesh* was also a remake of *Tarzan and Jane*, with Joe Dallesandro replacing Mead as the gay icon on the prowl in Hollywood. Some years later, looking back on this period in his book of poems, *Son of Andy Warhol*, Mead claimed, "I want to represent / The End of Show- / Business,"[21] and his performance here gives credence to his claim. But, Warhol wanted rather to renew the business, albeit on his own terms, and to make a place for himself in it. Jonas Mekas recognized *Tarzan and Jane* as a step in exactly that direction:

> I see new developments in the so-called underground cinema that is joining directly with the other, Hollywood cinema. A new entertainment cinema is developing. Andy Warhol's *Tarzan and Jane, Regained Sort Of* is one example. Uneven, sometimes good, sometimes bad, it is as good an entertainment as any half-successful Hollywood movie.[22]

During the next decade, underground film circled between the options instanced by Brakhage and Warhol, between rejecting Hollywood categorically and attempting to join with it. Brakhage periodically returned to Los Angeles, including one occasion in 1963 when, along with Kenneth Anger and Gregory Markopoulos, he judged the First Los Angeles Film Festival. In his overview history of the art of film, poet John Fles, the single most important promoter of underground film in the city who had sponsored the festival, claimed that "With Brakhage, then, we have reached the beginning of the birth of the new Masters,"[23] and his work remained the cynosure for experimental filmmakers. Later in the decade, the combination of the vibrancy of the city's underground film scene and the industry's desire to tap the youth cultures opened the way for many of the negotiations between the avant-garde and the industry to which Warhol aspired. But, when this happened, in films such as *The Trip* (Roger Corman, 1967) or *Head* (Bob Rafelson, 1969), the film styles used in industry films to figure the visual experience of hallucinogenic drugs and other forms of expanded cinema were those of Brakhage.

NOTES

1. The text of "Amateur Versus Professional" followed here, reproduced from the original carbon copy of the manuscript, was published in *Film Culture* 39 (Winter 1965), 45–46, some six years after it was written. "Planning by Eye," which appears to date from the mid-1950s, was first published in the same issue of *Film Culture*, 33–38. As detailed below, its use of the term *amateur* in film criticism is part of a tradition dating back to the late 1920s. By the mid-1960s, the amateur/lover etymology had developed wide currency in the American avant-garde; Jonas Mekas, for example, invoked it in his own formulation of amateur filmmaking in 1964, referring to it as "the Cocteau-Markopoulos-Tyler-Brakhage meaning." See Mekas, *Movie Journal: The Rise of the New American Cinema, 1959–1971* (New York: Collier Books, 1972), 134.

2. C. Adolph Glassgold, "The Films: Amateur or Professional?" *The Arts*, 15, 1 (January 1929), 56–59.

3. Glassgold, 56–57.

4. For a synoptic history of amateur filmmaking, see Patricia R. Zimmermann, *Reel Families: A Social History of Amateur Film* (Bloomington: Indiana University Press, 1995), 29. See also Alan D. Kattelle, *Home Movies: A History of the American Industry, 1897–1979* (Nashua, NH: Transition Publishing, 2000). Zimmermann distinguished four main phases in the history of amateur filmmaking: (1) 1897–1923, when amateur equipment was used by small numbers of technically minded hobbyists; (2) 1923–40, when the proliferation of 16 mm equipment made possible a popular practice that "was not distinct from or in opposition to professional film . . . [but] its accomplice in the dissemination of professional technical ideologies to consumers" (p. 57); (3) 1941–49, when "amateur-film technology and raw stock were framed within the discourse of patriotism, nationalism, and support for the war effort" (p. 90); and (4) 1950–62, when the postwar leisure market domesticated amateur film, transforming it into home movies, the "private production of and by the nuclear family," but which nevertheless privileged "a slavish conformity to Hollywood narrative visual logic" (p. 122). Her summary conclusion on this history is that, though amateur filmmaking did "in a very minimal way, democratize media production," overall "technical standards, aesthetic norms, socialization pressures, and political goals derailed its cultural construction into a privatized, almost silly, hobby" monitored and controlled by Hollywood and corporate interests (p. 157). Although Zimmermann's analysis is certainly judicious, she perhaps underestimated cases in which amateurs succeeded in developing real—if minor—alternatives to the industry.

5. The essays referred to below are Gregg Toland, "Realism for *Citizen Kane*," *American Cinematographer* (February 1941), 54–55, 80; Gregg Toland, "How I Broke the Rules in *Citizen Kane*," *Popular Photography* 8, 6 (8 June 1941), 55, 90–91; George Blaisdell, "*Citizen Kane*'s New Technique," *Movie Makers*, 16, 3 (May 1941), 120–21, 127; and John Mescall, "'Pan-Focus' for Your Home Movies," *American Cinematographer*, 22, 12 (December 1941), 576, 593.

6. *Movie Makers* 21, 12 (December 1946), 456. The same journal had previously carried a report on the Provincetown Playhouse screening, noting that her success had made her think that "there may be some hope for this sort of film work after all"; *Movie Makers*, 21, 4 (April 1946), 138.

7. See "Efficient or Effective," *Movie Makers*, 20, 6 (June), 210–11; "Creative Cutting," *Movie Makers*, 22, 5 (May 1947), 190–91, 204–6; and "Creative Cutting," *Movie Makers*, 22, 6 (June 1947), 242–43; and "Creating Movies With a New Dimension—Time," *Popular Photography* (December 1946), 130–40.

8. Stan Brakhage, "In Defense of Amateur" (ca. 1967), *Essential Brakhage: Selected Writings on Film-Making by Stan Brakhage*, ed. R. Bruce McPherson (Kingston, NY: McPherson and Company, 2001), 144; first published in *Filmmakers Newsletter*, 4 (Summer 1971), 9–10.

9. See "The Unsecret Life: A Warhol Advertisement," in David E. James, *Power Misses: Essays Across (Un)Popular Culture* (London: Verso Books, 1996), 153–171.

10. *Charles Baudelaire: A Lyric Poet in the Era of High Capitalism* (London: New Left Books, 1973), 171.

11. Gerald R. Barrett and Wendy Brabner, *Stan Brakhage: A Guide to References and Resources* (Boston: G. K. Hall, 1983), 14–15. Subsequent details from a personal interview with Brakhage in Boulder, Colorado, 5 February 1997.

12. In this respect, Harrington was following in the footsteps of his mentor, Josef von Sternberg; see his essay on von Sternberg, "The Dangerous Compromise," *Hollywood Quarterly*, 3, 4 (1949), 405–15.

13. George Landow, "Flesh of Morning," *Filmwise*, 1 (1962), 20.

14. For details on Mead's earliest acting in Los Angeles, see his "Acting: 1958–65," in *The American New Wave, 1958–1967* (Buffalo, NY: Walker Art Center, 1982), 13–17.

15. From Brakhage's own description of the film in a letter to Parker Tyler the year after it was made, cited in Barrett and Brabner, *Stan Brakhage*, 47.

16. *Telling Time: Essays of a Visionary Filmmaker* (Kingston, NY: Documentext, 2003), 84.

17. Smith never completed *Buzzards Over Bagdad*, but the footage from it he included in *Respectable Creatures* reveals that it was bona fide imitation, much closer to the original Montez films than his later transvestite burlesques and so very much in the vein of prewar amateur mimicking of industry styles.

18. James Stoller, "Tarzan and Jane Regained—Sort Of," *Moviegoer*, 2 (Summer 1964), 67.

19. *Popism: The Warhol 60s* (New York: Harcourt Brace Jovanovich, 1975), 40.

20. *Popism*, 280.

21. *Son of Andy Warhol* (Madras: Hanuman Books, 1986), 28.

22. *Village Voice*, 20 (February 1964), reprinted Jonas Mekas, *Movie Journal*, 121.

23. *Seeing Is Believing*, self-published pamphlet (Hollywood, 1964), 12.

CAROLEE SCHNEEMANN

It Is Painting

17 March 2003

How to type fast enough—waking dread, waking the dead (but the darling
kitten Minos poised by my cheek, his paw in my hand)—in advance of
all that will be destroyed, a five-thousand-year-old city, a cradle of
civilization, Mesopotamia, Bashra, Kirkut, monuments of the Goddess
withstanding thousands of tyrants, patriarchal tribes, the inversion of
sacral erotic worship. And cluster bombs? And smart bombs? And depleted
Uranium?

And so driving on the way to Bard—an intimate memorial for you—quiet
country roads, overtaken by sirens, police cars . . . River Road where
inexplicably sirens follow police car lights whirling in this first spring
afternoon to round the bend between the alley of black locusts, demarcations
of the Hudson River estates. There blocking the road, upside down, is a
huge shiny, red truck—was it a truck?—and police cars—upside down, it
covered the road symmetrically. Childishly one looked for little people who
had fallen out upside down . . . dead or alive?

Turning away to enter Bard past the decaying dormitory house,
where summer MFA faculty are given rooms redolent of mown grass,
mildewed carpets, rusted window screens. . . . Rushing down the familiar
steps into Preston film studies, originally the dining hall! "I used to work
here," I told Quasha . . . the raked little theatre is built over the dining
hall: The kitchen was over there, the huge steel sink where I scrubbed—yes,
we washed all the dishes by hand with bars of soap in steaming water—
and served the food on large round metal trays; the guys stealing lamb
chops from the girls.

Peter Hutton introduced our local group: Robert Kelly, John Pruitt, Joan
Retallack, Russell Richardson, Jennifer Reeves, Adolfas Mekas—vehement,
explosive "he was a difficult man! he was a difficult man! . . . but we are not
here to bury the man, it is the work, not the life." I would read from Phil
Solomon's e-mail that had arrived just a few hours before. Peter's Brakhage
film selection included two hand-painted films and a great surprise. So many
years since seeing *Desistfilm*, I'm astounded, stricken! Jim Tenney bursts
through the 1954 b&w film frame, raw, still adolescent, disgusting, a grinning
kid face—unimaginable that I would later adore him! And always for Stan
from this earliest film, the gesture of lived life, life of the thing the life the light
of the being its essence and to trust what is to reveal itself. Larry Jordan and
Windy Newcomb and Jim—the Colorado Kids (and the long-haired girl
unraveling the spool of twine, surrogate pre-visioned, that archetype would
soon shift my own life framing), even while I might have been scraping
grease from the Bard ghost dinner plates; rushing back to the paint tubes spread
on my window sill in the Albee dorm—alizarin, viridian, cadmium yellow,
thalo blue. In Denver, Stan films his restless crew of locked-in boy-men
in-desire, in-desist smoke-filled room tremulous trust of energy, dramatic and
suppressed, risk of motions, a mythological merge—the embedded narrative
is never not part of some deeply connected optical dance, flares to light.

Miraculous in the welter of worlds unknown unknowing, that I meet
my bedrock collaborator lover friend adventurer Jim Tenney in NYC. We
met on the stairs of the concert hall. He said, "I am a music student from
Colorado at Julliard. I treat sound as space." I said, "I am a painting student
from Pennsylvania, I treat space as time!" His closest friend, a poet,
filmmaker takes the Greyhound bus East. The night Stan arrived in NYC, we

converge at a Forty-Second Street dive, near the glittering movie houses he so loved, sharing a bowl of spaghetti. We dazzle, shine for each other. Stan believed you structured your art by going directly to meet the relevant, inspiring older artists and to live in their space! We followed you into the lives and work of Maya Deren, Joseph Cornell, Willard Maas, New York poets, and writers Parker Tyler, Edwin Denby, the Living Theater. Jim would bring us to meet older composers and a vortex of young musicians. His Tone Roads group, Phil Corner, Malcolm Goldstein (and also Terry Riley, Steve Reich, Phil Glass, LaMonte Young).

Willard Maas and Maria Menken offer us first realms of extended film experiment and sexual experiment! Willard asks you to join the enthusiastic guys up in the penthouse for Saturday's daisy chain. We ponder the ejaculatory of this phallic event. Marie is commanded to prepare whiskey, tea, coffee & snacks and sets a nice table for the re-emergence of the men. We met Warhol at Willard's—pale, rosy-faced, unspeaking—another kid. Jim and I introduce you to Robert Kelly, to Clayton Eshleman, Paul Blackburn, to David Antin & Jerome Rothenberg and New York-based poets to join the West Coast influences. Tenney brings us to John Cage, Chou Wen-Chung, Partch, Ruggles to Varèse (where he graciously employed me to sort the Varèse historic mess of clippings). And you lived at Maya Deren's—as a demanding, admiring acolyte expecting that she feed us— desperate as she was for funds for rent, for the lab to print her Haiti footage. She screened that original footage in her Morton Street studio while we smoked her cigarettes and drank her beers. Stan was offended, Jim and I puzzled by her lover, Teiji Ito, our age! A musician . . . how could a kid be a lover to an older woman consumed by her art. Even such a flaming beauty? And I struggled to understand the always anomalous aspect of the women artists. I warily observed that hand in hand with the men's evaluations, appreciations of the women's art were their maternal demands—the women were required to take care of the men and domestic functions.

After the Bard memorial for you, filmmakers gathered in a shadowy Tivoli bar talking of your great influence, the inspiration of a consecrated life, the immense beauty of the films, our sorrow to lose you and of the imminent destruction of another country, which sears our flesh, threatening the very flow of spring air newly, the haze of frost in the mellowing night (almost

Spring, reminder of the night I would first be with Tenney . . . and thinking of you poised in the grass with your old 8 mm camera focused as if hungrily as Jim & I embrace, turning in a harsh Colorado sunlight: The optic flow is physiological in *Loving*, sensuous camera, a painting in time, touch, gesture, drench of a vicarious wonder. You questioning what is love? Where do I find it? Do you represent it for me? Embodied? These earliest questions. . . .)

You film *Daybreak* and *Whiteye* in our little farmhouse apartment. The film captured Jim's writing to me in the frost on our door, "I love you." There I open DeKooning, Pollock, and Cezanne books. I would tell you, your "psycho dramas" will be a dead-end. You must look at painting, visual history and nature! And you study my paintings positioned for you against the walls of the peaked roof studio in South Shaftsbury . . . "Mill Forms" . . . "Personae" . . . while Jim played Ives for us, Ruggles at the upright piano.

Again you travel cross-country from Colorado to Vermont, this time with Jane. I prepare curtains for the little room facing the hillside. As hosts & guests, we struggled over who empties overflowing ashtrays? How do we share? Who shops? Cooks? Washes up? You announce a profligate devotion to having babies though you had no way to support them. You rage at my abortion: "That baby belongs to Jim and to me" . . . I had to paint! For *Cat's Cradle*, you insisted I wear the silly apron Jim's mother had sent for Christmas. I painted Jane—magnificent, naked—her first pregnancy. . . . You protested, "You made her look like a trapped animal." If I bought paints, we couldn't do the laundry, if Jim bought the piano bench we would be short on the rent. But we packed works, sleeping bags, and Kitch in our old station wagon and traveled West to see the first babies, to see sections of *Dog Star Man*, to have you hear Jim's sound collage *Blue Suede Shoes*, his Ives Concord Sonata, or the Webern piano works. . . . We slept in our cars cross-country . . . we ate sardines and stopped in desolate diners for coffee and toast at dawn. You were an advocate, holding infant Marina up to my landscape paintings: "She will absorb these colors, rhythms" . . . our travels to each other meant the richest discussions, a rigorous cultural history, which we studied, analyzed, probed. Graves, Nicholaides, Focillon, Proust, Baudelaire, Pound, Woolf—we exchange these books.

Our rule was that nothing should deflect the work, that all forces against this concentration were the enemy, evil. We were embattled to protect, to sustain

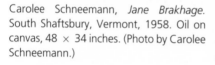

Carolee Schneemann, *Jane Brakhage*. South Shaftsbury, Vermont, 1958. Oil on canvas, 48 × 34 inches. (Photo by Carolee Schneemann.)

Mary Jane Collom Brakhage. South Shaftsbury, Vermont, 1957 (?). (Photo by Carolee Schneemann.)

Jane, Stan, and C.S. South Shaftsbury, Vermont, 1958, (Photo by Jim Tenney.)

Stan, baby Myrenna, Jane, C.S., Jim Tenney. Sidney, Illinois, 1960. (Self-timed photo by Carolee Schneemann.)

Jane, Stan, C.S. South Shaftsbury, Vermont, 1958. (Photo by Jim Tenney.)

the vision, envisioning, even as the struggle for income remained relentless. You impoverished, fighting to create film works and a family with Jane. And as well, we unleashed hysterical joy, mystical affinities, emotional nightmares.

And in those years, your objections to my despair over women artists as marginal, tokens—though you championed Stein, Deren, Menken, H.D. You and Jane burnt the copy of Simone de Beauvoir's *The Second Sex* I sent for a revelatory (I hoped) 1959 Christmas present. You were outraged by my notes on gender exclusions. My letters to you were cut up and burnt so that only certain acceptable paragraphs remained in a scrapbook... (but that I only learned much later when your letters to me and my notes of response to you were stolen in 1971 from here, this old house overlooking the Mohonk ridge where *Fuses* was filmed in 1965, in response to *Window Water Baby Moving*—I wanted to see "the fuck," lovemaking's erotic blinding core apart from maternity/paternity).

Radical. How unprecedented out of still life, the narrative fracture of poetry, the intimacy of paintings—to explore to make focus the forms, actions of actual lived life and its decay—*Sirius Remembered*—as death homage, optical duration, dissolution of the intimate dog body. Did they all forget this was forbidden! "Trivializing" and shocking for a male artist to embrace actual lived experience as source of perceptions. At early screenings of *Window Winter Baby Moving*, there were men who threw up, rushed out of the theater in revulsion and panic. (While *Fuses* was censored from 1965 up into the 1990s! despite the Yale film award and critical regard.) We confirmed each other within the energies of visualized embodiment and changing definitions of taboo. Very slowly we entered into the changing dynamics of academia, released from years of menial jobs. (Although it was only in the mid-80s that you began to "see" my films. Remember you told me they were "not really films": *Fuses, Plumb Line, Viet-Flakes, Kitch's Last Meal*... what are they then? Something else. By the 1980s, your women film students had asserted their regard for my film works: You changed your estimation.) In the 1970s, I could bring your films into programs for students in painting, drawing, expanded arts, new media.... Receptive worlds slowly built anchored East by Jonas Mekas (following the radical devotions of Amos Vogel and Cinema 16), Steve Anker and the Cinematheque in San Francisco, Tom Luddy and Pacifica, Robert Haller and Sally Dixon, programs at Pittsburgh.... Gene

Youngblood, Scott MacDonald, critical writers committed to independent film. Howard Guttenplan's Millenium, Mekas' Anthology and the solid honest artists' film cooperatives. By the 1970s the struggle to work and the struggle for a context for our works had entered a receptive force field. And you brought me to Telluride Film Festival 1977 for that incredible event "Erotic Films by Women." (But that's another story.)

Again we were traced together when Bruce McPherson, in 1976, prepared to publish *More Than Meat Joy*. As we created our relationship, we explored my cultural history. I became a bridge to your writings and Maya's. McPherson publishes *Divine Horsemen* and *Essential Brakhage*. In the 1980s & 90s, you and I write each other from our achieved worlds evolved flowed forward irreducible, troubling, inspiring, demanding. Across our fixed geographies we remain linked, extended from the small intense nucleus of 1958 when there were only 300 radical artists and we all knew each other. Our context now so wide and dense that we signal to each other within a vertiginous history.

. . .

12 December 2002

The radiation treatments are murder. You are desperate to leave Boulder. Marilyn has found a house in Vancouver. Will you have the strength to get there? Will customs stop your family and the cat? You say you should die to relieve Marilyn of all she endures suffers to take care of you. You are fearful that your illness confounds your young sons. I insist that you must accept her love, her devotions—that the pain is draining your spirit, the ceaseless ordeals. . . . That Canada will be restorative. . . .

13 February 2003

We spoke last night—between your fragile shifting awareness—exhaustion, intimations of an immense unendurable pain masked by 900 mg morphine every four hours. You told me of relief to have left Colorado: that Marilyn and the boys now finally feel safe at the new home in Vancouver. Her family is there. You relish the peace, the house, gulls flying. And your wish that your life with them could be prolonged, "I just want to see the boys grow up, to be here for them." Sitting in bed you work on films, writing, but strangely—all the morphine?—you cannot read—watching television, in the background, hysterical intonations. "It is unbelievable! Do you have your duct tape and plastic against the biological attacks?" Our incredulous, ironic grief at the insanity sweeping consciousness, the death wish of the militarists, deformed patriotism. You told me of your belief in God. I joked, "Well I always knew about your angels and I suppose God can't function without them." "Yes, like the secretaries who made everything run properly."

11 January 2003

All those early years, such hypochondria, invoking protection of angels to sustain you against "betrayals," malign "presences" (including friends in any disaffiliation), "forces" which brought on dramatic attacks of stomachaches, eye aches, headaches, backaches. Now your immense courage, endurance through years of this cancer's advance. (Three of us—that tripod— each having cringed in the cellular sparks of cancer's unique particularity Jim surviving lung cancer—allopathic treatment; my non-Hodgkin's lymphoma— alternative therapy). These invisible cells, micro-invaders, the chemical chain attacking its luxurious host body. Will your lymphocytes gather power to erode the protein sheath disguising cancer cells—to shrivel them into cellular dust— particles of pesticides . . . oxygen depletion . . . the moon. . . the stars.

. . .

3 March 2003

You tell me you are scratching into film with your nails, incised strokes, rhythms in duration replace the aniline dyes stained-glass intensity. No one said aniline dyes could be a chemical trigger for bladder cancer. Art Toxicity. Fiery liquid color, your thousands of luminous brush strokes frame by frame—did you lick the sable brushes to thin the ink? We discussed the nightmare loss of constitutional freedoms—that political cancer.

Max the family cat deeply asleep, devoted to you. You say, "He is large you know. He is sleeping and will have dinner and when we all fall asleep, he sleeps again through the night with us." At the American Museum of the Moving Image memorial—among your last films Max, we see his great sustaining eyes fixed upon you—as camera lens and emulsion become viewers face in place of yours—imprinted, you filming Max seeing you.

You tell me you are not afraid of death—you always have had guardians—the angels, the spirits. And, "I only wanted to make beauty as justice."

. . .

Extracted text from e-mail correspondence between Phil Solomon & C.S.

—Original Message—
Subject: Re: Stan
Date: Mon, 17 Mar 2003 12:18:28 -0700
From: Phil Solomon

Dear Carolee,
    I just returned from Victoria last night—I was just there in February, so it was a strange, sad, poignant return trip. I would like to make public some of my observations about the service, the day, the family, and Stan. . . .
    His service was simple, and during the morning of the funeral, the heavy clouds over Victoria parted for the sun, which streamed in through the stained glass to create a text of light on the wall . . . and we had a tape of 6-year-old Stan singing Ave Maria, which rang through time, as if he were praying over himself across a lifetime—it was terribly moving and gave me a great sense of closure.
    As for your epiphany, I fully believe it, as many marvelous things happened to me on this trip. The best was that when I was getting dressed and ready to leave the hotel, one of my CD cases fell over (I'm assuming . . .) in my camera bag and hit the start button on my portable CD player by itself—which was connected to headphones. I started to hear this voice coming from nowhere, very faint, very lovely—and it was a CD I made of young Stan, singing in my bag, "When You Wish Upon a Star" . . . I just sat down on the chair and stared at my bag until he was

finished, and knew he was winking at me, then having one of his grand laughs, echoing through the heavens . . .

best to you
Phil

. . .

Subject: Stan
Date: Mon, 17 Mar 2003 13:05:09 -0500
From: Carolee Schneemann

Dear Phil,

Thank you so much for reaching into the film community with details of Stan's death. . . . It is such a shattering loss. We were friends for most of my life, and I have been preparing an image text piece for David James with photographs of Stan from the 1950s. It will remain an anguish not to be able to speak to him—that marvelous voice, the unreeling thoughts always in their vital flow of insight.

On the desk downstairs there is a small mechanical bird constructed by my sculptor friend Maura Sheehan[1]; it was made with a motion sensor and a battery several years ago and had lost its charge. Yesterday at 2 pm it suddenly began chirping—not its normal few chirps, but a continuous warbling. I ran in from the other room to see what might have affected this mechanical object. Of course, not even a cat was nearby. I sat down and as it continued to chirp, I was overwhelmed with the presence of Stan, that he had entered this bird as a sort of angel through which to sing his presence and departure.

Lemuria, 1 November 2003

NOTE

1. The year before he died, Stan visited M. M. Serra at The Clocktower in downtown New York City, the new home to the Filmmakers Cooperative. Ken Jacobs followed with his camera as M.M. led Stan to the rooftops view of Lower Manhattan. Entering the Tower itself—a large symmetrical square area, Stan commented: "This would be a great place for a revolving projection." He did not know Maura Sheehan had previously created just such a work of projection—running horses circling the space. (Brakhage and Sheehan had never met.)

R. BRUCE ELDER

Brakhage

Poesis

I

Stan Brakhage believed that a being larger than the individual self was the maker of his artistic works. He famously summed up that idea on the title page of his *Metaphors on Vision* when he stated that the phrase "by Stan Brakhage" on his films should be understood to mean "by way of Stan and Jane and the children Brakhage."

A tension that permeated Brakhage's filmmaking is that between the image conceived as representing the content of consciousness and the image conceived as a form that embodies the energies of a greater field of being. This tension is often figured as a struggle to break out of solipsism. *Unconscious London Strata* (1982), *Nightmusic* (1986), *Glaze of Cathexis* (1990), *Crack Glass Eulogy* (1992), *The Harrowing* (1993), *Paranoia Corridor* (1995), and *Polite Madness* (1996) suggest the terror and sadness of solipsism, while the *Pittsburgh Trilogy* (1971), *The Governor* (1977), *Christ Mass Sex Dance* (1991), and the *Visions in Meditation* series (1989–90) halt the slide into solipsism through observation of the world outside consciousness. *Dog Star Man* (1961–4) and the Vancouver Island films suggest the resolution of the tension through the self's identifying with a larger matrix.[1] The self's isolation results from a disconnection from the "greater field of being" and the absorption of the subject into the phenomena that consciousness itself produces. Brakhage's well-known interest in hypnagogic images, and his refusal to distinguish among perception, memory, and hallucination ("Allow so-called hallucination to enter the realm of perception . . . accept dream visions, day-dreams or night-dreams, as you would so-called real scenes, even allowing that the abstractions which move so dynamically when closed eyelids are pressed are actually perceived") makes solipsism a perpetual threat.[2]

The unhappy consciousness is a consciousness locked inside the circle of its own being, isolated from the greater field. In late September 1966, while he was making *23rd Psalm Branch*, Brakhage wrote to the poet Robert Duncan explaining the role of consciousness in producing the images for that very troubled film. Those images, he wrote, represent "child's views of images of war"

> to be of the very rhythm the optic nerve pulses in its firing forth these pictures dredged from memory fund, and to be of the orders of that act of remembering . . . this is the closest I am enabled to come, at this time, to make visible the *being* of war's *cause*. You do inform me well as to why the TV screen will *not* yield material for this insight, tho' I would hope, in time (as I become attuned to my own nerve's impulse in the immediate sensory receiving of images—as distinct from memories' receipt) to break thru even the subversion of "the Advertiser."[3]

Time and again in his comments on his films, Brakhage returns to the position that the optic nerves themselves (which serve for him as a meto-nym for the physiological processes that condition our experience of visual phenomena) produce the disturbances that beset consciousness.

Brakhage longed to break out of the circle of consciousness by climbing out of the memory images and the hypnagogic images produced by the "backfiring" of the optic nerve. In his note on *Delicacies of Molten Horror Synapse* (1991), he identified the "molten horror" of the title as the TV, or even the film itself, with its four superimposed roles of hand-painted and negative television imagery since the film represents "the hynagogic process whereby the optic nerves resist grotesque infusions of luminescent light." We might be tempted, in trying to interpret this comment, to take consciousness as the pristine good entity, defending itself from the bad external (TV) object, but the film itself (with its strangely symmetrical images) more suggests the terror that besets a consciousness trying and failing to break out of its self-enclosure by identifying with a creative being that is both beyond and within itself. Films such as *The Process* (1972) and *The Harrowing* (1993), I believe, confirm these conjectures about the solipsistic pole in Brakhage's oeuvre.

In his 1995 article, "Having Declared a Belief in God," Brakhage dealt explicitly with the terror of the self-enclosed consciousness. He accused the traditional conception of God of simply projecting the self to all levels of being (or being-as-represented), from the microcosmic to the macrocosmic:

> If the external be subject to one's self, and if self be, thus, possessed by oneself, then all explative [sic] becomes such muttering as an echo-chamber might be said to engender: the visual corollary to this word-trap would be mirror-reflecting-mirror's imagery to some supposed infinitesimal microcosm. . . . I see myself seeing myself infinitely from a felt base-stance in diminishing, albeit solid-seeming, variations which, at sight's limit, opt, naturally enough, to be imagined and to be variably imaginable. The inverse of this imagined variability of one's diminished self, would most reasonably be a macrocosm in which one's self-shape didn't exist at all, coexistent with an imagined BEING, larger and ever larger, multiply amorphous shape-shifting of oneself: this, then, is the classically baroque romance of self and God which Western aesthetics have engendered.[4]

If the traditional conception of God is, as Brakhage said, "subject to one's self," it is locked within the circle of the self. It therefore lacks the power to release one from solipsism—for it is nothing more than the image of the self projected at larger and larger magnification into the beyond. In the sixth century B.C.E., Xenophanes proposed that "if horses or oxen or lions had hands they could draw with and accomplish such works as men, horses would draw the figures of the gods as similar to horses, and the oxen as similar to oxen, and they would make the bodies of the sort which each of them had," and even that the characteristics of the gods revered by a particular group reflect the human characteristics of that group's members: "Ethiopians say that their gods are snub-nosed and black, Thracians that theirs are blue-eyed and red-haired."[5]

I have suggested that a struggle between a solipsistic sense of the self and a sense of the self as embedded in, and ultimately identified with, a larger matrix is fundamental to Brakhage's filmmaking. The importance of this tension in Brakhage's work, and the centrality of the aspiration to identify with this larger force, makes it worth asking about the character of this "greater maker" that uses Brakhage as its instrument. In 1944, Jackson Pollock famously proclaimed to Hans Hofmann his reason for not painting from nature: "I AM nature."[6] That Brakhage's aesthetic credo shares many tenets with that of the abstract expressionists makes it tempting to infer that Pollock's assertion is one that could also have been made by Brakhage, and that nature is the greater maker of Brakhage's films.

There is much to recommend that view. Certainly the iconography of *Dog Star Man* could be cited in its defense, for that film identifies macrocosmic and microcosmic nature and represents consciousness as an effect of the energies that permeate the cosmos. Astronomical footage showing flares leaping from the sun's surface is rhymed with images of the internal body (a pumping heart, blood surging to and fro in the veins) to reinforce the comparison between the human and the cosmic scale and to imply, by this microanthropic/macro-cosmic identification, that the universe is a giant organism whose being is no different from the Dog Star Man's body. Furthermore, that work is a series of fragments, and the effort of the film is an attempt at reparation for reality's sundered condition by embodying a worldview that mythopoeically identities every part with the whole.

However, other films and other statements by the artist make clear that we cannot simply identify the greater maker with nature. Take *The Dante Quartet* of 1987, in which the problematic we are considering is central: The effort to rise out of the personal, limited self and to identify with the greater, creative self is its main theme. Of course, that theme is key to the Dantean original, too: At the opening of *Paradiso*, Beatrice chides the Poet: "You make yourself obtuse with false imagining; you cannot see what you would see if you dispelled it" (*Par.* I:88–90). The first canto of *Paradiso* tells us that the Poet underwent a "trans-humanizing" (*trasumanar*) change that words could not convey.[7] Through this change the Poet came to recognize, as Beatrice explains, that a universal instinct penetrates all things, endowing each with a principle that carries it on its individual course through the vast sea of being (*Par.* I:103–41).

The power that changed the Poet is crucial: Dante had beseeched "buono Appollo": "Enter into my breast, within me breathe the very power you made manifest when you drew Marsyas from his limbs' sheath" (*Par.* I:19–21). A breath that a god breathed into the poet transformed him.

Brakhage's *The Dante Quartet* concerns the hell of false (solipsistic) imagining and the release from that hell by identifying with something higher—something higher that also breathes within him. Brakhage outlined the parts of *The Dante Quartet* in an interview:

> The four parts are *Hell Itself, Hell Spit Flexion, Purgation* and *existence is song.* ... I made *Hell Itself* during the breakup with Jane and the collapse of my whole life, so I got to know quite well the streaming of the hypnagogic that's hellish. Now the body can not only feed back its sense of being in hell but also its getting out of hell, and *Hell Spit Flexion* shows the way out—it's there as crowbar to lift one out of hell toward the transformatory state—purgatory. And finally there's a fourth state that's fleeting. I've called this last part *existence is song* quoting Rilke, because I don't want to presume upon the after-life and call it "Heaven."[8]

Most parts of *The Dante Quartet* are painted over photographic imagery that sometimes peeks through. *Hell Itself* is the only section that lacks photographic imagery. Thus that section suggests the self isolated from the greater field of being. Despite the textual basis within the Dantean original for the transhuman identification that the final section of *The Dante Quartet* figures, that section, as Brakhage noted, takes its title from Rilke. The title comes specifically from the *Sonnets to Orpheus* I, 3. The phrase that appears in the poem is actually the reverse of the title—it is "song is existence" (*Gesang ist Dasein*); in the poem, the phrase opens a gulf between the human and the divine, as experiencing the equivalence of song and existence is "an easy thing for God" but, presumably, for humans it is more difficult.[9] Thus the poem highlights the need for a transforming change such as Dante's Poet refers to.

Gesang ist Dasein could also be translated "singing is reality." It was probably the sonnet's expression and affirmation of the lyric nature of reality that piqued Brakhage's interest in Rilke for the idea of song had long been important to him; in the late 1960s, he created the *Songs*, a major serial work; in the 1970s, he titled a work *Tragoedia*, alluding to the etymological origin of the word *tragedy* in "goat song"; and, more recently, he called a pair of films *Self Song* and *Death Song*. He named another *The Earth Song of the Cricket*. The poem that inspired *The Dante Quartet* is a series of *canti*, and in this film Brakhage reached, through Rilke, an identification of existence (reality) itself with singing. With all this evidence, it seems certain that what Brakhage thinks about song will tell us something about the greater being through which he escapes solipsism.

Rilke's poem asserts that it is not longing or passion that will enable humans to learn the true music for true singing comes from a different breath, a breath about nothing, a gust within God, a Wind.[10] True singing results from abandoning desire, turning one's inner being nearly into nothing. True singing results not from identifying the self with nature, but from allowing the self to dissolve in a greater nothingness. That is the view of singing that Brakhage evolved toward. In Brakhage's later work, song represents the greater maker with which the filmmaker strived to connect to break out of the circle of consciousness.

But that view of song is not the only one that Brakhage offered. He sometimes identified song more strictly with nature, rather than with a supernatural nothing. He said in an interview:

I believe in song. That's what I wanted to do and I did it quite selfishly, out of my own need to come through to a voice that is comparable with song and related to all animal life on earth. I believe in the beauty of the singing whale; I am moved deeply at the whole range of song that the wolf makes when the moon appears, or neighborhood dogs make—that they make their song, and this is the wonder of life on earth, and I in great humility wish to join this.[11]

Brakhage, then, offered two views of the nature of song. Though both treat song almost as metaphysical principle, the two views are contradictory. Sometimes he spoke as though he believed that nature embodies lyric reality, and at other times he treated lyric reality as something less material. His conception of the reality that is song is similarly conflicted: Sometimes he conceived this greater maker to be nature, and at other times he conceived of it as almost nothing—a gust of wind, a breath, pure movement, a nothing.

A similar tension between the conception of the greater maker as nature and as air, as breath or a nothing occurs in the work of the poet Charles Olson, a key influence on Brakhage's art. Olson refers to this larger dynamic that produces objects as "the field."[12] In his famous manifesto, "Projective Verse," Olson wrote that if a man is "contained within his nature as he is participant in the larger force, he will be able to listen, and his hearing through himself will give him secrets objects share."[13] This conception of the field was influenced by Alfred North Whitehead's attempt to develop a philosophy of organism, a metaphysical system that would accord with the modern scientific world view.

Whitehead had a major influence on Olson. Viewed from this aspect, Olson's poetics are really a deliberation on Whitehead's idea of concrescence, that is, the process of becoming concrete or actual, which consists in coordinating environmental influences in an intelligible, harmonious way. Thus, Olson wrote of the field as though it were the activity that, through concrescence, brings about the entities that constitute reality.

But there is a complexity in Olson's idea of the entities that make up reality—a complexity that derives from, but extends, Whitehead's philosophy. Olson sometimes treated these "entities" in a fashion that is not entirely true to Whitehead (as when he expounded his objectist convictions): He sometimes wrote of them as though they were the ordinary objects that make up the furniture of reality. At other times, he was truer to Whitehead's philosophy and proposed that the ultimate constituents of reality are activities that possess no simple location—they are not enduring substances with definable properties but are processes with an identity that cannot be traced to a single point in space and time. Construing the field in this more Whiteheadian way, as energies that ingress on these processes ("actual events"), moves Olson closer to Rilke's sense of reality (*Dasein*) as a nothing, a gust within God.

> The late plays of Shakespeare are aerodynes, in which, by a series of baffles (the verse, with its emphasis on quantities), they have their power straight from the element they move in, that they displace, and they go in speed from zero to as fast as sound. They are motion, not action—by power of vacuum, they use it and occupy.... They go in the air, that's all.... These things (*Winter's Tale, Tempest, Two Noble Kinsmen*) are forms of power not known.[14]

The development of Brakhage's oeuvre suggests to me that Brakhage sensed the tension in Olson's conception of the field, and that while he began by largely accepting the naturalistic conception of a greater being that holds all beings (processes) together in a nexus of relations, he moved gradually toward the more enigmatic, Rilkean sense. In the early films (and writings), the larger field that consciousness identifies with is nature. In the later films, it is, increasingly, something other than nature. Discussing art-making with Ronald Johnson, he revealed that he had come to reject a principle he had long espoused: "No ideas but in things." About William Carlos Williams's teaching, he remarked

> I work with ephemera. . . . I did try very hard, and took the kinds of pictures that would be . . . inspired by . . . "No ideas but in things," but in fact it's not that applicable to film, whose nature is to be fleeting and moving on. It's a weave of light, that's forever dissolving.[15]

Or, according to another metaphor, "a breath, a nothing, a gust inside God. A wind." When Brakhage came to reflect on films he had left unprinted for several years, he described them in terms almost identical to those Olson used of Shakespeare's late romances:

> A picture is (as I define it) a collection of *nameable* shapes framed (i.e., in interrelated composition). But it is almost impossible to name the *motions* of these shapes-as-things in other than the most general way ("fast, slow," "up," "down," "jerky," "smooth," "right," "left," and so forth).[16]

Brakhage described similarly a work he shot just before submitting to cancer surgery (and thus when he was on the cusp of a possible death) as "a kind of 'last testament,' if you will . . . an envisionment of the fleeting complexity of worldly phenomena."[17]

Brakhage expressed this sense of reality as ephemeral—as a composition of velocities—in various ways. In his article, "Having Declared a Belief in God," Brakhage alluded to the greater field of being as "a *moving* at-oneness" or as "a feeling of movement, of being so much at-one with an intricacy of cosmic rhythms, with felt radiant particle/waves (as Niels Bohr would have it) in cancellation of chaos and stasis at one once forever."[18] In the larger society, Bohr's name stands for the idea that reality is coreless—it ephemeralizes into energy and so has no more substantial reality than light.[19] Brakhage's later writings suggest a dynamic metaphysics in which the reality of objects dissolves into the movement of light.

Thus in his later works, the greater being, the greater maker, is not so much nature as it is an absence—a transcendent Nothing. Brakhage included the following snippets of text from Novalis' first *Hymn to the Night* in his own *First Hymn to the Night—Novalis* (1994): "the universally gladdening light . . . As inmost soul . . . it is breathed by stars . . . by stone . . . I seek to blend with ashes." In the same year, he made *Naughts*, which he described as "a series of hand-painted, step-printed films, each of which is a textured, thus tangible, 'nothing.' A series of 'nots,' then, in pun, or knots of otherwise invisible energies."[20] That reality, that airy nothing, can almost be characterized as pure flux, as the Vancouver Island films suggest. But it is the painted films, and especially those that moved beyond conveying the dynamics of "moving visual thinking," that are the principal vehicle of that view. If over the past fifteen years Brakhage's remarks on the cinema became increasingly critical of "picture" (by which he means representations of nameable things), it is because more and more the reality that he strived to suggest is nonobjective, nonmaterial, elusive, unstable—an airy nothing. Conveying the energies of deeper layers of thought—Brakhage's own explanation of the shift toward "abstraction"—may be a factor in his ever more strongly asserted critique of picture, but it is hardly the whole story, for that explanation could account for a slide into an ever deeper solipsism, the condition that Brakhage's abstraction sought to avoid (by connecting him with the lyric reality that is the greater maker of his films).

It is true that Brakhage's work, by and large, evolved from representation to abstraction. *The Dante Quartet* is a key to this evolution. The work was made in a time of crisis, when his first marriage had dissolved and his life was in a shambles. But, it is often the case that moments of crisis are moments of artistic breakthrough, and so it was with *The Dante Quartet*. *existence is song* shows Brakhage evolving not only toward "abstraction" but also toward a sense of field reality similar to that which Olsen sees in the late plays of Shakespeare—a sense of the field as more like a gust of wind, an airy nothing, a composition of speeds and slownesses, pure flux.

The idea of reality as empty, as coreless, was instrumental in pushing many early twentieth century artists to develop abstract painting or to embrace it. Two painters for whom Brakhage expressed admiration, Barnett Newman and Mark Rothko, used darkness and pure, nonrepresentational color to suggest deep silence and the infinite void of religious experience, the Unmanifest that lies beyond the manifest. For many twentieth century artists, abstract art had as its goal the destruction of appearances (the physical world) so that the spiritual might emerge—and that reality was tantamount to void, to "nothing."

Brakhage engaged me in a prolonged discussion on the status of picture; he proclaimed my work as a summa of the values of picture, values he forcefully excluded from his own work. We have trod different paths. Yet, as this brief discussion makes clear, Brakhage's remarks on picture (and on my films) have led me to reflect on what would bring an artist to attempt to expel representation from what is, after all, a photographically based medium. At last, I come to the answer: "Nothing."

II

We lived far apart, he in Boulder, Colorado, United States, and I in Toronto, Ontario, Canada; the expanse that separated us (as well as the modern oddity of long-distance friendships) were realities he often lamented. We saw each other whenever we could, but mostly we conducted our friendship over the telephone. The telephone calls often went on at length, and we would talk about many things: always the movies (a great topic with Brakhage, though I am afraid I was never much good in sharing in that enthusiasm), often the tribulations that an artist faces in making a living in the academy (a topic on which I was considerably better informed), usually fatherhood, but often the conversation got around to poets and poetry, our deep, shared interest. Over the years, we talked about many poets, a few living, most dead. Sometimes he read poems to me over the telephone (to ensure my renewed familiarity with them); sometimes we talked about what each of us remembered of a poet's works; and sometimes he would tell me anecdotes about the poets. He could tell me much about the lives of poets for Brakhage was an avid reader of literary biography: I was often struck by the fact that he recounted the tales of writers from the eighteenth and nineteenth century in exactly the same manner that he recounted tales of poets with whom he had a close personal acquaintance. Clearly, through reading, he could imagine the person's presence in the world, their conversation with friends, their generosities and rivalries and jealousies and kindnesses, almost as vividly as he experienced the conversation of flesh-and-blood people he knew.

Sometime in 1989 (I imagine), when the conversation rolled around to poetry, he posed the question whether I owned copies of the published portions of Ronald Johnson's long poem *ARK*.[21] I allowed that, despite my awareness of his, and Guy Davenport's, enthusiasm for the work, I did not. Within a week, the volumes arrived in the mail; they were obviously new copies, and I wish that I had thought to ask him whether he had gotten them from Johnson himself. A while later, a typescript arrived in the post, with a note written on the top: "Dear Bruce—This/ 'Spires' by R.J. (from Kansas also by the way) much mixed with sea and sand and sky, of the mind, midst whir of camera, catching light with Marilyn and Anton, 'up island' [at Parksville, on Vancouver Island].... hoping it moves you too. Blessings, Stan Aug', 1990." The typescript contained "Spires 50 to 66" from Johnson's *ARK*. Brakhage soon called to give me the telephone number at the motel where he and the family were staying: He wanted us to be able to talk about the new Johnson poems.

At that time, Brakhage was shooting *A Child's Garden and the Serious Sea*, one of the masterworks of his later years. In his catalogue entry for that film he wrote:

> In poet Ronald Johnson's great epic *ARK*, in the first book *The Foundations*, the poem "Beam 29" has this passage: "*The seed is disseminated at the gated mosaic a hundred feet/below, above/long windrows of motion/connecting dilated arches undergoing transamplification:/*'seen in the water so clear as christiall'/(*prairie tremblante*)" which breaks into musical notation that, "presto," becomes a design of spatial tilts: This is where the film began; and I carried a Xerox of the still unpublished *ARK* 50 through 66 all that trip with Marilyn and Anton around Vancouver Island. As I wrote him, "The pun 'out on a limn' [a line from *ARK* 56], kept ringing through my mind as I caught the hairs of side-light off ephemera of objects.[22]

My relation with Brakhage was fairly complex and receiving a gift like the completed parts of *ARK* illustrates that complexity: I write on avant-garde cinema, and his sending me this text could be an effort on the part of the artist to inform the critic about his motivations; it could also be the effort of a person to share his enthusiasms with a friend, and since I also am a filmmaker, his gift could also be effort at imparting inspiration. Complicating this tangle of possible reasons is the fact that *ARK* belongs to the lineage of Pound's *Cantos*, Williams's *Paterson*, Olson's *Maximus*, or Zukofsky's *A*—all works that I love deeply, as much as works produced in the twentieth century; so Brakhage may have speculated that *ARK*, too, would come to be (as it has) a work close to my heart.

Further, Brakhage consistently celebrated my cycle of films, *The Book of All the Dead*, as a special achievement in a long form—and he may have believed that I would feel a special affinity for *ARK* since it also is a recent achievement in a long form. Moreover, Ronald Johnson's early work was allied with the Black Mountain school, and I have a fondness for poets of that provenance; further, Johnson's work was also rooted in the poetry of such great visionaries as Whitman, Blake, and Dante, poets for whom, as Brakhage knew, I feel deep passion. Johnson's early poetry owes much, too, to Charles Olson's notion of projective verse, a topic on which I was writing at the time, in connection with Brakhage's work, so he could have been encouraging me to further explorations of that mode (and his place in it). These possible motivations for sending me this gift are not mutually exclusive, and I suspect that all were factors; but their number makes the reasons for the urgency that Brakhage felt to share Johnson's work with me all the more complex to fathom.

Right now, however, it is the question of what Brakhage was trying to tell me about his own work that interests me most. Some affinities between Brakhage's films and Johnson's poetry are obvious. Brakhage and Johnson are both among the rare contemporaries committed to the visionary strain in art. Like Brakhage's films, *ARK* is a paean to process, a hymn to light (the concrete that Johnson offers in "Beam 13" brings the ideas of process and flux together as compactly as any of Brakhage's films).[23] Further, *ARK* begins with "a long time of light"; light evolved vision, so Johnson offers a Brakhagian account of Vision near the beginning of *ARK* that proposes the eye is the sun in another form, which finishes, almost, with the assertion "there began to be eyes, and light began looking with itself."[24] In *ARK*, matter produces consciousness: Its straining for music produces Bach (this occurs in "Beam 7"), then, in "Beam 14," generates

he who
obsessed by light,
possessed by sight.[25]

(One wonders whether Brakhage might not have taken this to refer to himself, though for Johnson, of course, it referred to the poet.)

Both Brakhage's and Johnson's art lean toward the cosmological (the title of one of Brakhage's films, *Stellar*, is, but for initial capital, the concluding line in Johnson's "Beam 14"), and in both artists' work, attention to detail, to the immediate particular, viewed with a Zukofskian objectivist clarity, balances their cosmological interests. There is, too, a complex relation between the concrete and the visionary (the optical/cosmological) in Johnson's writings, as there is in Brakhage's filmmaking.

Those who know Brakhage's writing or lectures on Gertrude Stein will know how often he referred to the famous "[a] rose is a rose is a rose," especially in its original presentation, closed in a circle: Brakhage was fond of pointing out that that concrete contains references to "a rose," to "Rose," to "eros" (love), to "rows" (death), and to "arose" (resurrection). Johnson offered similar comments on his concrete,

earthearthearth
earthearthearth
earthearthearth
earthearthearth
earthearthearth
earthearthearth[26]

He noted: "Earthearthearth is a linkage of ear to hear to heart. Art and hearth are also hid in it. All is at the core of fall. Even the stones here have overtones and the clouds may speak."

ARK (to say nothing of Johnson's other works) is an extraordinarily diverse collection—the poems it draws together range from concretes to lyrics (e.g., the Palms, relatives of the biblical Psalms, in "The Song of Orpheus") to collage works (*ARK* 26) to prose poems (*ARK* 12) to found poems (*ARK* 14), to works that, by including imitation bird song (another enthusiasm Brakhage shared with Johnson and with the composer Olivier Messiaen), incorporate natural forms; among recent poets, only Kenneth

Patchen and Louis Zukofsky, it seems to me, have a similar range. But Brakhage's films display a similar range: I can't think of another filmmaker whose films span so great a range as that between *Anticipation of the Night* and *The Dante Quartet* or between *Rage Net* and *The Mammals of Victoria*.

A further affinity: Brakhage desired to ground his cinema in the unique person that he was. He partook of that Emersonian desire to undo the deforming influence of culture and to return to the authenticity of the self-reliant individual. Johnson held similar beliefs; in "A Note" on *ARK*, he wrote "I knew I'd my own tack to take. If my confreres wanted to write a work with all history in its maw, I wished, from the beginning, to start all over again, attempting to know nothing but a will to create, and a matter at hand."[27] Pound had defined the epic poem as "a poem containing history" and made it his business to write an epic; Johnson separated himself from that ambition, wanting to get behind the distortions of history and back to the authentic individual. So did Brakhage, even while I, as a filmmaker, continued to seek the Historical Sublime (so Brakhage's sending me the completed portions of *ARK* may have been to suggest to me the error of my ways).

For Emerson, the experience of immediate moment and the immediate particular was the means to get back to the authentic self. Thus, in "Self-Reliance," Emerson wrote that "These roses under my window make no reference to former roses or to better ones; they are for what they are; they exist with God to-day. There is no time to them. There is simply the rose; it is perfect in every moment of its existence." In *ARK* 50, "Adamspire," Johnson writes

> *never were there such roses in*
> *under the banner of summer.*

similarly affirming the utter uniqueness of the immediate particular (when seen in this paradisical frame). And Brakhage, in *A Child's Garden and the Serious Sea*, finds himself in an (imagined) child's garden, looking closely at the flowers.

Just slightly later in *ARK* than the concrete we quoted above, and just before the point in the ARK at which, Brakhage says, "the film began," Johnson stated: ":the mind become its own subject matter:"(*ARK* 25). Turning to "the mind's reflection on itself" is certainly Brakhage's method.

"Beam 29," where, Brakhage wrote, *A Child's Garden and The Serious Sea* "began," contains the lines

PIVOT means the-man-who-will-become-himself-centers-a-
valley-through-which-circles matter. . . . Voices begin in the waters.

(but will not unfigure the cut-glass prism
frozen in sunshaft)

Around the time he was shooting *A Child's Garden and the Serious Sea,*
my wife and I received a charming snapshot of Stan in Parksville, Vancouver
Island, sitting in the seawater like a baby in the bathtub, his attention focused
on his Bolex movie camera, like a baby's on his rubber toy—and attached to
the Bolex is a cut-glass prism.[28] What he was filming, off Vancouver Island was

'seen in the water so clear as christiall'
(*prairie tremblante*)[29]

The Child's Garden, The Mammals of Victoria, and *The God of Day Had
Gone Down Upon Him,* films shot on Vancouver Island, all embodied
Brakhage's reflection on himself; it was

AS IF

IN THE DEPTHS A MAN COULD SEE HIS OWN REFLECTION
ripple-counter-ripple[30]

The ripples are surfaces on which the ephemeral appears to arise and
vanish into nothing.

ARK 30 is entitled "The Garden" and begins with the line "To do as
Adam did," a line that epitomizes both Johnson's project in *ARK* and Brakhage's in his filmmaking: Like Brakhage's films, the poem suggests analogies between light, life, and physics; moreover, *ARK* as a whole draws analogies
between the human body, the macrocosmic universe, and the microcosmic
universe (much as Brakhage's *Dog Star Man* did). In conversations, Johnson
referred to his delight in finding the garden outside oneself, but this is surely
part of the feeling that is suggested in Brakhage's use in *A Child's Garden and
the Serious Sea* of photography, an art that then depends on discovering
the self in the world outside the mind. Johnson's poetry, like Brakhage's
filmmaking, belongs to that moment in the English poetic tradition that
was committed to uncovering the exquisite identity of consciousness and
nature—a moment we call *Romanticism.*

"Spires 50–66" contain lines that equally well suggest the film:

> *never such*
> *beautiful hullabaloo*

From *ARK* 50, these lines certainly put one in mind of the fair to which film gives such prominent place. *ARK* 51, "Rungs I, the Pencil Spire," contains such lines as

> bent luminous one giant flower

and

> glass spied big as all outdoors & more

and

> imaginations shone
> august

that evoke the film.

ARK has a diurnal structure: "The Foundations" begins at sunrise and ends at noon, while "The Spires" go to sundown; "Spires 50–66," the section of *ARK* that Brakhage tells us he was reading while shooting *The Child's Garden and the Serious Sea*, are the concluding cantos of "The Spires," and so represent late afternoon and early evening. Brakhage entitled the third film in the Vancouver Island series *The God of Day Had Gone Down Upon Him*, and one might well conjecture it may relate to the third ("The Ramparts") section of *ARK*, which Johnson refers as "a night of the soul."[31]

In *ARK* 34, "Spire on the Death of L.Z.", one of my favorite cantos, is an elegy for Louis Zukovsky, Brakhage would have read

> this is paradise
> this is
> happening
> on the surface of a bubble
> time and again

fire sculpt of notwithstanding
dark

The appearance of Lord Hades in that verse means that Johnson's art has a new adversary: He must combat oblivion. That accords with the tone of the films that Brakhage photographed on Vancouver Island—and more than all the others, of *The God of Day Had Gone Down Upon Him*, which seems so elegiac, as are Johnson's "Arches" (cantos 69–99 of *ARK*), the poems that come after eventide in the work's diurnal structure.

NOTES

1. Of course, the ambiguity that is an aspect of the complexity of all of Brakhage's filmmaking makes these categories suspect; thus, films that suggest the sadness of solipsism may also suggest that beauty of the mind's creativity (as *Nightmusic* does), while films that celebrate the wonder of the world of concrete particulars may also convey some terror at experience of that world (as *Vision in Meditation 2: Mesa Verde* and *Vision in Mediation 3: Plato's Cave* do).
2. The quotation is from Stan Brakhage, *Metaphors on Vision* (unpaginated).
3. Stan Brakhage, "Correspondences," *Chicago Reader* 47.4/48.1 (Winter 2001, Spring 2002), 23–24; ellipsis and italics in original. The reference to "the Advertiser" relates to Brakhage's fear that this film was turning propagandistic.
4. Stan Brakhage, "Having Declared a Belief in God" was originally published in *Musicworks* and reprinted in *Chicago Reader* 47.4/48.1, 53.
5. Xenophanes of Colophon, *Fragments: A Text and Translation*, with a Commentary by J. H. Lesher (Toronto: University of Toronto Press, 1992), Fragment 15 (pp. 25 and 89); Fragment 16 (pp. 25 and 90).
6. The story, which Pollock's wife, Lee Krasner, reported, is legendary; it is recounted in, inter alia, Steven Naifeh and Gregory White Smith, *Jackson Pollock: An American Saga* (New York: Woodward/White, 1998), 486.
7. "…/Trasumanar significar per verba/non si poria" (*Par.* I:70–71).
8. Suranjan Ganguly, "Stan Brakhage—the 60th Birthday Interview," *Film Culture* 78 (Summer 1994), 26.
9. The German original "Sonette an Orpheus" I, 3 can be found in Stephen Mitchell, ed., *The Selected Poetry of Rainer Maria Rilke*, ed. and trans. Stephen Mitchell, introduction by Robert Haas (New York: Vintage Books, 1984), 230; to better highlight how Brakhage might have taken the poem, I have not followed Mitchell's (fine) translation but made my own.
10. Loc. cit. These descriptions appear in the last two lines of "Sonnette an Orpheus" I, 3; see ibid., 230.
11. Suranjan Ganguly, "All That is Light: Brakhage at 60," *Sight and Sound* 3, 10 (1993), 23.
12. In fact, Brakhage actually acknowledged Olson when he made the remarks that closed the *Metaphors on Vision* interview: "The best definition I can give you for soul-in-action, rather than at center, is Olson's 'Proprioception' in *Kultur* No. 1."

13. Charles Olson, "Projective Verse," in *Selected Writings of Charles Olson*, ed. and introduction Robert Creeley (New York: New Directions, 1966), 25.

14. Charles Olson, "Quantity in Verse, and Shakespeare's Late Plays," *Selected Writings*, 32.

15. "Another way of looking at the universe," (a transcription of Stan Brakhage and Ronald Johnson conversing). *Chicago Review* 47.4/48.1 (2001/2002), 34.

16. Stan Brakhage, "The Lost Films," originally published in *Musicworks* and reprinted in *Chicago Review* 47.4/48.1, 68. Emphasis in original.

17. Note on *Commingled Containers* (1997) in Canyon Cinema Film/Video Catalogue.

18. *Chicago Review* 47.4/48.1, 53–54.

19. For Kandinsky, too, the discovery of the coreless nature of subatomic reality brought home to him that reality is essentially empty—and this helped impel him toward abstraction.

20. Note on *Naughts* in Canyon Cinema Film/Video Catalogue.

21. Ronald Johnson, *ARK: The Foundations* (San Francisco: North Point Press, 1980); *ARK: Spires 34–50* (San Francisco: North Point Press, 1984), unpaginated.

22. Brakhage's note does not italicize the first four lines of the passage from *ARK*; however, they are in italics in my editions of *ARK* (so I have quoted them that way). Brakhage wrote on a typewriter, not a word processor, and he may have omitted the italics/underscoring for convenience.

23. Ronald Johnson, "Beam 4," from *ARK* (Albuquerque, NM: Living Batch Press, 1996), unpaginated.

24. All the phrases cited in this sentence appear in "Beam 4," *ARK* (unpaginated).

25. "Beam 14," *ARK*.

26. "Beam 24," *ARK*.

27. Johnson's note on *ARK*, "A Note," can be found near the end of the Living Batch Press edition; the edition is unpaginated.

28. *ARK* 95, "Arches XXIX" is dedicated to Stan Brakhage: It contains the lines, "(filmed sea unveil sky/up to chest, camera in hand/Paradise *sans* lens)." Reading this poem, which was written after Brakhage had filmed *The Child's Garden and the Serious Sea*, I wonder whether Johnson had seen another copy of the same (or similar) photograph; if he had (and if this is the source for the image), then that would tell us much about Johnson's cinematic approach (the transfiguration of the commonplace). At any rate, Johnson's interest in the commonplace is surely one of the reasons for Brakhage's enthusiasm for his poetry.

29. "Beam 29," *ARK*.

30. "Beam 29," *ARK*.

31. Johnson described this way "A Note," which appeared in the Living Batch Press edition of *ARK* (the text is unpaginated). In many ways, though, the tone of *The God of Day Had Gone Down Upon Him* seems more fitting to twilight (which would be the opening part of "The Ramparts").

Of course the title of Brakhage's film also alludes to Dickens, *David Copperfield*; in the eleventh chapter of that novel, Mr. Micawber is arrested early one morning and taken to the King's Bench Prison. As he went out of the house, he remarked to David that the God of day had now gone down upon him, and David thought that Micawber's heart was broken, and his, too. In February 2003, Pip Chodorov videotaped Brakhage, who was then dying of cancer, as he delivered an introduction for a program of films to be shown in Paris; Brakhage mentioned Dickens as a source for the title (though did not identify the work). Brakhage's childhood, in many ways, was not unlike David Copperfield's, and he might well have thought that an allusion to the Dickens character in a work that he must have known was (in some regard) a valedictory work would round out the tale of his life.

Recollections of Stan Brakhage

n December of 1959 a screening took place at the Living Theater, corner of Fourteenth Street and Sixth Avenue, New York City. A program of five or six films was projected. One of the films was Stan Brakhage's New York premiere of *Window Water Baby Moving*. Stan was the projectionist for the evening. After the screening of Stan's film, Maya Deren came before the audience to declare, very emphatically, that giving birth was a very "private matter," and it shouldn't ever be made into a public affair. "Even the animals, when they give birth, retreat into a secret place," said Maya. I do not remember Stan replying to Maya. He was in very low spirits that evening. He was hungry, broke, and depressed. What follows is a piece I wrote for my *Village Voice* "Movie Journal" column. The piece, however, was misplaced at the *Voice*, and it was never published. I found it some years later. Here it is.

Movie Journal

Down the stairs stumbles a policeman. "Avant-garde films!" he curses angrily. "I felt there was something queer going."

A huge crowd is milling inside. No more tickets. In the auditorium the screen is almost dark. A few reflections, a beam of light. Suddenly, a doorway appears, a cup, a hand, a shadowy face. All reality broken, destroyed, no realism.

"Bravo!" shouts a man. "Boo!" shouts another voice. "My bravo was louder than your boo!" retorts the first voice. Again a silence. Now the shadowy figures are embracing, in the huge, animal darkness.

There is a man on the stage now, before the screen, talking something, half drunk, half inspired. "Willard Maas . . ." a voice whispers. "He was not drunk when he made his two films," whispers a youth leaning by the wall. He came from New Jersey to see the films.

In the lobby a man pulls from under his coat a huge can of film and passes it to a young man with a mustache—this is a free exchange market of the avant-garde, both, ideas and stock. Boultenhouse, whose first film poem was just screened, is surrounded now. He has to answer questions about cameras, someone is in the middle of making a film, another one is searching for a cameraman.

On the screen: a dark blob is eating a yellow blob. "What cute things!" shouts a mountain of a woman from the back. "Marie Menken . . . she made the film . . ." a voice whispers. The black strange thing finishes devouring the yellow thing, and creeps on the window.

On the screen: A young man looks at his hand. It trembles. It jumps. A hand of inspiration, not a real hand. A hand of a poet. A fist. "Cocteau!" shouts a bearded man. He tries to walk out, in protest. He steps over the heads, gives up, cannot pass, sits on the floor. In the back, by the wall, somebody applauds violently the birth of a new film poet.

On the screen: a wild party. A few youths, drunk, exulted with adolescent nonsense, stare at a couple kissing. One jumps up, and runs to the couple, sticks his face close to them. "Ha! Ha!" he laughs loudly—and he runs wildly around, laughing, with a face drunk and crazy and ablaze.

On the screen probably for the first time ever in film history: a woman gives birth to a child. We see it all. The woman is ecstatic. And so is the father. The audience is totally totally silent.

In the backstage, high upon the ladder, the projectionist, author of the film, Brakhage. It is cold there. A cup of stale coffee besides the machine. "It is bad. I have ten more films ready. But no money for printing. This is the

end. Nobody wants to help experimental film," he talks to another man,
sitting on the end of a garbage barrel—
    at the Living Theater, last Monday.

February 8, 1999

Dear Stan:
This Sunday we sat at Anthology,
some fifty of us,
watching your latest creations,
painted, scratched, filmed from
nature and imagination,
dreams and things very very
real, on this thing called film,
film strip; and all the camera
work, and lenses, and forms and
shapes,

ah, we all felt great—I know it,
because there wasn't a single
sound, cough, or anything that would
disturb, interfere with the
images—to tell you the truth,
I was the only one there making sounds
with my throat, same sounds I've been
making since age five or
around there, especially this special
sublime evening, since I had
an extra bad cold.

And yes, I was amazed, as we all
were, how good you are, in your
amazing work, and how you never stop
and just keep going ahead and
ahead making new and new
work—

You know what? Just the other day,
actually late night I read this

guy Origen, a book called *On First*
Principles, and the back cover note said
"He left behind a massive body of
writings numbering close to
a thousand titles." Now, that was
in the beginning of the Third
Century! Imagine that? But I was really
thinking, when I read that, was ah,
on what kind of material was he writing all
those 1000 volumes—no Guttenberg
was there, and no nothing,
but he did it, and was no doubt
obsessed with it all
like you are,

but you are still far from 1000
titles! so good wind to you!
& keep going—
& gods bless you!

June 27, 2002

Dear Stan:
A huge rain storm just passed by. Thundering
heavily. Disturbing my cats. Some old music
on radio, don't know what but very pleasant.
Pleasant when you are cooking something for your
supper, like me, some potatoes with sour-
kraut . . . that primitive . . . I just had a craving
for it.

Haller calls. Tells in a concerned voice all about
your troubles.
Ah, that word, chemotherapy . . .
How many of my friends had to deal with it . . .
Susan. George. Annette. I have been lucky
so far, cross your fingers. I just had some
straight radiation stuff—but even so

I walked the streets and I thought I was
transparent and everybody could see through
me.

Ah, Stan, I wish I could pass to you some of my
farmer boy's health. I am drinking right now a glass
of Veltliner, Peter's favored Vienna wine, to
your health, feeling guilty that I am still
here and comparatively in good shape despite
some threats that were immediately radiated
out—luckily—but I want to drink to you
this evening—not that it's of any help
to you but somehow the fate has brought us
together so I feel we are sort of related
one could even say brothers of sorts

so I wish you strength and endurance and
faith and humor and trust persistent trust
in angels & everything that really matters and
frees and opens and heals & yes, yes, poetry
poetry of being

I am with you, Stan, although I seldom write
or call—my own life last ten years hasn't been
bread and honey—and even that is not the
right image: when I was ten, I was by a river, under
a bridge, small river—I was eating a piece
of bread my mother had given me, with honey on
it—it was my graduation day—Primary
School—and this girl comes and sprays sand
on my sandwich. . . . I don't know what it means
but I have never forgotten it—it comes back to me
at least once a year, this memory: why did she have
to do it!

Yes, Stan, I don't know what anything really
means, but I know that friendship means a lot
to me, and knowing that you are there in Colorado
doing what you are doing—things that have meant

so much to me—ah, forgive me, Stan, that I have
been so rare in calling or writing or saying
things that I should be saying—always so busy,
always running, always on the way, so rarely having
time to stop and take breath—I don't know
why I got into this—but that's how my life
has been—so forgive me, Stan,

Anyway—I think you should go out and have a
Bushmill or something and no matter what
pep up & boost & drown it all and I wish I could
be there now with you to keep you company and
drink with you—because Robert he said you feel
very low and are about to give up on chemotherapy &
leave it all to angels—

whatever happens, whatever is the decision,
I am with you this evening—this rainy thundering
and very very hot evening writing you this
long line letter with a glass of Veltliner next
to me which means I am thinking also about Peter
and P. Adams besides you—which means, the present
is mitigated—as Peter would say—with the
past.

We are all still here, separately but
together—

NICKY HAMLYN

The *Roman Numeral* Series

In this essay, I examine the relationship between focus, form, color, and
spatiality in Stan Brakhage's *Roman Numeral* series (1979–80). In
discussing these films, I touch on *Text of Light* (1974), in which focus
and defocus are central to the work's character, and examples such as
Delicacies of Molten Horror Synapse (1991), in which layering of the image
creates a synthetic spatiality in contrast to that of the organic space of the
Roman Numeral films. I also compare Brakhage's exploration of color with
that of Michael Snow's in *Wavelength* (1967).

An initial impulse to writing was the challenge of trying to give an
account of what may be read as some of Brakhage's most ineffable works.
In contrast to the films discussed by P. Adams Sitney in his book *Visionary Film*,[1] many of which have identifiably extra-cinematic themes (birth,
childhood, war, eschatology, and so on), the *Roman Numeral* series exhibits
a relatively purist concern with color and shape, playing on the tension
between image as indexical/referential and as abstract. Brakhage's own initial description of them as "imagnostic" invokes the mystical tradition of
Gnosticism, in which knowledge comes through subjective reflection, as
opposed to adherence to an external set of theological doctrines.[2] The myth
of a transcendental divine spark or light that the gnostic must discover

within himself is central to the tradition and crucial to the attainment of knowledge within it. There are obvious parallels here with Brakhage's ideas about closed-eye vision and the reversal of the role of the camera as a recording device: "I began to feel all history, all life, all that I would have as material with which to work would have to come from the inside of me out rather than as some form imposed from the outside in."[3]

The retreat from a hostile outside world implied by this statement chimes with the reception of his work as expressionistic. However, I am not interested in discussing Brakhage's work in this way, not least because I find the idea of Expressionism unproductive. It seems, inevitably, to lead up the blind alley of who, or what, exactly, is being expressed (among other blind alleys). Neither am I concerned with the films as diaristic or autobiographical, however strongly they may be rooted in a family life. It is more productive to see how the films' formal operations work toward the dissolution of a related set of antinomies: matter and form, focus and defocus, rhythm and a-rhythm, montage and continuity, contrast and sameness, monochromy and poly-chromy, the last of which occurs more between the films than within them, and which is thus one of the rationales for their being a series. Overarching these is the opposition between representation and abstraction (a dichot-omy Brakhage refused, specifically in relation to these films: " 'abstract,' 'non-objective,' 'non-representational,' etc. I cannot tolerate any of those terms and, in fact, had to struggle against all such historical concepts to proceed with my work"[4]). This last hangs on the distinction between subject (profilmic) and apparatus, the fundamental distinction—spatial, formal, conceptual—whose dissolution is entailed in all the foregoing antinomies and the one that char-acterizes the vast majority of his films.

The questions raised by these antinomies are what are examined here, as well as the role and nature of color in time-based work and how it is different from the way color is used in painting, a medium to which the films gesture strongly. What is the relationship between form and color and how and why does it tend to get hierarchized? Can there be color films that are neither abstract (Paul Sharits's *Ray Gun Virus*) nor use color decora-tively (Oskar Fischinger's arrangements of color patterns to music) or in-formationally (as in Steven Soderbergh's *Traffic*, in which several different story strands are color coded to help the viewer orient within the narrative) but in which color achieves a relative independence from form and function to become a thing in itself.

The films were completed in 1979 and 1980, interspersed among his production of the *Duplicity* (1978–80) and *Sincerity* (1973–80) series. They all run at eighteen frames per second, apart from the first, which is at twenty-four. They were shot on Super 8, then blown up to 16 mm. This results in strikingly coarse grain, something that Brakhage explicitly explored in some of the films. However, they have the feel of 16 mm in that the image is more full bodied and stable than it would be if seen in Super 8. At the same time as making the *Roman Numerals*, Brakhage also made a Super 8 to 16 mm blowup of the two parts of *23rd Psalm Branch*, partly to preserve the film from disintegration but also, as he said, "because I fear the war-inclination of this society at this time once again."[5] Compared to these epic works, the *Roman Numerals* are modest in length and intimate in tone. In their painterly qualities, one can also sense how they look forward to the hand-painted films of the mid-1980s onward.

In these films particularly, form is always in a process of becoming: With the exception of a couple of key, but inconclusive, moments, representation is held at bay, a characteristic that distinguishes them both not only from obviously representational works such as the *Riddle of Lumen* (1972), but also from *Text of Light*, which stays resolutely within the physiomorphic world conjured from the light refracted in a glass ashtray. In collapsing many of the aforementioned antinomies, the films pose questions about some of the presuppositions we bring to bear in our routine watching of moving images.

For example, in discussing these films one inevitably resorts to expressions like "out of focus," yet such expressions are already problematic. First, and most obviously (and not just in relation to Brakhage's oeuvre), the phrase is value laden in ways that will be familiar to anyone who is familiar with experimental film. It assumes a normative and narrowly drawn understanding of vision as focused and stable. In questioning the instrumentalism of dominant cinema's use of film technology, experimental filmmaking must involve a rejection of ostensibly technical terms that turn on unexamined or assumed correlations between focus, clarity, objectivity, and good practice/craft. Such questioning is not unique to Brakhage's oeuvre, of course, but his work constitutes, with a few exceptions, a consistently sustained attack on the dichotomy of focus versus unfocused.

The concentration on focus raises productively ambiguous questions about the place of vision in a hierarchy of the senses. The films extend the idea of vision by including the out of focus as equal, if not superior, to the in focus, yet in the act of defocusing there is also a denying of vision in its place as a superior or dominant empirical tool. The interrogation of focus furthermore is crucial to Brakhage's breaking down the distinction between objects and light formations into phenomena, a move with an aim that seems to go beyond the obvious sense in which all film and photographic images are made of light, to comment on our relationship with the world we inhabit: a world we can experience as a scintillating interplay of complex optical phenomena but that we nevertheless describe and classify as static or moving objects situated in a determinate space and time. Defocus is also a way of liberating color from its coextensivity with form without completely setting it adrift so that it becomes merely decorative.

In many of the films there is a key tonality, or degree of lightness or darkness, as well as a predominant color with varying degrees of saturation. In some of the films, color contrasts, such as green/red, are key, but in most a single hue pervades.

The first film: *I* (1979, six minutes) has a predominant scheme of off-white through salmon pink to deepish mid-red. A camera circles over a knot of fuzzy, reddish lines. Underneath (or beyond?) these light, caressing moves, presumably lies an unidentifiable object, but it is just as easy to see this knot as a spatial array because it is neither enclosed by a contrasting border that would locate it in a putative space nor does it appear to be cropped by the camera's framing. As such it has no perceptible depth but neither does it obviously lie on the picture plane. The familiar octagonal refracted images of the lens diaphragm, formed when light enters the camera directly, are rendered circular by the lack of focus and form an integral part of the image. Could this be because the object is a light cluster—incident light—and not an object, which would help it to harmonize with the light/lens refractions, or is it simply that defocusing blurs, literally, the distinctions between objects and light or rather between reflected and incident light? Here are the first of the many cinematic antinomies that are dissolved in the film, between the profilmic and the apparatus, between conventionally wanted and unwanted optical phenomena.

Periodically, we see what appears to be a zoom, but into what? The idea of zooming supposes a final target detail in a predefined field, but when that field is already undefined—insofar as it is defocused—there is little against which to measure the zoom's progress, and thus the distinction between wide and close loses its purchase. What we have in effect is a kind of reframing or, better still, a pure cinematic movement, one that is not dependent on a preestablished profilmic that retains itself as a function of the apparatus, but a new kind of abstract movement that progresses, or evolves, the image.

In a number of the films Brakhage inserted black spacing, but in each case the function and effect of this is different. In the first film, there is a run of similar-looking shots; in each the first one or two overexposed frames have been retained. This overexposure is an effect of the Bolex taking a frame or two to run up to speed. Each of these frames is preceded by one frame of black, which serves to heighten by contrast the flash of the first, light frame. Thus, a purposeful, precisely calculated shot (one frame of black) is placed next to an incidental effect at the beginning of a shot, something that would normally be discarded. The equal validity of both intentional and unintentional features is thereby signaled.

A sequence of closely similar shots follows in which editing has at least two distinct functions in different parts of the film. The cuts serve to enliven the material by imparting a rhythm to what would otherwise be a near-unvarying sequence of red forms, although even when there is little perceptible movement or difference from one shot to the next, a (jump) cut is always a reminder of the exact extent to which a shot has evolved. At the opening of the film, the impression is that the camera was moving over its subject, but later the editing creates a sense that the camera was passing through its subject, or that the subject was parting to make way for the camera.

In *II* (1979, eight minutes, forty-five seconds) there is a stronger sense of shapes held within the frame and hence a greater separation between camera and subject. The color is darker but less saturated, and the image has the appearance of being created from superimpositions. Prismatic light clusters move in front of each other, but it is hard to tell whether the layering of these images is caused by their being superimpositions or an effect of defocusing. Things seem to come into focus, but they are not distinguished, spatially or formally, from the more out-of-focus areas of the picture. When we say "comes into focus," what we often mean is textures sharpening, lines or edges forming out of the flux. But what if there are no edges in the frame? These comings-into-focus encourage us to read the image as being of objects in a determinate spatial relationship to each other; in other words, they stimulate our reflex recourse to gestalts to fill in or anticipate what we think we are going to see. Here, however, while there is a definite sense of things resolving (into objects), we are still unable to read the whole scene as an image of objects in a space.

Long, stable shots are then interspersed with bursts of rapid cutting, with more dramatic changes from shot to shot than in *I*. There is a definite sense that image mutations are being produced by focus pulling, yet without the degree of out-of-focusness seeming to vary, and thus also avoiding the terrible cliché of focus pulls as seen on TV wildlife programs, when an alienated moment of disinterested formalism—free camera play—is self-consciously inserted into the stream of narrational camera work.

At five minutes, thirty-seconds, a bright, asymmetrical, tombstone shape sharpens momentarily in the lower right corner, dramatically coalescing out of its antithesis, a greenish fuzz in the center of the screen. Where does this shape come from and how, given that the fuzzy shape from which it emerges remains unchanged? If this were a simple focus pull, the whole shape would change; instead, two antithetical shapes seemingly emerge from a single source, which itself remains unchanged. This event throws no light on its own process: It is a challenging mystery. On the other hand, such moments teach us to beware of our easy familiarity not only with the phenomenal world, but also with that world as mediated by the cinematic apparatus, about which we just as easily make (knowing, sophisticated) assumptions.

A clue to the above may be provided by a later sequence in which a veiled, but sharp, shape is seen through a kind of gauze. This gauze could be literally that, or it could be an out-of-focus foreground object. The tomb-stone shape could be akin to the gauze, but that would still not explain the fact that the "background" fuzzy shape remains unchanged as the tomb-stone shape emerges. Alternatively, the latter could be a refracted aperture light disk, as in the first film, but seen beyond an interposed object that alters its shape.

III (1979, one minute, fifty-six seconds) is polychromatic, and the colors are mixed within the frame, not sequentially, so there are opportunities for color overlaps to produce secondary hues. Thus, colors are mixed in-camera, rather like paints are mixed on a palette or, rather, directly on the canvas. In this way, there is both a subjective process—Brakhage mixes his colors by framing things in certain juxtapositions—and an objective process, in that color mixing obeys certain chromatic laws, so that, for example, red and green overlaps produce a pale yellow. But this yellow mutates as the overlap shifts, so that there is never a fixed color. In fact, mysteriously, a pale blue appears as if on top of the yellow, suggesting that green and dark blue primaries are also

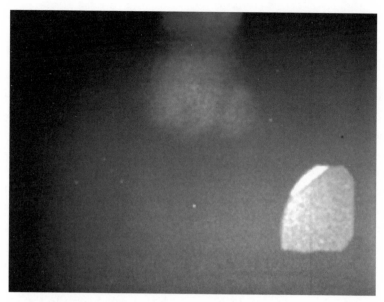

Stan Brakhage, *II*.

impinging into the scene. All this points to an inversion of the primary and secondary hierarchy in additive color mixing.

Color values are relative, as Michael Snow demonstrated in *Wavelength*, a film with color balance and contrast that constantly shift through the placement of color filters in front of the camera lens, changes of film stock, and variations in light levels and color saturation. People often mention the yellow chair in the loft space where the film was made, its presence out of all proportion to its significance, even when it blends into the wall behind when a yellow filter is applied. Perhaps even more remarkable, however, is the way white is relativized. White—the color of the loft wall and that from which all colors derive—is shown to be wholly context dependent, appearing as cool or warm, never neutral, even when there are off-whites with which to compare it and even, thereafter, when it appears neutral next to other seemingly neutral whites in the scene, such as the exterior signboards of Canal Street, where all the other colors fall convincingly in around a strong pale white. Eventually, one's whole sense of neutrality comes adrift: What appeared to be neutral whites at one moment seem, retrospectively, to have been colored.

The *Roman Numeral* films thus far have had a certain murky quality, albeit punctuated by bursts of brighter color. They establish themselves tentatively, working up to a slow climax before dying away slowly in longer, darker shots. By contrast, *IV* (1980, two minutes, five seconds) bursts onto the screen, a large radiant block of brilliant golden yellow, like a field of flaming wheat, before falling back somewhat into a lower key. Eventually, this turns into one of the darkest of the set, with forms half-emerging out of heavy grain in a manner that recalls Peter Gidal's *Room Film 1973* (fifty minutes, 1973). Gidal's camera strategy is intended not as expressive, but aims to create a producer, as opposed to a consumer of the film, that is, a self-conscious, reflexive viewer: "A film practice in which one watches oneself watching is reflexive; the act of self-perception, of consciousness per se, becomes one of the basic contexts of one's confrontation with the work."[6] Shifts of focus and the interaction between grain and image shift the viewer into a state of constant revision of knowledge and understanding of what is being looked at as it is being looked at and hence to engender an ongoing state of epistemological uncertainty. Gidal's project works to displace the author into the apparatus and hence is ideologically hostile to the idea of Brakhage's oeuvre as a vehicle for sustaining a transcendent authorial voice and the concomitantly adulatory spectator thereby constructed. He is also critical of the role of the image in the production of spectator consciousness: "The Structural/Materialist film must minimize the content in its overpowering, imagistically seductive sense."[7] There are, nevertheless, moments in Brakhage's work that, if one will detach the oeuvre as a whole from its reification of Brakhage as the subject and origin of the work, pose similar kinds of epistemological problems to the viewer through a strategy of withholding representation in such a way that the spectator must reflect not only on the conditions for knowledge, but also on the assumptions they bring to bear on a given image. The foregoing should not be seen as an effort to reconcile what are two clearly opposed positions simply to state that a given kind of film can be understood as sometimes functioning in a way that aligns it with work to which it is in principle hostile.

Perhaps the most notable event in *IV* is the projection outward, directly toward the spectator, of an abstract shape. One seems to have been looking at the picture plane, insofar as the image does not position itself back in space, yet this object now protrudes out of that place into an undefined, yet nearer, space. In his book on *Psycho*, Ray Durgnat reminds us of the important but usually overlooked fact that there has to be a space between the camera and the profilmic.[8] The profilmic cannot come right up to the camera, as it were, and when it does occasionally come close, as in some shots in movies, the effect is disconcerting. The suicide shooting at the end of Hitchcock's *Spellbound,* the close-up of a woman's ear in Bertolucci's *Before the Revolution,* or in *Citizen Kane* when objects in the extreme foreground lie immediately next to distant ones, all achieve this effect by collapsing the sense of comfortable distance that characterizes most movie shots. It is akin to the discomfiture one feels when the person to whom one is talking stands a little too close. This is what happens in the middle of this fourth *Roman Numeral.* The object exists in a space that is unreadable, perhaps because it flattens the space, annihilates it, or occupies a space that was ever there but always looked through. The sensation is something like the effect of moving one's fingers right up to one's face to the point at which they go out of focus. They no longer seem to be spatializable, even though they must be somewhere. Yet, why should one experience a similar sensation when watching this in a film, given that the screen itself is away from one's face, in the familiar space of over there?

As the film develops, the golden opening image reappears, transformed, along the margin of the frame, itself forming an incomplete frame around a gradually darkening, indistinct shape. Thus, a dialectic between object and frame emerges, gold being the common element that unites the two opposing functions. Partly by virtue of the common color link back to the work's opening shot, we are inclined to see this framing shape as the edge of a larger form that is edging into frame, rather than seeing it as frame-shaped. The shape appears successively, bearing down from above, pushing up from the bottom, squeezing the sides, while the central form remains constant. Despite the sense of the golden shape being much larger and therefore mostly off screen, these films do not ever create a strong sense of off-screen space, perhaps because on-screen space is never adequately staked out, yet here, if anywhere, one might have expected such a thing.

There are a number of transitions in this short film, mostly confined to one section, that are impossible to classify. They are concealed, not in the way that cuts are concealed in narrative movies through various kinds of across-the-cut continuity, but through purely visual formal operations. Sometimes, the screen image seems merely to shift or rapidly mutate, or there is a kind of "action cut" as the camera swings from side to side, but this is not like continuity editing since there is no strongly apparent move within the frame that continues across the cut.

Stan Brakhage, *IV.*

In *V* (1980, two minutes, thirty-six seconds), we see for the first time shapes that are probably generated from pro-filmic objects, in other words, things that do not look like light effects, although, as always, one cannot be entirely sure. The main image is a kind of eclipselike semicircular line that partially encloses a roundish shape. The color scheme is blue and yellow-green, and there are long black pauses with color flare-ends that fall in the middle of the frame. Thus, each black stretch is announced with a momentary flash of brilliant red/yellow and ends with the same, creating a kind of overhang (as opposed to an afterimage) into the next shot.

This film is more self-consciously composed and measured than the preceding four, but even the sections of black spacing announce themselves as shots, not just pacing devices, through the color flare-ends. The flares imply that the black has some kind of meaning beyond its rhythmic/pacing function. This may be nothing more than the intention to dramatize the contrast between black (colorless and lightless) and red-yellow (colored and light). In this respect, it relates to the single black frames in the first film. The sense of high contrast is continued within images, as opposed to between

Stan Brakhage, *V.*

them. These are followed with some low-contrast sections that are very different in character from the high contrast ones. Low-contrast imagery, which in itself would seem to be intrinsically undramatic, is dramatized by juxtaposition with the other material in the film. What is it that invites us to think of high-contrast imagery as dramatic? The cut between one such image and another, similarly contrasty but formally different, can be dramatic in that it draws attention to itself in its formal disruptiveness and so seems momentous. But, could not subtle shifts in low-contrast imagery, which gain in detail what they lack in punch, be just as dramatic in their own way?

Within this film, there is heterogeneity of color and image, so that it looks more like other Brakhage works. Yet, one is not eased, but plunged into this familiar territory because of the manner in which it is reintroduced, against a background of four films that have been strikingly homogeneous in color and restricted in imagery.

VI (1980) is the longest at nearly twelve minutes. The colors are green and pale red: not pink, but a desaturated red. Immediately, one is set to think about the relationship between hue, brightness, and saturation, factors that are in turn complicated by the brightness of the projector bulb and variations in the color temperature of white. Pinkness is a product of white being added to the mix and is, given that white is opaque, therefore an opaque color itself. But, the whiteness in a film pink comes from the projector lamp shining through a certain density of redness, so how is a color like pink even possible in film? (There is something here about a disjunction between film as colored translucent shapes and film images as simulacra of real objects). Furthermore, opaque colors tend to look flat, that is, nonshiny and hence chromatically homogeneous. Yet in films, unlike flat-colored graphic design images, say, there is always an impurity of color, and a certain depth at the grain level, since the film image is a composite of colored layers of grain held in a plane with a depth of field that is so minutely shallow that even grain has a modicum of perceptible depth.

In the *Roman Numeral* films the (Super 8) grain is very coarse, so that even at moments when there are large blocks of color, the multicolored grain structure supporting them is clearly visible as such (a reaffirmation here, at the technological level, of Brakhage's statement on the child's perception of "green" in *Metaphors on Vision*, perhaps: "How many colors are there in a field of grass to the crawling baby unaware of "Green"? How many rainbows can light create for the untutored eye?"[9]). And, of course, each grain appears to contain more than one color, in contrast to video, in which each colored gun fires only a single color, so that the image is visible as a regular grid of red-green-blue lights in a way that the film grain structure is not. In video, mixing takes place on the retina, but in film, and notably here, Brakhage creates a red on the screen that is at the same time visibly supported by complex interactions of primary colors. In video, then, there is a more clear-cut distinction between the red-green-blue on the screen and the apparent color that is mixed in the retina, whereas in film the distinction is blurred: In a sense, the eye meets the image.

This film in the series is closest to *Text of Light*—scintillating and crystalline—but more animated, with faster cutting: *Text of Light* must be Brakhage's most leisurely work. In this *Roman Numeral*, there is a more obvious sense of the camera bringing things into being and thus a stronger existential reference back to the maker. There are things that look more obviously like night lights—shop windows, street lights, vehicles?—yet their sources remain unobvious because unrecognizable. There is also a greater presence of lens refractions, and sometimes the familiar octagon shape is the only thing on screen, set against a midblack field of grain.

In becoming detached from its source—the presence of the sun is usually evident to some degree when these light rings appear—the octagon takes on a curious status. It is epiphenomenal, yet here, in isolation from its cause, it becomes phenomenal in the sense of primary, or sole: Its metaphysical status changes, but its physical state does not. The lens refraction image is abstract yet recognizable, indexical, yet transient.

The juxtaposition of red and green is notably strong, and it produces something like new colors. One sees the source colors and at the same time the colors produced by the interaction of those sources. The whole experience is somehow one in which color borders and definitions are superseded by something like new colors that do not fit onto the color wheel. It is akin to the experience in music of a work like Morton Feldman's long composition for piano, *Triadic Memories* (1981), in which the sustain pedal is held down continuously, producing slowly decaying clusters of adjacent notes that mingle to produce new kinds of unpitched-sounding sounds, even as they are initiated out of pitched ones.

At the end of the first part of *Psycho*, as Marion Crane's car sinks into the swamp, there is a fade to black. Ray Durgnat points out: "The *speed of fade* and the *time length* of the black reminds us that movies aren't moving *pictures* only: structurally, they're time-based *graphics* (like a black screen), some of which aren't pictures at all."[10]

The single black frames and prolonged spacings that appeared in the first and fifth *Roman Numeral* films, respectively, appear again here, now in blocks of four or five frames, separating long sections of pale imagery. There is a consistency about the way Brakhage uses these black spacings in the films not only to increase the contrast, and hence the impact of shot changes, but also to put some variety and dynamism into what could otherwise become overly homogeneous material. Yet, there are also differences in the effect and meaning of the blacks in each case. In *I*, a black "flash," or a moment of darkness, emphasizes the adjacent light flash frame of the following shot, whereas in *V* the blacks may be understood as shots: This is implied by the color burst at the beginning and end of each one. In *VI*, black is more like a momentary interruption to the flow, the briefest pause, separating a sequence of continuous imagery, turning it into quasi-disconnected shots, subduing the montage, as it were.

The grain is coarser in this film than in the others, so that the aforementioned effect of "single" colors emerging out of fields of pointillist, multicolored grain is reiterated even more strongly. Furthermore, because of the grain's mobility, and hence the surface's relative autonomy, camera movements appear as animators of kinetic events: They make the grain dance rather than seeming to pass across objects as in conventional pans.

VII (1980, four minutes, forty-five seconds) begins with what appears at first to be a TV roll bar, but it soon becomes apparent it is not: Its movements are too discontinuous. It is actually a black bar on a white ground, and its position shifts arbitrarily, yet there is surely a comment on TV here. Brakhage's dislike of both broadcast TV and video as a medium have nevertheless inspired some of his best films, including *23rd Psalm Branch* (1966–67) and *Delicacies of Molten Horror Synapse* (1991), with its extraordinary ghostly TV textures and images in negative, overlaid with looped, hand-painted material. In the Roman film, the comment seems to be more on the violence of the electronic process by which the TV image is constructed and disseminated, a disruptive, arrhythmic emission, a direct assault, in contrast to the reflected light of film.

The color scheme is further extended to include green/orange, gold, blue, white, and black, and there are lens refractions in which all of these colors are simultaneously present. The black sections get longer throughout the series, and here, as in *VI*, they have color flare-ends of red-yellow, but cutting to blue, so that the red-yellows impinge on the blue shots and become quasi-attached to them without becoming detached from the black. There are also shots with strongly contrasted color and black areas, such that one's eye conjures complementary-colored images in the black part of the frame.

Diminishing the aperture size of a camera lens extends the depth of field—the spatial axis between the lens and infinity—so that "stopping down" brings things into focus that were out of focus when the aperture was wide open. Stopping down concomitantly darkens the image as progressively less light reaches the film. Brakhage makes repeated use of these principles, creating fades to near-black from out-of-focus beginnings, so that shots come tantalizingly into focus just as they fade away. One says "fades to black," but in fact the device as used here is not really a way of fading, more a strategy for shifting emphasis within the image, in effect altering the hierarchy of elements within the scene, or "leading the eye around," to borrow a phrase from painting. Darker areas, of course, are the first to go, and highlights are the last, so that at a certain point in a given shot, the image will shift from being a variegated, multicolored field to a dark, modulated one with a constellation of soft highlights.

A key image in this film is steam, although like the epiphenomenal lens refractions in *VI*, it is detached from its source, so that it functions not only abstractly, but also as a kind of veil across something that is itself obscure. Given this obscurity, the veil comes to function less as a veil and more as a translucent texture overlaying a colored ground, but without us ever losing the sense of it being interposed between us and the veiled scene.

In *IX*, the final film in the series (1980, two minutes, nineteen seconds), black spacing comes to dominate even more.[11] The film has a "hot spot" at its center, as if it has been refilmed using a crude back projection system. Focus pulls are deployed extensively, notably to change the shape of clusters of starlike highlights, which morph into horizontal bar shapes and back again; hence, motion and mutation are achieved through focus pulling. An alternative approach to such cinematically created movement, that is, movement as the product of camera strategies, not pro-filmic movement, is rigorously elaborated in Wilhelm and Birgit Hein's film *Structural Studies* (1970). Where the Brakhage films are restless and animated, the Heins's is cool and methodical. It may be compared, in its taxonomical rigor, to the photographic work of Bernd and Hilla Becher, who photograph industrial buildings in a meticulously uniform manner. This is not to say that their work is not also about the apparatus in important ways, but there is a settled equilibrium in their pictures between the apparatus and its subject that in Brakhage's films is always precarious and unstable.

This brings me back to my starting point, which was to see Brakhage's films as interesting for the ideas that are raised through the operations of the apparatus, as opposed to discussing them in terms of the way they deliver Brakhage as the "existential subject of the work," to borrow a phrase from Malcolm LeGrice.[12] This second approach seems ultimately futile and un-productive because either the work is seen as heading into an ineffable realm where nothing can be said about it or, if seen as a reflection of its maker, leads backward into untenable metaphysical ideas about soul, origin, and genius, from which discussion is displaced into vague, ahistorical notions about oneness/affinity with nature and so on, none of which gets at what makes these films work on their spectators as films, what, in other words, makes them successful as art and amenable to critical analysis.

What is most interesting about this body of work is how it can make us rethink a number of assumptions we bring to viewing film: not only about focus and defocus and its role in the creation of representations, but also representations of what? About space: what kinds of space do out-of-focusness create, and what happens to those spaces when focus is pulled/aperture closed or opened? Concomitantly, what happens to form/space dichotomies when space becomes form and forms are dispersed into fields of color? What about the opposition between blackness and image, in which blackness can be image and vice versa, that is, image, if one includes color flashes as such, becomes spacing or a modified kind of pause? These kinds of formal/conceptual issues are at the heart of this series of films and are what distinguish them from the more widely discussed mythopoeic body of work, in which many of the formal innovations for which Brakhage is rightly acknowledged are nevertheless working in the service of larger, often noncinematic ideas. In the *Roman Numeral* series, these innovations function as ends in themselves, so that the films' themes are neither existential nor mythopoeic, but formal/philosophical. This is also what distinguishes them just as clearly from the hand-painted films that followed soon after, in which the camera is abandoned, and thus the problematic indexical and iconic connections to an evasive yet evident profilmic, are severed.

NOTES

1. P. Adams Sitney, *Visionary Film*, 2d ed. (New York: Oxford University Press, 1979).
2. Brakhage dropped "imagnostic" in favor of "deja vue" after the fourth film in the series.
3. Stan Brakhage, introductory interview to *Metaphors on Vision*, Film Culture, 30 (Autumn 1963), cited by Sitney, op. cit., p. 147.
4. Stan Brakhage, *London Filmmakers' Co-op Distribution Catalogue Notes* (London: London Filmmakers' Co-op, 1993), 11.
5. Notes to *23rd Psalm Branch: Part II*, Canyon Cinema Film/Video Catalog 7 (San Francisco: Canyon Cinema, 1992), 53.
6. Peter Gidal, "Theory and Definition of Structural/Materialist Film," in *Structural Film Anthology*, 2d ed., Peter Gidal, ed. (London: British Film Institute, 1978), 10.
7. Gidal, ibid., 2.
8. Ray Durgnat, *A Long Hard Look at Psycho* (London: British Film Institute, 2003).
9. Stan Brakhage, *Metaphors on Vision*, Film Culture, 30 (1963), n.p.
10. Durgnat, op. cit., 153, Durgnat's italics.
11. In researching this essay, I have, for various reasons, not seen the eighth film, *VIII*, in the series, so a discussion of it is omitted.
12. Malcolm LeGrice, "The Truly Modern: Prototypes for the Non-Linear," paper delivered at the conference *The Future of Experimental Film*, University of Central Lancashire, Preston, England, 4–6 July, 2003.

   Thanks to the staff at Lux, London, Brakhage's U.K. distributor, for the provision of viewing facilities.

BRUCE BAILLIE

Letter re: Stan

Hello David,

    Very nice having a talk on the phone the other day, seldom hear from anyone these days outside of the Navy (my alter-occupation). The CFIDS [chronic fatigue and immune dysfunction syndrome] has pretty well put me out of action since '67. Unfortunately, it is not terminal.

Don't know if I'll have anything to say here, pretty tired, and prospect of normal energies not in sight; however, like to respond to your letter re: Stan, his life and work, etc.

Like Stan in his high mountain retreat of earlier years, I am at this moment of writing engaged in conversation with our four-year-old, Keith Baillie, over the whereabouts of some cherry-flavored candy. I recall during that visit of some years past Stan's describing his method for managing work, in between the raising of children and the usual mundaneries (of everyone's) life. He referred to a small room upstairs...later in our film exchanges during the 60s he sent me *Scenes From Under Childhood*, conceived in the darker corners of that place, which had some of the same "pre-birth" stuff of my own work, *Quick Billy*, of the same period.

En route from Houston where I had been filling in for James Blue at Rice, I stayed in my tent near Stan and Jane's place with my dog Bill. During the nights, we were joined at times by a great white, part wolfdog who ran wild up in the Rollinsville, Colorado, woods. (I sent an 8 × 10 for publication in Paris a year or so ago of myself naked high up in those mountains with the two animal companions.) One night the wolfdog came into our tent with a nose and mouth full of porcupine quills. I recall waking Jane, and with a pliers we blindfolded our wild friend and pulled out the quills, one by one throughout the night. He was one of those mythic "persons" who wander through our histories, finally shot by some retired general or somesuch, a neighbor of the Brakhage's. Possibly the same who may have sent the awful IRS agents up to Rollinsville. One of their least favorite experiences, so Jane said.

There were numerous exchanges between us later, or was it earlier? I sent him my "Rolls" (post *Quick Billy*) as they emerged—without "apology" (i.e., written explanation) or narrative context. For example, my face was distorted with poison oak, along with having just suffered a major case of hepatitis—the film can was by chance marked, "Poison," with skull and crossbones, apparently alarming Stan (who then contacted James Broughton about my "situation"). He in turn sent me long written responses to a series of Rolls as the months rolled by. And I believe he, like Will Hindle, came up to my temporary spot by the sea in Ft. Bragg (CA—there was a follow-up letter re: his perceptions of my "farm" as a sort of artifice—I can't recall the essential focus of this particular letter, but it was to be one of several observations on his part of what was—as Paul Arthur recently put it—my latest masquerade. I believe he had divined "the farm" to be a sort of fabricated illusion on my part, in that the illness was, characteristically, a death experience.

As well as filmmaker, father, and friend, Stan, I think, has been for all of us—this curious non-occupation of the film composer or poet—a mentor, or at least commentator, perhaps historian and even biographer, tending to a willful flock of disparate geniuses—not unlike a Cocteauian roll in the flowering of earlier 20th Century French arts. His place among us has reminded me as well of Henry Miller as in a sense Dean of Letters, or Defender of The Arts; recalling our occasional return to a running dialogue/ argument regarding "transcending the arts"—a particular theme I have thrown into the historic stew of our era or arena.

Anticipation of the Night. Dog Star Man. Mothlight (I have an 8 mm copy in my magic tower). Beautiful eyes. I can always see his eyes that during the Chicago lectures failed to identify a questioner in the last row: I was there by chance doing some sort of visit to the Art Institute, staying in the same hotel. Stan was emerging from a long and brilliant paragraph on, as I recall, the horrors of the life of the poet/artist/filmmaker—not, however, so-phrased ... but he was in fact the only person I have ever heard offer a definitive explanation of the phenomenon. At any rate, I concocted an inane question and threw it down toward the stage, receiving in turn a gentle and tolerant reply, which was not always the case during that singular lecture series. Later, I admitted to being the questioner in the top row.

During that time, Stan inspired me into becoming a Johnny Carson fan. I was surprised to hear from him during that stay in the downtown Chicago hotel that he always watched *The Tonight Show* when touring, a habit I eventually picked up.

So it has been. An occasional phone call, a postcard, photographs exchanged. "How are you?" "Still here." Like that.

Camano Island

CRAIG DWORKIN

Stan Brakhage, Agrimoniac

Je me voyais me voir.—PAUL VALÉRY

Loud Visual Noises

Unglassed Windows Cast a Terrible Reflection, asserts the title of Stan Brakhage's early 1953 film, challenging the very view that William Blake famously let pass unnoticed. Blake confesses: "I question not my Corporeal and Vegetative Eye any more than I would Question a Window concerning a Sight. I look thro' it and not with it."[1] As in the old saw that the eyes are windows on the soul, the window has long been figured in this way as the very model of a transparent, unimpeding conduit. However, as Brakhage's title suggests, there is a counter tradition that not only recognizes the interference of even the most pellucid material medium, but also casts a shadow of doubt on the dream of any unmediated vision at all. In Leon Battista Alberti's *De Pictura,* the probable source of Blake's figure and the most famous instance of the metaphorized window, the representational space of the panel painting is figured as an unglazed "window on the world" (as Joseph Masheck has noted in an erudite textual analysis, Alberti's reference is quite explicitly to an open [*aperta*], rather than a paned, window). Moreover, as Fernand Braudel reminds us, "fifteenth-century window glass was not very translucent and was anyway uncommon....What glazed windows there were would hardly have revealed an undistorted, transparent view."[2] Regardless of the view through Alberti's window, he would have had its orthogonals corrected by the *lucinda*, a "how-to-do-it apparatus of a thin 'veil' (*velum*) of semi-transparent cloth . . . for translating, as with Dürer's famous gridded frame in the next century, three dimensions into two."[3] In similarly optical terms, Louis Marin describes pictorial representation as the dialectic between the veil and the window. Given

1. The painting as material medium does not exist: human vision is not filtered by any grid or interpretive screen in order to comprehend the natural world.
2. In order to be able to represent the natural world, the painting as material medium exists: the accurate partitioning of reality comes about on and by that material medium. The human eye takes in only the double of the world.

Marin concludes:

From these propositions it follows that the material *canvas* and the *real* surface must be posited and neutralized in the technical, theoretical, and ideological assumption of its transparency: the invisibility of the material medium is the very condition of possibility for the visibility of the represented world. Transparence is the technical/theoretical definition of the opaque screen of representation.[4]

That "grid or interpretive screen" of representation returns in the anti-retinal, but still devotedly optical, art of Marcel Duchamp. One might, for instance, read the craze of cracks kept as design elements on the surface of the *Large Glass* in this light, and the "opaque screen" of the grid is an even more central subject of his witty *Fresh Widow*, which translates the pain of a wartime French widow into the glass panes of a miniature French window. In Duchamp's sculpture, those panes are veiled in a mourning black of leather, which would, presumably, block any morning light. Literalizing Alberti's metaphors, Duchamp puts punning pressure on the single silent *l* (with its ghost of the homophonic "elle," the putative widow) that differentiates the Latin of Alberti's *velum* (veil) from *vellum* (leather). The word-play of the English title further triangulates Duchamp's sculpture between the English word veils and the paragogic French word *œils* (eyes), and with those veiled eyes, *Fresh Widow* offers an alternative model for the eye as window: the eye in its carnality, and understood not as a clear windowpane but as what Guy Davenport has called a "flesh window," or to return to Blake, a "little curtain of flesh."[5]

To replace Blake's transparent ocular window with the curtain blinds of a corporeal eye, to insist on the opacities of vision and see *with* rather than through the eyes, has been central to the later films of Stan Brakhage, who has worked to occlude the illusion of a transparent vision and to recognize instead the fleshy materiality of sight.[6] Against the dream of a "transparent Eye-ball" (to borrow Emerson's famous phrase from the first chapter of *Nature*), and in contrast to the habitual and mechanical registration of external images, Brakhage's later films manifest that even the gross and vegetative "Eye sees more than the Heart knows."[7] Understanding that the "eye is not a passive mechanism for intercepting the image of objects," Brakhage's films lead their viewers to differentiate, like Ludwig Wittgenstein, between the alternate demands made by the rigid idealism of the pellucid "mental" or "geometric eye" and the inescapable carnality of the corporeal "physical eye."[8] Attempting to "untutor" that geometric eye, Brakhage posits a vision free of the social disciplining that conditions us to ignore certain material and retinal information and to regard the eyeball as some kind of transparent window on the world. His often-quoted opening to *Metaphors on Vision* formulates that defamiliarizing position in these terms:

> Imagine an eye unruled by man-made laws of perspective, an eye unprejudiced by compositional logic, an eye which does not respond to the name of everything but which must know each object encountered in life through an adventure of perception.[9]

In following Brakhage's "adventure of perception" in this essay, I do not want to suggest that we mistake his reconfigured or expanded conceptualization of vision for something closer to "true" sight or as the wholesale replacement of one model with another. Rather than imagine the return to a prelapsarian and prelinguistic visual utopia, I want to understand the project of optic untutoring as a reconfiguration of the codes of visuality and an opening of the visual field to multiple, competing, and contradictory "scopic regimes."[10]

In reconfiguring those codes, Brakhage has explored damaged vision and ophthalmological aberrations. The punningly titled 1994 film *Black Ice*, for instance, is named after the sight loss that followed from slipping on unseen ice and suffering a concussive blow to the head, just as *Through Wounded Eyes* (a 1996 collaboration with Joel Haertling) takes its inspiration from a detached retina. Moreover, Brakhage has also insisted that even the healthiest vision is less clearly transparent than we typically imagine, and he exploits the characteristics of his medium to produce filmic equivalents of the optical phenomena he refers to as "closed-eye vision."[11] Rapidly intercut clear and colored leader, for instance, creates flashes and flares that dramatize the visual renewal of the blink. The micromontage of sequences of only a very few consecutive frames in length, for another example, replicates those eidetic images that flash suddenly and briefly before the unwilling mind in "the hypnagogic process whereby the optic nerves resist grotesque infusions of luminescent light," just as the inclusion of solarized images, superimpositions, and the printing of black-and-white negatives from color reverse suggest figure-ground reversals and make manifest the normally unrecognized optical phenomenon at the heart of motion pictures: the persistence of vision in afterimages.[12]

Similarly, the rhythmic twists of the anamorphic lens in a film like *Pasht* exaggerate the fatigue of the ciliary muscle and the flattening of vision beyond the *fœvea*. Moreover, the rapid jerky movements of Brakhage's trademark camera work, in handheld 8 mm, can be seen as an equivalent of the eyes' saccadic movements or their constant drift and tremor. The treatment of that 8 mm stock by bleaching and baking to bring out the emulsion grain (which is already more visible than in 16 mm), as well as an embrace of the lower definition created by optical printing, suggest the halation of retinal saturation and the subtle but incessant pixilation of the visual field.[13] Furthermore, the dust, hair, and scratches visible after that printing—like the surface manipulations of paint flicked from a brush onto the surface of the film or scratches etched into the emulsion—all simulate the flinch and drift of entoptic imperfections that cast shadows on the retina as debris floats through the vitreous fluid.

Above all, Brakhage's manipulations of the surface of the film—through overpainting, scratching, and the inclusion of foreign particulates in printing—suggest the luminous dance of phosphenes: those scintillating patterns and specks of light that are "subjective images generated within the eye and brain rather than by light from outside."[14] In Brakhage's hand-painted films, the isolated flecks, dripped trails, shaped smears, and layered washes of ink and paint all nictitate in bursts of patterned color against richly black ungiving grounds, flaring and disappearing with a rate that often renders them difficult to retain, or at times even to perceive clearly with any certainty. Indeed, unable to arrest the precession of fleeting color forms, the viewer comes to measure their pace with the body's own optical clock: the literal blink of an eye. With more or less fit and disjunction, the sequences of stepped and staggered patterns stutter in certain films with a crude animation, appearing at times to move or rotate in a mutating motion. In other films, static images are held and replaced at a more meditative pace, but never long enough that their perception is unthreatened by the shutter of the viewer's blink.

In the eye itself, the phosphenes that these filmic effects approximate can be elicited by a range of physical and neurological trauma, but they are most familiar from simply applying pressure to closed eyes. The bodiliness of these visions are, appropriately, further underscored by the rich carnality of Brakhage's reds, the biomorphic suggestiveness of the paint's viscosity, the brush bristles' hint of dermal prints, and the frequent impression of diagnostic slides: surgical cross sections of flesh, flayed and dyed for microscopic analysis. By revisioning phosphenes in these ways, the pellicule of organic material comprising the substrate of Brakhage's films mimics the body's own translucent and photosensitive membranes and permits, through its very opacities, an illusion of transparence that allows the opacities of the human membrane—glimpsed in tentative flickers and transient shadows—to be seen. Brakhage's films, in short, momentarily replace the illusion of the eye's transparent clarity with a clear view of its materiality. His films, like the bodily experiences they imitate, frustrate the idealization of vision by documenting the obstructions and impediments that the eyes themselves present, and they remind us of the corporeal ground for resisting those ideologies that have attended myths of unmediated transparency.[15]

Brakhage is certainly not the first artist to focus attention on such phenomena. Phosphenes, in fact, have a surprisingly long history in the modern French literary tradition. They appear at key moments in Arthur Rimbaud's "Les Poètes de Sept Ans," Samuel Beckett's *Watt,* Robert Desnos' *La liberté ou l'amour!,* René Crevel's *Babylon,* René Daumal's extraordinary essay "L'inérrable expérience," and Francis Ponge's "La Crevette," in which they swarm before the eyes of the reader like particles of type. Nor is Brakhage alone in making films that emphasize the illusion of clear vision or that propose the distinctly ecstatic pleasures of obscurity. The examples from Brakhage's own works are quite numerous, but one might note, by example, the empty sockets in the autopsied skull in the *Act of Seeing With One's Own Eyes*, the emulsion scraped from the image of the eyes of the man in *Reflections on Black*, or the images of a cloud-veiled disk of the sun: that object which permits the very vision that cannot directly comprehend it.

These figures of the threat and inevitability of blindness take their place in the long tradition of ocular aggression in avant-garde cinema—an aggression always implicitly aimed at the open eyes of the viewer. Most famous, of course, is the razor scene in Luis Buñel and Salvador Dalí's *Un chien Andalou*, but one might also recall of the equally disturbing operation in Paul Sharits's *T,O,U,C,H,I,N,G*, or the enucleation in the final moments of Pier Paolo Pasolini's *Salò: o le centoventi giornate di Sodoma*—all of which foreground sharp metal slicing instruments to suggest an allegory of cinematic splicing and thematize precisely that formal method by which they achieve their emotional and narrative effects: montage. Similarly, the crashed rocket in Georges Méliès's 1902 *Voyage a la lune* projects from the wounded lunar eye like an impacted telescope: an analogue for the cinematic tool of successive close-ups that gives the illusion of thrust and motion to the preceding scenes of the rocket approaching the moon. Such scenes, in fact, date back to the inaugural moments of cinema; the first copyrighted film, William Dickson's 1894 *The Edison Kinetoscopic Record of a Sneeze*, presents a physiological event during which one cannot physically keep the eyes open.

A powerful sneeze, like the one melodramatically recorded for Edison, is also one of the numerous conditions, including loud noises, that can induce phosphenes.[16] Not coincidentally, Brakhage specifically refers to the latter stimuli in his short 1986 film *Loud Visual Noises*, the title of which was suggested by its dedicatee, Paul Lundahl. Related to contemporaneous works like *Fireloop* (part of the "Caswallon Trilogy"), *Loud Visual Noises* is a looped and erratically hand-painted film in which the projected paintings create foudroyant displays and sudden, intense bursts of visual pyrotechnics. When the film was included in a video collection of four of Brakhage's hand-painted films from the 1980s, producer Joel Haertling paired its "visual music, a 'music' for the eyes" to which Brakhage aspires, with a soundtrack of darkly ambient postindustrial music montaged from Die Tödliche Doris, Hafler Trio, Nurse With Wound, IHTSO, Haertling himself, and :Zoviet-France (represented by an excerpt from the composition "Cair Camouflet," which was originally released on an album entitled, significantly, *Look Into Me*).[17] The selections that Haertling chose for inclusion prominently incorporate a range of untuned radio signals; the crackle, hiss, and screech of electromagnetic tape; and a wide sampling of audio static. Indeed, beyond the high-decibel audio stimulation that can provoke neuoptic flares, "noise," in its information-theory sense, is all to the point for closed-eye vision. Phosphenes "presumably reflect the neural organization of the visual pathway"; that is, they are part of the noise in the optical channel.[18]

A film like *Loud Visual Noises* reminds us that we can see even in the complete absence of light because there "is always some residual neural activity reaching the brain, even when there is no stimulation of the eye by light."[19] *Loud Visual Noises* thus provides the optical equivalent to John Cage's aural revelation that even in the absence of external sounds "there is no such thing as silence." Brakhage, as it happens, studied briefly with Cage, who contributed the soundtrack to Brakhage's short 1955 film *In Between*. A few years earlier, Cage claims to have come to his realization about the absence of silence during a purported visit to a soundproof laboratory:

> For certain engineering purposes, it is desirable to have as silent a situation as possible. Such a room is called an anechoic chamber, its six walls made of special material, a room without echoes. I entered one at Harvard University several years ago and heard two sounds, one high and one low. When I described them to the engineer in charge, he informed me that the high one was my nervous system in operation, the low one my blood in circulation.[20]

To listen to that high-pitched drone and low percussive rhythm in the anechoic chamber, or to view phosphenes, is to experience the operation of the nervous system as it records itself rather than any external stimuli.[21] As Henri Bergson realized, even after eliminating all "the sensations that come...from the outer world" one still registers "the organic sensations which come from the surface and from the interior of the body."[22] Or, as Brakhage described his films, with an echo of Valéry's *La Jeune Parque*:

You are seeing yourself seeing. You're seeing your own mechanism of seeing expressing itself. You're seeing what the feedback of the mind puts into the optic nerve ends that cause them to spark and shape up like that.[23]

These correlations are not only interpretive but also bear on the overall generic status of Brakhage's films. By recording that "act of seeing," Brakhage insisted that his works are documentaries rather than mere expressionistic abstractions or imaginative and fantastic inventions. I want to qualify his assertion further and propose that his films are intimate physical portraits of their viewers; they hold up a mirror—albeit a *speculum obscurum*—of the glaucous, carnal eye looking at its fragile fleshy self.[24]

> *The stars are sparks of lightning. . . . Big dust motes*—STAN BRAKHAGE

To Have Apprentice in the Sun

In his extraordinary *Boite verte* of 1934, Marcel Duchamp left the note: "To raise dust on Dust-Glasses for 4 months. 6 months. which you close up afterwards hermetically = transparency—Differences to be worked out."[25] Which may help explain Man Ray's famous 1920 photograph of "dust breeding [*elevage de poussière*]" on the *Grand verre* (large Glass), but Duchamp's enigmatic note might equally have come from the lab books of Georg Christoph Lichtenberg, a scientist at the University of Göttingen experimenting with electrical generators and "working out the differences" of "dust breeding" as early as 1777. After carelessly leaving the laboratory equipment uncovered one night, he found that the cakes of resin being used as inductors were coated with tiny stars of dust. The rather aptly named Lichtenberg realized that when light had reached the photoconductive resin, it charged the surface, attracting dust along the branching lines of its electrostatic fields (*du champ*, as it were). Such stochastic electron patterns are still known to scientists as "Lichtenberg figures," but his discoveries had far-reaching industrial and commercial consequences as well. A century and a half later, just as Duchamp was breeding his dust and working out the mechanized reproductive technologies of the bride and the bachelors, with their glass plates and chemical sprays and heat exchanges—a project he sums up by saying "I wanted to get back to a completely *dry* painting"—the young American poet and inventor Chester Carlson was developing Lichtenberg's findings and creating his own version of chemically heated reproductive machines, with glass "beds" and a "dry writing" that he would translate into Greek with an invented word to name his invention "xerography."

In the modern copier, Lichtenberg's patterns of electrostatically charged dust reappear as the dry carbon dust of toner, negatively charged and attracted to patterns of conductivity made by reflecting light off of an image (the document to be copied) and onto a coated drum. The toner is then transferred to a piece of paper or some other support and fused to it with heat. Or, at least that's how it is supposed to work. In a twenty-four-hour Kinko's store in Boulder, Colorado—not far from where Brakhage was making *Loud Visual Noises*—Jay Schwartz, a young poet studying at the Naropa Institute's Jack Kerouac School for Disembodied Poetics, was investigating the potential of the Xerox machine to malfunction. Exploiting the fact that color copy toner fuses at a lower temperature than black and white, he found that color copies reinserted into the bypass tray of a black and white copier had their surfaces altered not because of any image copied but because the higher temperatures of the black-and-white machine would melt the color toner into messy runs and leave residues that then transferred to any subsequent sheets sent through the same feed path. Similarly, a Federal Express envelope could be cut into 8.5 × 11 inch pieces and sent through the bypass tray to melt and have the images copied on it fracture over the facture of its crust of blisters and wrinkles. As Schwartz laconically remarks in a letter describing his experiments and encouraging further investigation:

> The copier might say there is a paper jam. In fact, the FedEx material has melted in the fuser. If this happens, open the copier and extract whatever you can from the fuser (near the end of the copier where the paper comes out) and close the machine. Don't tell the employees. They'll be angry.[26]

The visual results of such procedures cannot be predicted or controlled, and these works offer one version of what it would mean to realize Duchamp's proposal to "make a painting of happy or unhappy chance (luck or unluck)."[27] Nonetheless, in a confirmation of Marshal McLuhan's hypothesis that superseded technologies are ripe for artistic appropriation, the resultant "displacements and deformations" are striking, and often surprisingly beautiful.[28] The pages emerge caked with partially fused color toner baked in a thick impasto that cracks as it cools and dries and dislodges in flakes. Passed back through the machine, the sheets also return with adhesive, decalcomanic prints, and the residue of burns, or with smears and tears that pattern and disfigure the original image.

The streaks and smudges of ink in particular recall the expressive abstractions of midcentury gestural painting. Indeed, several of the found images seem to be drawn from the illustrations to an art history text, and their vandalized results—like the defacement of tourist snapshots and amateur photo portraits—appear like nothing so much as indifferently executed versions of Asger Jorn's détourned paintings, the mediocre realist paintings he picked up second-hand and overlaid with his signature drips and runs and splatters. Moreover, Schwartz's aggressive modifications of ready-made images, distorted and stretched with elongated smears from their subjection to heat transfers and the rollers' flattening, also evoke Duchamp's proposal for making a "reciprocal readymade" by using "a Rembrandt as an ironing-board."[29] "It's rather hard on the Rembrandt," as one of Duchamp's interviewers noted, to which he replied: "It is, but we had to be iconoclastic back then," signaling not only the typically outrageous dadaist gesture of outrage but also the image breaking—*ikono klastes*—of his anti-retinal program. "Perhaps," as Duchamp wrote to himself while working on the *Grand verre*, "look for a way to obtain superimposed prints"; accordingly, ghostly geometric forms float in shadow over some of Schwartz's pages in a complex layering, while other pages are cancelled with series of thickly inked black boxes punctuating the Xeroxed Polaroids, computer printouts, time cards, commercial charts, and pages from industrial manuals that Schwartz had gathered from the shop's recycling bins: misaligned, misfed, or misregistered sheets; unwanted duplicates; pages that had been rejected for no apparent reason; and pages that had been copied in the first place for reasons one could not imagine.[30]

For all of their ruined beauty, Schwartz's Xerox works have less to do with their final look than with the process of their modification. Indeed, like Anthony McCall's *Line Describing a Cone* or Ernie Gehr's *History*, they are photographic works that investigate the nonimaging properties of the photographic apparatus. By using "the copier only for its heat, pressure, and chemical properties, rather than its ability to create new versions of the 'original'," Schwartz's investigations measure a machinic climatology and record the humidity, temperature, pressure, and electrical storms of the machine's interior atmospherics.[31] Similarly, with their streaking smears and tears and shadows, they map the feed path and the interior architecture of the machinic corpus: its internal organs and skeletal system and endocrinology. Multiple exposures, for instance, track the relative time of the source page's movement through the feed path in relation to the timing sequence of the illuminating scan, registering the systolic reflexes of the machine and creating a "painting of frequency."[32] Similarly, the geometric blocks that ghost over the pages record machine parts usually hidden from view or interior spaces in fact inaccessible to view; such structures and spaces are of no consequence when the paper is on the glass, above the focused light of the copy cycle, but when the toner is charged from below, as the paper passes through the unshielded, interior areas of the machine, they are imaged in a shadow painting as their forms are unintentionally illuminated by the flash of copy light from somewhere above. They are "the negative apparition" on pages where "the picture is the apparition of an appearance"—an attempt to "determine the luminous effects (lights and shadows) of an interior source" and to "make a picture of *shadows cast.*"[33]

Once again, the implications of these formal effects are generic; Schwartz's works, in short, are portraits. But unlike Brakhage's films, they are *self-portraits*: reflections of the photocopier looking at itself. Where Brakhage put the mechanisms and materials of film in the service of representing the body, using opacities in order to *look at* opacity, Schwartz's procedure is much closer to the radically nonrepresentational cinema proposed by Peter Gidal in his "Theory and Definition of Structural/Materialist Film": a "non illusionist . . . demystification of the film process" in which the film is neither a representation nor a reproduction.[34] To this extent, Schwartz's images have less in common with most "photocopier art" than with a musical composition like Steve Reich's *Pendulum Music,* in which microphones are hung over a loudspeaker with an amplifier arranged so that feedback is generated only when the microphone and loudspeaker are in alignment; the microphones are then set swinging along their parabolic pendular paths, honking and whooping briefly each time they pass the speaker with a rhythmic logic that follows from their harmonic motion and ends in an inevitable augmented drone.[35] Similarly, Matmos's *Always Three Words* sets a four-channel tape recorder running with no input and then passes two walkie-talkies over the recorder, both handsets in transmit mode but again without any input, thus producing an audible interference that can be manipulated with gestural sweeps.[36] As with Cage's bodily music in the anechoic chamber or Schwartz's Xeroxes, these compositions are examples of a system recording itself recording. Moreover, like Brakhage's techniques of presenting closed-eye vision, or Schwartz's exploration of the inutile capacity of the machine to record the nonphotoreproductive aspects of its functioning and structure, they are examples of recoding the presumed utility of machines by redirecting and emphasizing characteristics of media that are normally ignored, avoided, or considered as incidental errors.

By obviating the uniform reproducibility that is the dream of the Xerox machine in favor of irreproducible singularities, unique dispositions of unstable materials, and a host of exceptions, accidents, and errors, Schwartz's work is decidedly 'pataphysical. In Alfred Jarry's formulation, 'pataphysics is "the science of the particular," which "will examine the laws governing exceptions" to form a "science of imaginary solutions."[37] One of the more serious versions of 'pataphysical thought can be found in Ludwig Wittgenstein's *Philosophical Investigations*, which in contrast to the rigid, single-minded totalizing of the earlier *Tractatus*, repeatedly explores multiplicities and "the fact that there are other processes, besides the one we originally thought of."[38] With reference to mathematics, for instance, the "point is, we can think of more than *one* application of an algebraic formula."[39] Ridding himself of the illusion of a single logical necessity for decoding a formula— what he calls "the hardness of the logical must" that seems to attend a mathematic computation—then leads Wittgenstein, interesting, to the figure of the machine.[40] He argues that, as with mathematical formulas, the utility associated with machines induces us to forget that they might equally perform other functions and be used in different ways. Moreover, he argues that even the conventional, utile operation of the machine contains the latent potential for other functions and activities. In a passage that anticipated the work of Jay Schwartz with an uncanny accuracy, he writes: "We talk about a machine as if its parts could move only in one way, as if they could not do anything else, while we forget the possibility of their bending, breaking off, melting, and so on."[41]

Such malfunctions, paradoxically enough, get at the essence of the machine. Expanding on T. E. Hulme's recognition that "the grit in the

machine" is an integral part of the machinic essence, Gilles Deleuze and
Félix Guattari theorized that "breaking down is part of the very functioning
of desiring-machines," a concept that Guattari later abstracted to the claim
that malfunction is in fact "the fundamental element of the machine":

> The maintenance of a machine is never fail-safe for the presumed
> duration of its life. Its functional identity is never guaranteed. Wear and
> tear, precariousness, breakdowns, and entropy, as well as normal func-
> tioning, require a certain renovation of a machine's material, energetic,
> and informational components, the last of which is susceptible to
> disappearing in "noise" . . . In fact, wear and tear, accident, death, and the
> resurrection of a machine in a new "example" or model are part of its des-
> tiny and can be foregrounded as the essence of certain aesthetic machines
> (Cesar's "compressions", Metamechanics, happening machines, Jean
> Tinguely's machines of delirium).[42]

One could update Guattari's example with the mention of Mark Pauline
and the Survival Research Laboratory, as well as more recent projects from
Eric Paulos and the Experimental Interaction Unit at Berkeley or Bill Vorn
and others at the Laboratory for Interactive Technology in Quebec; the
techno-parasites of Erik Hobijn and Andreas Broeckmann, the Center for
Metahuman Exploration, and all of those techno-anarchist 'pataphysicians
interested in disrupting the smooth, unthinking interaction between humans
and machines. Indeed, as Guattari continues, "Machines speak to machines before speaking to humans, and the ontological domains that they
reveal and secrete are, at each occurrence, singular and precarious." The
compositions by Reich and Matmos let us overhear what machines say to one
another as they speak, and Schwartz's work gives us a corresponding example
of what nonhuman vision might look like. His works of machine vision
propose concrete examples of what the Xerox machine might see if it were
freed from the service of looking for us and instead looked at itself.

We are surrounded with examples of vision machines, from contact
lenses to closed-circuit cameras and digital scanners, from the medical
technologies of x-ray and magnetic resonance images and computed axial
tomographic scans, to the military technologies of infrared binoculars, radar
screens, and the sorts of "intelligent" missile systems so luridly displayed in
the first Gulf War. All of those machines, however, are prostheses of human

vision; they extend or modify information that is inflected in a circuit back to the human vision, with which they are interfaced by way of the screen, the lens, the printout, or the photocopy.

In Schwartz's work, on the other hand, in which the conventional imaging properties of the machine are incidental, we can begin to glimpse the sort of mutant evolutionary transfer of characteristics from the human to the machinic phylum that Deleuze, Manuel de Landa, Paul Virilo, and others have recently theorized: "a vision machine" that will "automate perception" and establish a "sightless vision," to use Virilio's terms.[43] Such a machine vision, he argues, will "remove us from the realm of direct or indirect observation of synthetic images created *by the machine for the machine*," so that "blindness is thus very much at the heart of the coming 'vision machine.' The production of sightless vision is itself merely the reproduction of an intense blindness."[44] That sightless vision is registered in the blinding flash of the copier's light, at which one cannot directly look, and which gives us, finally, the photograph Duchamp proposed but never achieved: "avoir l'apprenti dans le soleil [to have apprentice in the sun]."[45]

The "sightless vision" of Virilio's inhuman vision machine throws the humanism of Brakhage's machine vision into sharp relief. Suspecting that film itself "*is*, as eyes have it, *at one* with the synapting Human nervous System," Brakhage, as we have seen, recognizes that the "background [medial] noise of motion picture systems is very much like that of the eye-brain."[46] Counter to the tradition of rationalizing the eye in the terms of a geometrically perspectival rationalist machine, Brakhage's films envision their technology in terms of the corporeal eye and its own reserves of sightless, scotoscopic, closed-eye vision. Understood in the light of Schwartz's erring machine model, Brakhage's defamiliarization of our habitual understanding of vision reminds us of the limits of the metaphors at work in those technologies of vision that increasingly occupy and regiment our surveillance culture. Moreover, his defamiliarizing techniques return us to our bodies and to a sense of their failings and fragility. Perhaps unexpectedly, the very tenuousness of our bodily mechanisms (our "soft machines" understood in Wittgenstein's sense of a machine that will err unpredictably and break down) will in fact be the ground of its strength in resisting the seamless interface between body and machine. Furthermore, the reconfigured eye, like the reconfigured understanding of the metaphor of the machine, is one step toward dismantling the "myths of necessity, ubiquity, efficiency, of instantaneity" required by the dark age of intelligent machines prophesied by Virilio and De Landa.[47] We should learn to see for ourselves while we still can, to see for the last time—in this last instance before the age of the vision machine—as if it were for the very first time. That is, to see without ceding any of the modes of the optical operation: with a fraught vision replete with all its imperfections, distortions, opacities, and sightless displays. Perhaps then we can see our sight as model of how to engage the world, and one another: with the full experience of the body, and not through the proscriptions of the well-tutored mind.

> *The blinding film shall part,/And . . . the eyes/In recognition start.*—ARTHUR HUGH CLOUGH

NOTES

I would like to thank Lyn Hejinian, who first introduced me to Brakhage; Ty Miller, who gave me the opportunity to present a portion of this work; and P. Adams Sitney, who has given me encouragement and discouragement in well-timed succession—this essay is for him.

1. "A Vision of the Last Judgment," in *Complete Writings*, ed. Geoffrey Keynes (Oxford, UK: Oxford University Press, 1966), 617.

2. Quoted in Joseph Masheck, "Alberti's 'Window': Art-Historical Notes on an Antimodernist Misprision," *Art Journal*, 50, 1 (March 1991), 36. Masheck quotes from *Capitalism and Material Life: 1400–1800* (New York: Harper and Row, 1973), 121, 214. Confer Braudel's *Civilisation materielle, economie, et capitalisme: xve–xviiie siecle* (Paris: A. Colin, 1979), 257–8; translated as *The Structures of Everyday Life: The Limits of the Possible*, Vol. 1 (New York: Harper and Row, 1979), 296–7.

3. Masheck, "Window," 37.

4. *Détruire la peinture* (Paris: Éditions Galilée, 1977), 61. The original reads:

> 1/ Le tableau come surface-support n'existe pas: le regard humain n'est filtrÉ par nulle grille ou tamis interprétatif pour se saisir du monde naturel.
>
> 2/ Pour pouvoir représenter le monde naturel, le tableau comme surface-support existe: sur et par lui s'opère l'exact dédoublement de la réalité. L'œil humain ne reçoit que le double du monde.
>
> D'où la nécessaire position et la nécessaire neutralisation de la «toile» matérielle et de la surface «réelle» dans l'assomption technique, théorique, idéologique de sa transparence: c'est l'invisibilité de la surface-support qui est la condition de possibilité de la visibilité du monde représenté. La diaphanéité est la définition technique-théorique de l'écran plastique de la représentation.

Compare Marin's description of pictorial realism with Ron Silliman's description of literary realism, which aspires to have the page and any sense of "the word as such" disappear before a reader absorbed in "content" ("Disappearance of the Word, Appearance of the World," in *The New Sentence* [New York: Roof Books, 1987]). Moreover, this double sense of material grid and transparent window come together in the projection "screen," which Charles Bernstein discusses in an argument sympathetic with my own: "The movie screen becomes, through the magic of cinema, a window onto a world behind it" (*Contents Dream: Essays 1975–1984* [Los Angeles: Sun and Moon, 1996], 93).

5. Blake, *Writings*, 130. Davenport, "Two Essays on Brakhage and His Songs," *Film Culture*, 40 (1966), 10.

6. Blake, *Writings*, 433. Without elaborating on Blake's idealist or spiritual argument— a visionary poetics and optics of apocalyptic transcendence that Brakhage counters by literalizing—I want to emphasize the vocabulary, if not the sentiment, of Blake's visionary optics; he derides the "Corporeal and Vegetative Eye" earlier in *A Vision of the Last Judgment* (614), and he repeats the prepositional distinction, explicitly in terms of transparency, in "The Everlasting Gospel": "This Life's dim Windows of the Soul/Distorts the Heavens from Pole to Pole/And leads you to Believe a Lie/When you see with, not thro', the Eye" (753). The full couplet from the "Auguries of Innocence" reads: "We are led to Believe a Lie./When we see not Thro' the Eye" (433).

7. Ibid., 189.

8. Bernstein, *Content*, 135; Ludwig Wittgenstein, *Preliminary Studies for the "Philosophical Investigations," Generally Known as the Blue and Brown Books* (Oxford, UK: Blackwell, 1969), 63–64.

9. "Metaphors on Vision," *Film Culture*, 30 (Autumn 1963).

10. Though it may now be more familiar from Martin Jay's appropriation of the term, *scopic regimes* comes originally, of course, from Christian Metz's *The Imaginary Signifier: Psychoanalysis and the Cinema*, trans. Ben Brewster, Alfred Guzzetti, Celia Britton, and Annwyl Williams (Bloomington: Indiana University Press, 1981).

  For more on the dream of undisciplined vision, see John Ruskin's *Elements of Drawing*; (London: Herbert, 1991), as well as Ernst Gombrich's refutation that "the innocent eye is myth," *Art and Illusion* (Princeton, NJ: Princeton University Press, 2000).

11. In *Light Moving in Time: Studies in the Visual Aesthetics of Avant-Garde Film* (Berkeley: University of California Press, 1992), an inspiring and superb study of the visual aesthetic of avant-garde film to which I am greatly indebted, William C. Wees provides a more patient and sustained account of Brakhage's attempts to "give sight to the medium" of vision; his book is requisite reading for anyone interested in Brakhage and avant-garde film.

12. Brakhage, screening notes to *Delicacies of Molten Horror Synapse*.

13. For the swoop of the handheld camera as an equivalent of the saccade, see Wees, 85 et seq. Brakhage explicitly relates "the grainy shapes of closed-eye vision" to the emulsion grain of film, *Brakhage Scrapbook: Collected Writings, 1964–1980*, ed. Robert A. Haller (New York: Documentext, 1982), 48, 51; cf. 115, 120.

  For more on the pioneering use of 8 mm and the "inherently radical" political import of Super 8 and the "utopian alternative" it presented to wider gauge strips, see J. Hoberman, "The Super-80s," *Film Comment* (May–June 1981), 39–43.

14. Gerald Oster, "Phosphenes," *Scientific American*, 222, 2 (February 1980), 83. See also Otto Grüsser and Michael Hagner's historical overview in *Documenta Ophthalmologica*, 74 (1990), 57–85.

15. One might extend a reading of Brakhage's interest in the carnal eye to the general bodiliness of vision and the optical implications of the body as a whole since even the most blunt and gross movement through space changes our relation to sources of light and its reflection. As Bruce Elder summarizes, picking up on a passage from Henri Bergson: "Corporeal changes register in perception, altering its form"; see *The Films of Stan Brakhage in the American Tradition of Ezra Pound, Gertrude Stein and Charles Olson* (Waterloo, Ontario, Canada: Wilfrid Laurier University Press, 1998); see also Bergson, "The Image and Reality," in *Matter and Memory,* trans. Nancy Margaret Paul and W. Scott Palmer (London: George Allen, 1950), 43–44.

Jonathan Crary has attempted to historicize the shift from the body as "a neutral or invisible term in vision" to "the thickness from which knowledge of the vision was derived" and an understanding of the "carnal density of the observer" ("Modernizing Vision," in *Vision and Visuality,* ed. Hal Foster [Seattle: Bay Press, 1988], 43). See his expansion of this summary in *Techniques of the Observer: On Vision and Modernity in the Nineteenth Century* (Cambridge, MA: MIT Press, 1990), as well as the related arguments presented in *Suspensions of Perception: Attention, Spectacle, and Modern Culture* (Cambridge, MA: MIT Press, 1999).

16. Albert Rose, *Vision: Human and Electronic* (New York: Plenum, 1973), 46.

17. "Inspirations," *Essential Brakhage: Selected Writings on Filmmaking* (New York: Documentext, 2001), 211.

18. Oster, "Phosphenes," 83.

19. Wees, 3; R. L. Gregory, *Eye and Brain: The Psychology of Seeing,* 2d ed. (New York: McGraw-Hill, 1973), 81.

20. "Experimental Music," in *Silence: Lectures and Writing* (Middletown, CT: Wesleyan University Press, 1961), 8. Cage frequently repeats the anecdote elsewhere.

21. Cf. Brakhage, *Scrapbook,* 134.

22. Henri Bergson, *Creative Evolution,* trans. Arthur Mitchell (New York: Henry Holt and Co., 1911), 278. I am grateful to Branden Joseph for drawing my attention to this passage; he makes the immensely significant discovery that Cage was paraphrasing a passage from Henri Bergson, whom Cage had been reading ("White on White," *Critical Inquiry,* 27, 1 [Autumn 2000], 90–121).

23. From lecture at Hampshire College, summer 1972 (audiotape 23, Media Study, Inc., Buffalo, NY); quoted in Wees, 93. Brakhage makes similar comments elsewhere (*Scrapbook,* 48) and frequently repeats his Helmholzian rhetoric, speaking, for instance, of neural activity as a "short circuit," *Scrapbook,* 134.

In *La Jeune Parque,* the persona exclaims: "Je me voyais me voir [I saw myself seeing myself]." Other lines, such as "Quel éclat sur mes cils aveuglément dorée,/Ô paupières qu'opprime une nuit de trésor" and "Mon œil noir est le seuil d'infernales demeures!" are equally suggestive, and the whole of Valéry's poem, with its rhetoric of internal visions, haptic sight, and palpable luminosity, might be productively read in the light of Brakhage's films.

24. For Brakhage on the "documentary" nature of his film, see *Scrapbook,* 188, and *Dialogue on Film,* 2, 2 (1973), 10. Charles Bernstein makes a similar point in terms of the conventions of realism: "As for realism, from the point of view of reproducing the material conditions of seeing—including diffusion, distraction, fragmentation, blurring—works by Snow or Brakhage, and the like, are probably more deserving of the term" (*Content's Dream,* 103).

25. Marcel Duchamp, *Salt Seller/Marchand du Sel: The Writings of Marcel Duchamp*, ed. Michel Sanouillet and Elmer Peterson (New York: Oxford University Press, 1973), 53.

26. Undated correspondence (ca. 1998), author's collection.

27. Duchamp, *Salt Seller*, 23.

28. Ibid., 35

29. Ibid., 32.

30. Ibid., 38.

31. Schwartz, undated correspondence (ca. 1998), author's collection.

32. Duchamp, *Salt Seller*, 25.

33. Ibid., 71.

34. *Studio International*, 190, 978 (November/December 1975), 189–96.

35. Written in 1968, the piece was premiered near Brakhage's home in Boulder by Reich and William Wiley and given a famous performance at the Whitney Museum in 1969, with Reich, Bruce Neuman, Michael Snow, Richard Sierra, and James Tenney performing. Two recent recordings are available from the Ensemble Avantgarde (Wergo 6630-2) and Sonic Youth (SYR4).

36. *Quasi-Objects* (Vague Terrain 001), 1998.

37. *The Exploits and Opinions of Dr. Faustroll, 'Pataphysician*, Book II, trans. Simon Watson Taylor (Cambridge, UK: Exact Change, 1996). For more on 'pataphysics, see Christian Bök's indispensable *'Pataphysics: The Poetics of an Imaginary Science* (Evanston, IL: Northwestern University Press, 2002).

38. *Philosophische Untersuchungen/Philosophical Investigations*, 2d ed., trans. G.E.M. Anscombe (Oxford, UK: Blackwell, 1997), section 140.

39. Ibid., 146.

40. Ibid., 437.

41. Ibid., 193.

42. Gilles Deleuze and Félix Guattari, *Anti-Oedipus: Capitalism and Schizophrenia*, trans. Robert Hurley et al. (Minneapolis: University of Minnesota Press, 1983), 32 et passim; Félix Guattari, "Machinic Heterogenesis," in *Rethinking Technologies*, ed. Verena Andermatt Conley (Minneapolis: University of Minnesota Press, 1993), 22. See also "On Machines," trans. Vivian Constantinopoulos, *Journal of Philosophy and the Visual Arts*, 6 (1995), 8–12.

43. Paul Virilio, *The Vision Machine* (Bloomington: Indiana University Press, 1994), 59 et sequitur. For similar theoretical work by someone who began his career as an experimental filmmaker, see Manuel De Landa, *War in the Age of Intelligent Machines* (New York: Swerve Editions, 1991).

44. Virilio, *Vision Machine*, 62, 72–73.

45. Duchamp, *Salt Seller*, 24.

46. First quotation from Brakhage, "Manifesto," in *Essential Brakhage*, 205; second quotation from Leny Lipton, "A Filmmaker's Column," *Take One*, 4, 1 (1974), 46.

Annette Michelson finds Brakhage's conception of the camera as an extension of the eye a "highly questionable" equation that takes a useful metaphor too literally and "violates the camera's function" ("Film and the Radical Aspiration," *Film Culture* [winter 1966] 41).

47. Jonathan Crary, "Eclipse of the Spectacle," in *Art After Modernism: Rethinking Representation*, ed. Brian Wallis (New York: New Museum of Contemporary Art, 1989), 294.

Brakhage Package

Wedlock'd in a ranchero two step/writhing together in a fiery mating dance of long and lost embraces/one plugged into the other in a loop like a perpetual energy machine/we were/we are in a battle of furious glances/we, us, one/I am you are/one of us/me, you/ each of us/find the key and unlock this fucking door/and now it is intermission/king's x and coffee and cigarettes.

i remember Sirius/black dog/white dog/brown/speckled/dotted/longtail, short tail/long hair or not, ears up, down, nose to the air, into a hole, alert/ sniffing/dem bones, dem bones/drinking from the hose/the basso in the neighborhood choir imitating ghost dogs/the smell of him/shaking himself dry, ears flapping/oh yes, he is loved and cared for, he has a name, a telephone number and should not wander away, get lost, get picked up, get killed/late at night he scratches himself/and his dog tags tinkle and I am reassured/I love his cranky I am sleeping voice and matted fur, his thunder and loving grunts, his pretense of submission when he bows and rolls over on his back giving me access to his vulnerable underside/I know that what he really wants is a good rub on the belly and he indulges me/Sirius-ur dog fell down somewhere in the forest having found his secret dying place, or what was pushed, dragged, knocked down shot down and the life went out of him/the man finds him like that, and sniffs him, brother dog/and time and the elements return the animal to the earth/the man watches and re-members/I live in the city and I'm old now and my dead dog can't be left out to rot and be detected/he's too big for me to lift or drag where I can bury him on the hill in back where stones grow like potatoes/I call the dead animal pickup guys/they come and grind him up mixing his dear parts with a dead horse and the road kill of the day/but the dogman has told me how it happened to Sirius and how it will happen to me and to all of us and in a few days I have another puppy.

sunlight baby moving just beneath the surface of flesh mountain as she pounds out her song/let me out/and we get the message/in the dark waiting, the future pushes down and down and then the volcano erupts and it feels like molten lava/flowing flowing/punching through my body/the hot rude runaway river is devouring every feeling in its path except pain and I am burning alive giving life to the sun/and the river drops its cargo from my cunt with a thud and a wail/Jane takes the camera and films the man and he has fallen over/stun-gunned to the earth/the breath sucked out of him.

wings speeding through the night toward the light/thousands of ex-quisite aviators on a suicide mission/at dawn the mothman gathers up the dead, arranges them in fantastic patterns on transparent film, binds them in place with a path of clear tape and gives them to us/are those tiny petals and stems that he found while crawling bare assed, ecstatic, fuckplowing the earth, up the canyons, down creek banks, over boulders, through, through meadows, among the leaves where ur-dog died?/or are they broken wings among the whole ones, and slender legs and little faces?/and he shows it to us/this lit from behind cascade, flying without a net.

spread fingers over my eyes/just in case/in the act of seeing/peeking over the edge of the table where the dead woman lays in a cold room among metal knives, hammers, spreaders, hooks, tools handed down from the inquisition/this smooth skinned, long limbed, naked hunk of dead meat is soon adorned with its own skin turned inside out and peeled back/pearly skull cracked/revealing the essence of her/moist ribs exposed, opened up stern to stern and beautiful guts arranged modestly on her lovely thighs/there are questions to be answered here/i never did shut out the light with my waiting to be closed, just in case fingers.

crazy with images/starman/scar the film, paint it, bury it in snow, piss on it, bake it, see the forest with a baby's eyes, unlearn everything, hymn to nod/sunday comics with light blasting through Prince Valiant's armor/sun through the jelly jars, shadows on the mussed bed, morning through the window/the night/the cello'd storm/explosions of painted fire/forest trapped by the lens/majestic solitude/trying to remember what we cannot/what it was that we knew before context and memory

P. ADAMS SITNEY

Brakhage's Faustian Psychodrama

Most of Brakhage's energetic output of films in the eighties refracted the prolonged crisis culminating in the end of the marriage in which he had been so invested as an artist and polemicist since the late fifties. The key documents representing aspects of that agony would be *Tortured Dust* (1984), a four-part film of sexual tensions surrounding life at home with his two teenaged sons; *Confession* (1986), depicting a love affair near the end of his marriage (1987); and the *Faust* series (1987–89), four autonomous sound films reinterpreting the legend that obsessed Brakhage throughout his career.

Apparently, the filmmaker did not have a series in mind when he made the first part, *Faustfilm: An Opera* (1987), in collaboration with the composer Rick Corrigan. Joel Haertling, himself a composer and filmmaker, played Faust. There are three other players in the film: Gretchen (Gretchen LeMaistre) and Faust's Friend (Phillip Hathaway) and his Servant (Paul Lundahl). The narrative action is carried largely by Brakhage's voice-over, almost unique in the immense corpus of his films, while human action is nearly reduced to silhouetted figures in dark interiors. In the schematic episodes of the film, we see Faust drinking, masturbating, and playing the French horn. At the instigation of his Mephistophelean "Friend," his imaginary female companion materializes as Gretchen. The film concludes with Faust and Gretchen on a bed blowing bubbles while the naked Friend whispers in Faust's ear.

Brakhage quickly followed that film with a further meditation of Faust's erotic imagination, *Faust's Other: An Idyll* (1988). Haertling composed the music for this work. In it, we see him and his girlfriend, Emily Ripley (also listed as a collaborator for the use of her paintings in the film), alternating domestic chores with scenes of him playing music and her painting. The cinematic style is much more typical of Brakhage at this period than the static, nearly monochromatic imagery of the first Faust film had been: It has a rather rapid change of richly colored shots with regular shifts of focus, giving elaborate attention to details within the unfolding daily events.

The next section, *Faust 3: Candida Albacore* (1988) seems to be a dramatic rehearsal for a performance in which Ripley and Haertling are joined by other masked and gaudily costumed musicians and actors in a *"Walpurgisnacht* to Faust."[1] The series concludes with an extended, somber periegeton, or travel poem, *Faust 4* (1989), with minimalist, often-rasping music, once again by Corrigan. Occasionally, the editing reminds us that Faust (Haertling) is the subject of this episode, but otherwise it constructs its rhythmic force from nonstop moving camera shots, usually from an automobile, of a trip that includes the oppressive modernist architecture of Oral Roberts University in Tulsa, the decaying house in Winfield, Kansas, where Brakhage was born, and the monumental ruins of Mesa Verde.

Brakhage had begun the eighties with two related series of silent "abstract" films—modulations of color and light without identifiable imagery—The *Roman Numeral* series (1979–81), nine films "which explore the possibilities of making equivalents of 'moving visual thinking,' that pre-language, pre-'picture' realm of the mind which provides the physical *grounds* for image making (imagination), thus the very substance of the birth of imagery,"[2] and The *Arabic Numeral* series (1980–82), nineteen abstract films "formed by the intrinsic grammar of the most inner (perhaps pre-natal) structure of thought itself."[3]

I discuss the Faust series here as keys to the major achievements of the filmmaker's mature career. Brakhage told Suranjan Ganguly in an interview celebrating the artist's sixtieth birthday: "Faust, for me, is *the* major legend of Western man."[4] Permutations on the Faust story had been central to his education as an artist. In 1947, when he was fourteen and entering high school, three of the most influential authors in the world published versions of Faust. The gradual translation of two of them and the assimilation of all three would have occurred during the formative period of the precocious filmmaker. Thomas Mann's *Doctor Faustus* was probably one of the most prestigious novels published in his adolescence. He quotes elliptically from its climax in *23rd Psalm Branch* (1966): " 'Then, take back Beethoven's Ninth,' he said."[5] As a would-be dramatist with modernist convictions, Brakhage may have known that Gertrude Stein wrote *Doctor Faustus Lights the Lights* in 1938 and that Paul Valéry had written *Mon Faust* in 1940; both were published in 1947. Furthermore, from the time of its publication, William Gaddis's *The Recognitions* (1955) was acknowledged as a major achievement within some of the avant-garde circles of Brakhage's contemporaries; it repeatedly incorporates allusions to Faust in its narrative of forgery, disillusionment, and eventual redemption. However, he would have been less favorably disposed to Jack Kerouac's Faust, *Dr. Sax* (1959).

Yet above all other versions, Robert Duncan's *Faust Foutu* (1956) seems to have challenged the filmmaker's imagination during his formative period. Duncan's masque, "an entertainment in four parts," depicts the anguish of Faust as an abstract expressionist artist in a witty, plotless phantasmagoria: As he marks his canvases, he compulsively narrates to himself the personal associations his colors and shapes call to mind. It is apparent from his mention of Duncan's masque in *Metaphors on Vision* (1963) that Brakhage considered it to be a crucial statement of the limitations of "affection" and an instrument for understanding (and thereby overcoming) the first crisis of his marriage to Jane Collom. A year before that marriage, he had begun to write his own *Faustfilm* (1957) but never finished or filmed it.[6]

There may even have been a psychodramatic element in the association with Duncan's play at the time Brakhage returned to the theme of Faust. Duncan himself was a mentor, teacher, and at times a tormenter of Brakhage from the time he moved to San Francisco in the early 1950s. When the filmmaker James Broughton moved to Europe at that time, Brakhage rented his apartment, below Duncan's. Duncan became his model for the serious Artist, his poetic father, with whom he had an unresolved agon. Duncan's fascination with Gertrude Stein, whom he was studiously imitating at the time, became Brakhage's obsession. Her *Doctor Faustus Lights the Lights* may have inspired Duncan; certainly, it inspired Brakhage, who had his collaborators study it during the making of *Faust's Other: An Idyll.*[7]

When *Faust Foutu* was first performed at the Six Gallery in San Francisco in January 1955, Brakhage's high school friends, Larry Jordan, himself a distinguished filmmaker, and Yvonne Fair played the chief roles; Jordan was Faust, and Fair played Helen, the film actress Faustina, and other roles. Earlier in Colorado, Brakhage had shared Fair's affection, but ultimately Jordan prevailed in their erotic triangle. Therefore, if Duncan's inflection of the legend of Faust had once been interfused, for Brakhage, with his potentially traumatic displacement by Jordan, certainly as Fair's lover and more remotely as the subject of Duncan's recognition, his surprising return to the *Faustfilm*, at least in title and theme, after thirty years might be seen as a reengagement with the sexual and psychic tensions that immediately preceded his first marriage, for he started the Faust series during the severe crisis of the failure of his marriage to Jane and continued the series of four films through the period of his divorce, living in isolation in rented rooms in Boulder, Colorado, and into his subsequent courtship of Marilyn Jull. During that time, Robert Duncan died (1988).

Whereas Goethe's Faust contracted with Mephistopheles for youthful vitality, in *Faustfilm: An Opera* Brakhage's Faust asks for the advantages of age: The filmmaker, speaking in voice-over, identifies "his absolute wish that he, Faust, suddenly could have fulfilled his every last task without having to live through the intervening years of tedious accomplishment." Yet, nothing we see confirms this chiasmus. The initial *Faustfilm: An Opera* shows us a young man, sometimes accompanied by a boy, in his house. He plays the French horn, drinks wine, talks to another man, masturbates, and seems to make love to a woman with the friend watching, naked. It is the voice-over that informs us Faust is a divorced, solitary drinker, "estranged from the ways of God and men," raising his son in his father's house, and desperately seeking a confidant. Many of these details reflect Haertling's domestic situation. In the culminating erotic scene, Brakhage confirms the woman's passage from imagination to reality as, her voice-over continues, she "finally becomes flesh to his imagination . . . is real then as she always was somewhere."

Duncan had preceded Brakhage in dismissing Faust's will to be young again: His Faust, an abstract painter, proclaims near the end of the third act: "It was the tradition that Faust sold his soul to regain his youth. But *my* youth has lasted so long it is like a world-burden, a straightjacket of guilelessness."[8] But Brakhage's invention provides a double perspective to the psychology of his collaboration with the musicians and actors of his serial film: Literally, he projects onto his protagonist the desire to be like Brakhage himself, a senior and accomplished artist, but without the long and often painful labor required for such accomplishment, and in this way he points to his artistic achievement and its costs by indirection, elliptically attempting to reassure himself of the value of his lifework in the midst of his crisis. At the same time, he defends himself in the narrative fantasy against the very quest for renewal that he is blatantly putting into practice, both in associating—"collaborating"—with young artists and in returning to a psychodramatic mode of cinema he had abandoned at their age or younger.

Brakhage's earliest films had been influenced by the pioneering work in the 1940s of Maya Deren, Kenneth Anger, James Broughton, Sidney Peterson, Gregory Markopoulos, Curtis Harrington, and Willard Maas (and the even-earlier films of John Sibley Watson and Melville Webber). These filmmakers often used cinema as an instrument of discovery, frequently acting in their own symbolical dramas of sexual agony and illumination. Brakhage and Larry Jordan were the most important continuers of the psychodramatic mode in the 1950s.

Brakhage's evolution as an artist was quite rapid, even though it was slower than the spectacular starts of the major figures of the 1940s. By 1958, he had withdrawn the somnambulistic protagonist of the psychodramas from his place before the camera and fashioned a style of somatic camera movement and editing that made the presence behind the camera the center of a lyrical crisis film. This became the dominant mode of his mature work. It was massively influenced by that of Marie Menken, another of the great generation of the 1940s who never made psychodramas but often assisted her husband, Willard Maas, in making his. The transition from psychodrama to the crisis film essentially coincided with Brakhage's meeting and marrying Jane Collum in 1958. Therefore, his return to psychodrama at the end of his thirty-year marriage combined elements of regression, desperation, and the weight of the experience of a life of staggering prolific filmmaking.

Thus, the double perspective of *Faustfilm: An Opera* may be projected into the film through a double identification for, just as the filmmaker is obviously exploring his long-dormant empathy with the figure of Faust, he cannot have forgotten the motor principle of his entire mature oeuvre—explicitly stated by the actor of *Blue Moses* (1962): "We're not alone! There's the cameraman. . . . There's a filmmaker in back of *every scene.*" If, indeed, the man behind the camera is necessarily a primary character in every film, then Brakhage is also representing himself, tacitly and sinisterly, as Mephistopheles, or Faust's Friend, the voyeur and almost participant in his amours.

In fact, in casting Joel Haertling, a composer and filmmaker, as "the contemporary Faust I was looking for,"[9] Brakhage happened on a psychodrama with parallels to the legend: The shift from Gretchen of the first film to Emily of the second records the change of Haertling's paramours; by the third part, Haertling was feuding with Brakhage and suffering from a sense of artistic and erotic betrayal from another friend and collaborator. In these young artists and their music and theater companies, "Architects Office" and "Doll Parts," Brakhage seems to have found a situation similar to the society he knew with Jordan and Fair.

Sidney Peterson's film *Mr. Frenhofer and the Minotaur* (1947), the preeminent allegory within the American avant-garde cinema of artistic aspiration and its erotic consequences, preceded Brakhage's indirect evocation of the mature accomplished artist. In the collapsing of the fictional Frenhofer and the historical Picasso, Peterson invented an ironic model for the artist Brakhage's Faust desires to be, and in his reimagining Poussin as an art student he created something of a precursor for Faust himself. In filming the young "Gretchen," the sometimes-naked object of Faust's masturbational fantasy, Brakhage almost reenacts Frenhofer's pact with Poussin: Je will let him see his "unknown masterpiece" if he offers him his mistress, Gilette, as a nude model to compare his imaginary portrait with a supremely beautiful woman. Poussin's older friend, Porbus, plays a role similar to Brakhage's Mephistopheles, symbolically dancing with Gilette on a mattress before encouraging and witnessing her modeling for Frenhofer.

Therefore, it is not surprising that the first three parts of the Faust series are indebted and pay homage to the films of Peterson, with whom Brakhage had intended to study when he moved to San Francisco in the early fifties. *Faustfilm: An Opera* may derive from *Mr. Frenhofer and the Minotaur* in its use of voice-over, mise-en-scène (action limited to a few interior sets and emphasis on the gestures of unheard figures in conversation). There is even a comparable focus of visual excitement: an isolated circular disk—in *Mr. Frenhofer* the interior mechanism of a music box, in *Faustfilm* a prismatic mobile in the shape of a wheel. Yet, the most revealing allusions to

Peterson's masterpiece[10] are deferred to the second part, *Faust's Other: An Idyll*, in which the overall tone suggests Brakhage's early *Cat's Cradle* and even Anger's *Inauguration of a Pleasure Dome* more than *Mr. Frenhofer*: the co-presence of a female fencer and a cat, Peterson's uncanny displacements of Theseus and the minotaur. Furthermore, anamorphic cinematography, the dominant stylistic feature of *Mr. Frenhofer*, does not enter the Faust series until the third film, *Candida Albacore*, which owes much more to Peterson's (and Broughton's) *The Potted Psalm* (1947), a film without anamorphosis, than to *Mr. Frenhofer*.

In his chapter on Peterson, Brakhage praised his ability to "assume a woman's viewpoint," comparing him to D. H. Lawrence.[11] One of several elaborate ironies Peterson marshals in *Mr. Frenhofer* gives the organizing voice-over to a female art student and model who, moving across the threshold of sleep, imagines herself as Picasso's Ariadne and Gilette, the heroine of Balzac's *Le chef d'oeuvre inconnu*, Poussin's mistress and the model for Frenhofer's almost-Galatean portrait of the ideal woman. Brakhage's recognition of the perspectivism Peterson gained by creating a female protagonist may account for his odd note for *Candida Albacore*: "It is the modern Walpurgisnacht to Faust, but the daydream of 'his' Emily: It exists that a woman have, finally, something of her ritual included in the myth of Faustus...and that 'muthos'/'mouth' become a vision."[12]

However, the wit, so abundantly manifest in Peterson's works, is the very quality most lacking throughout Brakhage's magnificent cinema. In a tacit acknowledgement of that lack, he made it the central theme of the lectures on American avant-garde filmmakers that make up his book *Film at Wit's End* (1989). There, he offers the following observations:

> Wit is sharp and based in repartee. It is a statement in relation to a fact, a fact in the immediate environment or a fact in history or in one's own experience. Wit points out those things in life that are disturbing or incongruous.... American humor is greatly influenced by a sense of sport which, as with the Greeks, is almost a religion.... The American inherently struggles to be gentle and at the same time not to be taken advantage of.[13]

I cite these observations in the hope of grasping the tone of the third part of the Faust series, *Candida Albacore*. By far the weakest of the four films, it seems to depict the costume rehearsal of a performance glimpsed in embryo in *Faust's Other: An Idyll,* itself the most accomplished film in the series. *Candida Albacore* lacks the voice-over commentary that is crucial to the narrative comprehension of the other three films. In style, the film owes much to Peterson's *The Potted Psalm,* but it suffers in comparison to its originality and strangeness. Brakhage might as well have been commenting on the acting in his film when he wrote of the Peterson-Broughton collaboration:

> *The Potted Psalm* is, I think, one of the least seductive films I have ever seen, and that is rather a triumph Peterson stumbled into, although it is intrinsic to his work to be very flat with his wit, to be very clear and always to reveal his techniques and disguises. . . . It is at least an incredibly unique example of art that has little seduction and complete ambiguity [of viewpoint]. . . . Many viewers feel that . . . "the hero," can't act, that the women in the film can't act . . . people don't gesture like that. The truth of the matter is that they do.[14]

Can Brakhage possibly have taken the performance these collaborators are rehearsing in *Candida Albacore* seriously? The setting seems to be a basement in which economy-size boxes of disposable diapers are stored. The costumes call to mind last-minute masquerade party attire. The posing and gesticulation are painfully awkward, adolescent, provincial. So much so that, despite the note's claim of including a woman's ritual in the Faust myth, Brakhage may be turning against himself in disgust, forcing us and himself to confront aesthetic humiliation as the Faustian price he must pay for the social and, in some sense, erotic intimacy with youth. In such a reading, the visibility of large cardboard boxes of disposable diapers in the background, and the blatant setting of a suburban basement, would be "statements" of the filmmaker's "relation to a fact"—his complicity—in which he would feel "taken advantage of." In his *Caswallon Trilogy* (1986), he put together a hand-painted film he made to be used in a play his wife, Jane, wrote with fragmentary glimpses of its rehearsal and similar impressions and a dance performance into a credible, if minor, film in his characteristically elliptical mode, making an evocation of his perception and memory in which he did not register the embarrassments (or splendors) of the performances.

Peterson had made his best films under daunting restraint: He worked with the budget of a semester's workshop class at the California School of Fine Arts, with his students for actors and incorporating the props they brought to class. Brakhage does not follow the method of bricollage Peterson used, stimulated by the very incongruity of his raw materials. Instead, he trusts his camera eye to make the performance or rehearsal revelatory.

Some overview of the four-part progression of the Faust films is needed at this point, although the discrepancies of the legend, Haertling's psychodrama, and the filmmaker's autobiographical tangents force the narrative to the verge of incoherence. Keeping in mind the organic evolution of the series, we can see *Faustfilm: An Opera* as a potentially self-enclosed unit to which the three expansions were added. It differs substantially from all of the other elaborations Brakhage made of traditional stories in his long career for previously he had seized on a single incident or image, such as Jahweh's exposing his backside to Moses (*Blue Moses* [1962]), the blinding of Oedipus (*The Way to Shadow Garden* [1955]), or the Styx as threshold of the underworld (*The Dead* [1960]), but in *Faustfilm* alone he reenacted a narrative sequence: Faust's despair, meeting, and pact with his Friend, erotic fantasy and fulfillment, approximately corresponding to Goethe's *Faust, Part One.*

If, as Brakhage's catalogue notes indicate, *Candida Albacore* corresponds to the Walpurgisnacht (one in each of the two parts of Goethe's drama), *Faust's Other: An Idyll* would be his version of the Helena drama. Thus Emily, who replaces Gretchen of *Faustfilm*, would function as Helena, even though the narrative evaporates after the first film of the series. Brakhage does not repeat the death of Helena's child (Euphorion in Goethe and Duncan, Echo in Mann); the role of Faust's son simply withers away as the series goes on. Mephistopheles (called Faust's Friend) also disappears after the initial film, unless the title *Faust's Other: An Idyll* derives from the preface "To the Wary But Not Unwilling Reader" of Paul Valéry's *Mon Faust*: "The personality of Faust, like that of his fearful partner, has an indefinite right to fresh incarnations. . . . The creator of Faust, and of the Other, brought them to birth so that they might, through him, become instruments of the world's imagination."[15] In that case, we might say the Other moves behind the camera, recedes within Faust, or both. Without this questionable clue, the Other in the title would seem to be Emily, Faust's (other) companion.[16]

Faust's Other combines glimpses of domestic life with preparations for a stage drama—painting sets, making props, composing music—which presumably becomes the focus of *Candida Albacore*. It ends with Emily caressing

Faust as he holds a cocktail. In a 1955 scenario published in *Metaphors on Vision*, Brakhage had written: "The legend of Everest is Faust in reverse. . . . [His] flights of fancy are interfered with by . . . a young woman who loves him. The scene between them realizes that she has more claim to his body than he has. . . . Once the young woman has left him for a time, that time becomes a trial in torment. He is confronted with his own selfishness."[17] It remains a credible gloss on the connection between the second and fourth parts. *Faust 4* explores the landscape of the Rockies and the Southwest in a rhythmic mesh of images shot from moving vehicles with periodic reference to shots of Faust and Emily, now familiar from the second part. The fourth act of *Faust Foutu* may be the model for this conclusion, but Duncan goes even further in discarding his dramatis personae, replacing them with five independent voices. The whole series schematically suggests that the mastery Faust gains is a masturbatory self-deception; he gets the power to attract women seriatim, but his brief idyll of energy and connubial harmony only results in an artistic failure from which he flees or attempts to flee.[18]

Much more than a narrative sequence, the Faust films are occasions for the filmmaker to return to the scenes of his aesthetic origins and his artistic growth. The editing rhythm and colors of *Faust's Other* recall *Cat's Cradle* (1959), one of his breakthrough lyric films. In it, he refracts the tensions he and Jane, then newly married, brought into the home of his friends James Tenney and Carolee Schneemann—like Faust and Emily a composer-painter couple. Brakhage is speaking:

> By part 4 I had to work my way out because I knew by then that I had to free myself from psychodrama, and from the dramatics of *Faust* itself, and inherit the landscape again. Part 4 is the obliteration by single frame of the memories of the past in the swell of the earth and in the desert. Also, by this time, I had met and fallen in love with Marilyn, and the film resulted from a road trip we took during which I photographed the landscapes of the west and the midwest. So in Part 4 there is no story really—but a going to the desert to rid myself of these "pictures" and encompass the whole spectrum of sky and earth and what lies between the two.[19]

This statement echoes remarkably the interview-introduction of *Metaphors on Vision* conducted thirty years earlier, in which the young filmmaker described his growth as an artist as a function of ridding himself of psychodrama at the time he met and married Jane. The Faust series, as such, schematizes the movement of Brakhage's much earlier career: A narrative psychodrama provides the basis for a more complex, subjectively filmed psychodrama, and commissioned film precedes a liberation from both narrative and psychodramatic conventions in a crisis film of expressive camera movements. This crude outline would make *Faustfilm: An Opera* the counterpart of his first film, *Interim* (1952), and *Faust's Other: An Idyll* the equivalent of the more intricate and subjectively photographed psychodramas *The Way to Shadow Garden* (1955), *Reflections on Black* (1955), and *Daybreak and Whiteye* (1957) with elements from the early transitional lyrics *In Between* (1955), *Nightcats* (1956), and *Loving* (1957).

Candida Albacore can be called a commissioned film only insofar as it centers on the work of the company Doll Parts and may have benefited from a grant to support regional arts. In his development, the commission from Joseph Cornell to film the 3rd Avenue El in New York was a crucial spur to Brakhage's origination of his lyrical mode, even though the resulting film, *Wonder Ring* (1955), lacks the power of subsequent, more personal lyrics. Finally, with *Faust 4* he ended the series with a work parallel to his breakthrough film, *Anticipation of the Night* (1958), in which there are traces of a psychodramatic frame story—the shadow protagonist hangs himself at the end—but the originality of the work lies in his exquisite articulation of camera movement and contrapuntal montage.

The Faust films not only are an exorcism of the ghosts of his earlier career, but also reflect the themes and modes of the strongest films he made just before them and immediately after. The texts of their sound tracks are even the nuclei of Brakhage's theoretical writing in the nineties. Let me take the latter point first.

The voice-over of the first, second, and fourth films in the series is a radical departure for Brakhage; the only previous instance of it in his filmography had been the aberrant film, *The Stars Are Beautiful* (1974), in which the filmmaker recited a series of fanciful cosmologies. In *Faustfilm: An Opera*, the spoken narrative controls the film's plot, providing us with Faust's history, motivations, and thoughts. But, from the start of *Faust's Other: An Idyll* the voice-over enters a new, and a startlingly original, mode. Without mentioning Faust once or even alluding to the legend, the spoken text elaborates in dense poetic language a theory of auratic vision and its relation to affects. This prose poem on the process of isolating pictures from the field of vision eventually leads to a visionary analysis of love:

> All is a'tremble, the waves of light, the eye itself enpulsed and continuously triggering its moods, the jelly of its vitreous humor (the first bent of light), the wet electrical synapse of each transmission, the sparking brain; but then comes the imagination of stillness midst the meeting of incoming light and discreet sparks of nerve feed-back, the pecking-order of memory which permits cognizance of only such and thus such, and imposes-on each incoming illumination an exactitude of shape and separates each such with a thus/distancing in the imagination: It thereby creates, of the dance of the inner and incoming light, imaginary tensions. These tensions, then, in taut network containment of these shapes constitute warp/woof of mem-ories "pick" of shapes acceptable to the imagination. The entire fretwork of these picked shapes at "taught" distance from each other are/therefore, in the mind's eye, the composition of image. The moves-of-shapes within the elasticity of such networking is/are the gestalt of acceptably sparked picturing; and the whole-of-the-process is the domain of picture.
>
> The very air trembles with the electric possibilities of this dance. The vapors round the cells stance-dance. The synapse is arrested, or as-if arrested which stops all known-dance. Leaps of an as-if imagnosis opts for aura. Little threads-of-color are warp to the woof of shadow-aura-gateway then. The eyes in drowse-of-love be fit to blur these weaves to an as-if-enlargement, vibrant as plucked strings seen slow-motional as unwinded fog or psychological haze. Magic!

My punctuation of these passages and even the accuracy of some clipped or slurred words has been confirmed and aided by access to the typescript of *The Dominion of Picture*, a long theoretical text, unpublished at the time of this writing.[20] If, as we may reasonably conclude, *The Dominion of Picture* was written during the period of the making of *Faust's Other*, the context in the book of such passages may illuminate the perspective of the voice-over of the film. *The Dominion of Picture* is a long love letter incorporating the author's experience of lovemaking and masturbational fantasies in an ex-plication of the nuances of his optical epiphenomena. It is addressed to

"Dear Reader," although its tone forcefully suggests it was written initially for a particular lover, probably his future wife, Marilyn.

Unlike the voice-over of *Faustfilm*, there is no irony or authorial distance in these elaborations of aesthetic psychology. They become the free indirect discourse of Faust's thought. Yet, the structural irony of the four-part whole indicates that this collapsing of filmmaker and protagonist, vividly represented in the fusion of words and image, is the paradigmatic moment of error, a dangerous seduction. "Sound is crucial for psychodrama principally because there is a lack of, what I would call, vision," Brakhage said to Ganguly. "What is psychodrama after all but the drama that's in the mind, and the extent to which you approach dramas, even in the oblique way that I did in *Faust*, involves engaging with picture and continuity as well as a whole hierarchy of symbols. In the absence of vision sound becomes necessary to stitch the loose threads together and make it all bearable."[21]

The opening speech of *Faust 4* begins with a deep sigh, almost groaning:

This is the aura of Faust's vision in meditation and the error of all his envisioned meaning. This is the landmass that fed his flesh, the very marrow of his unformed bones, the raw electrical connects of all he was ever to have known. These, then, the symbols of human hubris that tricked him out, the engineered play of mastery over earth and all the glistening sea, the dread darks thereof, the very air, suns white and molten. These the synaptical sparks of Faust's brain dreaming finally of stars.

Lacking a printed text this time, I waver among printing the first noun as *aura, order,* or *error.* The ambiguity is consistent with the film. Even more elusive is the anaphoric use of the deixic demonstrative pronouns: this...this...these...these. Do they refer to a whole chain of images unfolding and to follow in the film? Or, is the filmmaker indexically referring to the very words he is using in this and the one other speech late in the film? What precisely is "the aura [order, or error] of Faust's vision in meditation" and "the error of all his envisioned meaning"? Does Brakhage intend envisioned meaning as an oxymoron, as if it were necessarily an error to make vision follow meaning?

There is only one other recitation in the film. Six minutes before the end, a short monologue suggests Faust's redemption in terms of death and rebirth, darkness and sight, being and knowing, with echoing reverberations of the syllable *own*:

> And all that was known is now newly known. . . . Multitudinous montane shapes vie with inner clouds' geometries so that *that*, that was, is now reborn one. To wear/the curve/of earth itself, be weave, bear black's intrusion on one's closed, known, old illusional buzz of being; what one was is now one's end-zone. Gone to ground being then the very saw-teeth of the comb sown between sky and mind. The wild mountains of eyes' irregularities and all that was known *be* now then one's own.

The catalogue note for the film reflects this language, while providing a synopsis much more explicit than the film itself:

> This is the imaged thought process of the young Faust escaping the unbearable pictures of his broken romantic idyll, mentally fleeing the particulars of his dramatized "love," Faust's mind ranging the geography of his upbringing and its structures of cultural hubris—the whole nervous system "going to ground" and finally "becoming one" with the hypno-gogically visible cells of his receptive sight and inner cognition . . . and all that I could give him of Heaven in this current visualization of these ancient themes.[22]

Actually, there is a concentration of images from *Faust's Other* during the speech near the opening, but visual echoes of it recur infrequently and separated by long intervals; they have disappeared totally by the time the second text is heard. Instead, the film is an elaborate mesh of shots from a moving automobile, often in superimposition. Synchronized to the phrase "symbols of human hubris" the image of a monumental sculpture of praying hands appears for the first time. The montage suggests the vanity of aspirations to permanence by associating this bronze inflation of piety with the mysterious ruins of Mesa Verde and the mournful look of the weathered house where Brakhage lived as a baby. The superimpositions of the ruins of Mesa Verde and the wooden house in near-dilapidation suggest that these (and other modernistic structures from the campus of Oral Roberts University) are icons of the error of envisioned meaning, from which Faust flees through the desert and past a body of water to a neutral, flat, rural land-scape. But, since the weathered house is, in fact, Brakhage's first home in Winfield, Kansas, the oscillation between filmmaker-narrator and subject continues at least in this obscure personal reference to the geography of his upbringing. From this opening, a melancholy tone dominates the film.

Ironically allegorizing the breakdown of their collaboration, Haertling told me: "Brakhage sent me to Hell, while he went off on a trip with Marilyn." The film, however, suggests that a more accurate description might be that Brakhage was extricating himself from the problematic psychodrama of his Faust project when he fell in love with the woman who would soon become his wife. It is as if he accented the melancholy—"Faustian"—dimension of the landscape at the very time that he was grasping a new, enlarged vision of it. Thus, *Faust 4* documents that extrication and sketches out his next project, the brilliant *Visions in Meditation,* a series of four films made in 1989 and 1990. It rekindled his confidence in the eloquence of the embodied moving camera and resolved the crisis that engendered the initial return to Faust.

In fact, the phrase "vision in meditation" first occurs in the opening commentary of *Faust 4.* However, the four periegeta that make up the *Visions in Meditation* lack the grimness of that film. Even the spectacular *Visions in Meditation 2: Mesa Verde,* which tries to articulate the horror Brakhage felt at the site, is an exuberantly beautiful, vibrant film. As he travels through Canada and New England (in the first), studies a "dust devil" or miniature tornado in *Visions in Mediation 3: Plato's Cave* (1990), or makes a pilgrimage to D. H. Lawrence's home in Taos (in the fourth section, 1990), Brakhage films and edits with renewed energy and acuity. The melancholy that pervades the Faust series and clings to the periegeton of *Faust 4* dissipates in these films; in its place comes a vital engagement with the landscape and a depth of wonder and visual intelligence unsurpassed in all of Brakhage's cinema.

NOTES

1. *Film-Makers Cooperative Catalogue No. 7* (New York, 1989), 63.
2. *Brakhage Films* [sales catalogue for 16 mm prints], Boulder, CO, undated [ca. 1989], 18.
3. *Film-Makers Cooperative Catalogue No. 7,* 58.
4. Suranjan Ganguly, "Stan Brakhage—the Sixtieth Birthday Interview," *Film Culture,* 78 (Summer 1994), 27.
5. Adrian Leverkühn renounced his Faustian gifts of musical talent and success in these terms in Mann's novel, after his beloved nephew died of a disease caught from him. I was unaware

of the quotation when I wrote *Visionary Film* and even misquoted the film from faulty memory. The attribution first appeared in William Wees's essay "Words and Images in Stan Brakhage's *23rd Psalm Branch*," *Cinema Journal*, 27, 2 (Winter 1988), 43.

6. A fragment of the script appears in Stan Brakhage, "*Metaphors on Vision*," *Film Culture*, 30 (1963), unpaginated.

7. Telephone interview with Joel Haertling, February 8, 1996.

8. Robert Duncan, *Faust Foutu* (Stinson Beach, CA: Enkidu Surrogate, 1960), 57.

9. Ganguly, 27.

10. Brakhage refers to *Mr. Frenhofer and the Minotaur* as Peterson's "greatest work" in "Sidney Peterson. A Lecture by Stan Brakhage, Art Institute of Chicago, 1973," *Film Culture*, 70–71 (1983), 35, from which the chapter in *Film at Wit's End* was edited. Brakhage did not discuss the film in detail in the lecture and allusions to it did not remain in the edited book.

11. Stan Brakhage, *Film at Wit's End: Eight Avant-Garde Filmmakers* (Kingston, NY: Documentext, McPherson and Company, 1989), 59.

12. *Canyon Cinema Film/Video Catalog 7*, San Francisco, 1992, 57. The claim of incorporating a female point of view reaffirms an earlier statement of the role Jane Collom Brakhage played in his filmmaking.

13. *Film at Wit's End*, 15–16.

14. Brakhage, *Film at Wit's End*, ibid., 55–56.

15. Paul Valéry, *Plays*, Bollingen Series xlv.3, trans. David Paul and Robert Fitzgerald (New York: Pantheon, 1960), 3.

16. Joel Haertling understands the title to refer to Emily; telephone interview, February 9, 1996.

17. Stan Brakhage, *Metaphors on Vision*, from "His Story" chapter.

18. See Benjamin Bennett, *Goethe's Theory of Poetry*: Faust *and the Regeneration of Language* (Ithaca, NY: Cornell University Press, 1986), for an illuminating discussion of the role of masturbation in Goethe's *Faust*.

19. Ganguly, 28.

20. Stan Brakhage, "The Dominion of Picture," 2, 16. Robert Haller of Anthology Film Archives made his copy of the typescript available to me in 1996. Brakhage retitled it "The Domain of Aura."

21. Ganguly, 29–30.

22. Canyon, 57.

WILLIE VARELA

Stan Brakhage

American Visionary

If you want to know what cinema is . . . it's Brakhage.

—P. Adams Sitney *in Jim Shedden's documentary film, Brakhage*

It would be impossible to do justice to Stan Brakhage's influence on the directions and potentials of cinema over the last fifty years or so. His example as an artist, theorist, and lecturer, not to mention his larger-than-life personality, all contributed to a presence that was the stuff of legend. Even though his relevance in the experimental film world fluctuated according to the prevailing trends at any given time (structural film, punk film, feminist film, conceptual film, etc.), his indefatigable energy and creativity always announced to all who cared about film as an art that here was a man who was devoted to a practice that in the end encompassed over 400 films, several books, countless lectures, and many lives touched. When Brakhage's life came to an end on 9 March 2003, a uniquely American sensibility was silenced.

Stan Brakhage not only was one of the greatest filmmakers in the history of the medium, but also one of this country's greatest examples of an energy that persisted, even thrived, in the face of an almost-criminal neglect by a society that never recognized his powerful genius. (I remember thinking what a moving gesture it would have been if, at some point during the 2003 Academy Awards ceremonies, some Hollywood director, say, Martin Scorsese, would have acknowledged Stan's passing. Sadly, predictably, no such gesture was ever made.) Still, societal and film industry neglect have done nothing to diminish Brakhage's gift to American arts or his status in the minds and hearts of all those who loved his films.

At a time when the American cultural landscape is littered with the detritus of a disposable popular culture and a dumbed-down "serious" culture, perhaps Brakhage's work has had its most-lasting resonance in the series of eight-millimeter films that he called the *Songs*. Consisting of over thirty films ranging in length from three minutes to over ninety minutes, these films elevated the home movie—a form that most considered either too trivial or too personal to be taken seriously—to an art. Long before the advent of the video camera, the Everyman's electronic sketchpad, Brakhage was pushing the capabilities of the eight-millimeter camera and color film to new heights. With such works as *23rd Psalm Branch*, a feature-length meditation on the Vietnam War and, by extension, its effects on his own domestic life, and *XV Song Traits*, another lengthy eight-millimeter work, Brakhage displayed a sensibility that was American to its core: contentious, dissenting, questioning, skeptical, critical, fiercely independent, fiercely individual. And, while Brakhage was not a politician per se, his body of work nonetheless was "political" in that it not only celebrated the best of what he was and what he SAW with those eyes, but also probed those areas of himself that were dark, duplicitous, and not very pretty. (I remember reading that his film *Murder Psalm* was inspired by a dream he had in which he had murdered his own mother.) Suffice to say that, like any major artist, he considered and engaged all the major issues of life: birth, sex, death, family, country, friendship, love, and the nature of existence itself.

Anyone who has done any reading on Brakhage's career knows that he initially wanted to be a poet who also made films, like Jean Cocteau. Brakhage soon came to realize that his true calling was not words (although his writings and lectures have formed a powerful body of work in themselves) but images. And yet, even as he pioneered the development of a new filmic sensibility, a sensibility built on rhythm, color, composition, and "signatures" (hand painting, in-frame collage, scratching text on the surface of the film, and the shake of his handheld camera shots), he struggled to develop a cinematic practice that went beyond language to a self-contained cosmology of the eternal present. The vast majority of his films could not be described in a conventional sense. One could not recite the sequence of events that would form a linear plot, such as one could at least describe the plot of a Hitchcock film. Instead, his films occupied a filmic space that was defined by light, rhythmic pulsation (like the human heart), color, depth, and a time frame that could not be held in check by memory. Indeed, a memory of a Brakhage film was closer to an aura, a dream, something that was paradoxically ephemeral and concrete at the same time. Of course, there were exceptions: the procession of sliced up bodies in *The Act of Seeing With One's Own Eyes*; the flicker of spiderwebs, twigs, leaves, moth's wings, in *Mothlight*; and the images of Brakhage himself looking fragile and vulnerable in the bittersweet *I...Dreaming.*

In these works, Brakhage looked at the world, and himself, with an honest, unflinching eye. Brakhage, in his freedom as an experimental filmmaker, was able to make work that transcended the shallow concerns of a popular culture that, for the most part, was intent on becoming more and more disposable even as it became more and more pervasive. (As I write this piece, in late November 2003, the self-proclaimed "King of Pop," Michael Jackson, is almost certainly headed for total ruin as a result of yet another series of accusations of alleged child molestation. Jackson's troubles are now dissected virtually round the clock on cable television, something impossible twenty-five years ago.) Warhol's prediction that in the future everyone would be famous for fifteen minutes has now come painfully true. Perhaps Warhol's pronouncement should have been treated more like a warning of things to come. Still, in a cultural climate that, over a period of fifty years, became more and more intolerant and idiotic, Brakhage conducted himself with dignity and intelligence.

It is important to remember that Brakhage started making films in the 1950s, a time almost always described as stultifyingly boring and conservative, a time when millions fled to the suburbs to inhabit "ranch-style" homes, who wore buttons that said "I Like Ike," when Commies could be found under every bed, and television was beaming live images into millions of American homes. And yet, the fifties were also a time when the arts were beginning to rise up and question the mindlessness of American culture, to protest for freedom of thought and speech, and to demand an end to conformity and an explosion of individuality.

Brakhage's contemporaries included Allen Ginsberg, Wallace Berman, Bruce Conner, Jonas Mekas, Lenny Bruce, Jack Smith, Robert Duncan, Jess Collins, and many others. Brakhage made a crucial contribution to the artistic and cultural revolutions that were to change American society in the 1960s and, in so doing, helped to pave the way for many other filmmakers who were

Stan Brakhage in Boulder, Colorado, August 2000. (From a videotape by Willie Varela.)

to emerge in the seventies and eighties, including this writer. Within this context, one other artist stands out: Jackson Pollock. Brakhage always acknowledged a deep debt to Pollock's work and his working methods, often referring to the trancelike state he would find himself in while shooting film as akin to Pollock's observation that he would also go into a trance when he was deep in the painting process. Two artists working in completely different media both revolutionized their respective practices. Both were uniquely American in their energy, their intense commitment to their visions, and their desire to leave a lasting legacy.

After Brakhage's marriage ended in the mid-eighties after thirty years, he went through a difficult period of adjustment, much like anybody would coming out of a long and intense relationship. (I recently rewatched Jim Shedden's documentary film of Brakhage and was struck by a deep sadness as I watched a young Brakhage talking about his theories of film and, in some old home movie footage, the young lovers Stan and Jane playfully poking each other at a kitchen table, Jane with long hair, Stan with a pipe, blissfully unaware of the long and dramatic life they were to live together.) In the early nineties, he remarried and started a new family. He had reinvented himself, was ready to make new work (much of it hand painted), and finally seemed to be at peace with himself and the choices he had made.

Brakhage had spit in the face of that old adage that said there were no second acts in American life. He was still teaching, still putting out significant work, still claiming his place in American culture, and went on to become a national treasure, as great an American artist as Edward Hopper, Jackson Pollock, Alfred Stieglitz, Georgia O'Keefe, Jack Kerouac, Bob Dylan, Allen Ginsberg, Robert Rauschenberg, Mark Rothko, Walker Evans, and a few others.

Brakhage was an American artist, and as the American Dream has turned into a national nightmare, his example will always remind us that as tragic and hard as it is to live, we are all obligated to grow up, to do the best we can with the gifts we are given, and to finally look Death square in the face and declare that it was all worth it after all. Goodbye, Stan. You gave me so much. And I will never forget it.

TYRUS MILLER

Brakhage's Occasions

Figure, Subjectivity, and

Avant-Garde Politics

Brakhage, Romantic and Avant-Garde

> *The romantic strain in film-making was most*
> *strongly maintained by the prolific and influential*
> *Stan Brakhage.*—A. L. REES[1]

Stan Brakhage's filmic art has often been characterized as "romantic," and
as my quotation from Rees's brief treatment of Brakhage in his *History
of Experimental Film and Video* suggests, this designation has indeed become canonical. Here, as elsewhere, however, the predicates of this putative
"romanticism"—whether thought to be primarily an aesthetic attitude or a more
encompassing aesthetico-political stance—are extremely variable and tend not
to resolve into a coherent description. They rather conglomerate in a loose,
indefinitely extendable catalogue of features. Some of the familiar elements of
such a catalogue include withdrawal from a historical present marked by technological modernity in favor of a celebration of nature or the past; insistent
emphasis on individual experience as a protest against impersonal, homoge-
nizing social forces; a channeling of social commitment through aesthetic experience and the practice of art; preference for subjective, intimate, lyrical

expressionism over naturalistic registration of social facts or realistic articulation of narrative; refusal of modern capitalism's technical division of labor and championing of precapitalist handicraft or independent guild work; a favoring of intimate communities of friends or traditional communal institutions over the large-scale institutions of modern societies; reduction of political thought to emotional reactions of acceptance and rejection; and so on.

In Brakhage's biography, artistic work, and programmatic writings, there are unquestionably examples and instances that could be correlated with each of these items in my catalogue. The much-noted figure of the infant, perambulating about the center of several key films in Brakhage's oeuvre, both embodies a Wordsworthian creature trailing clouds of glory from birth and enacts the natural possibility of an untutored, unnormalized vision for which the filmmaker's camera seeks miraculous equivalents. The romantic *politics* of Brakhage's cinema seem to follow like a syllogism from the oscillations of this infant-figure between the sight-site of that glorious subject and the pathetic seen-scene of its unavoidable sacrifice to social convention, when the visionary child falls eternal victim to repressions, reductions, norms—to the whole "matrix" of social power, cinematically reloaded.

Of course, to state the case thus not only replicates those parodic attributions of Brakhage's "social irrelevance" that were sometimes his critical fate but also offers little better than a parody of his most political acute (and often most aesthetically sympathetic) critics, including P. Adams Sitney, Annette Michelson, William Wees, and David E. James. These critics, while in various ways developing the picture of Brakhage as, in many respects, romantic, are equally informed by an awareness of the taut complications of a specifically modernist and avant-garde cultural politics that also form part of Brakhage's productive dilemmas. Brakhage's own complex consciousness of the social poverty and cultural richness of the avant-garde's social position, evidenced especially in his writing and teaching, further fuels the dialectical subtlety of their critical accounts of his work.

William Wees, for example, discerned in Brakhage a politics of exemplarity that might be most profitably compared to John Cage's anarchist exemplarity in his musical, textual, and performance practice (though Wees himself did not pursue the comparison[2]). This avant-garde exemplarity involves the artist's offering the work as an example of how one might begin to see, hear, or think in novel ways for oneself. The spectator or listener is not asked to imitate the *result* of the artist's act (the work) or even replicate the *method* by which it was arrived at (the technical process), but rather to accept the artist's invitation to a return of that "same" quality of newness of which the work constitutes a singular, unrepeatable instance (the creative process). The work might thus serve as the *occasion* rather than the instrument of personal, aesthetic, and political awakening for any given member of the audience.

This mode of "occasional" exemplarity, in my estimation, was *the* crucial way in which postwar avant-garde artists tried to get beyond the tragic political experience of the early twentieth century avant-gardes, which foundered on the rapid recuperation of their anarchist revolt or on the authoritarian temptations of fascism or Stalinism. The most politically canny artists of the postwar sought to rethink their political role as "exemplary," yet not "representative" (of a party, ideology, or institution). The work, accordingly, was presented to its audience as a mixture of direct sensuous experience (often highly disorganized, abstract, unformed) and implicit pedagogical intent, which could reinvest highly a-semantical or a-formal artistic materials with distinct contextual "senses." Dwelling on Brakhage's seemingly paradoxical search for technical "equivalents" of visual experiences not usually experienced by his viewers in the first place, Wees suggested an analogous pedagogical supplement in Brakhage's artistic-political practice: "Here is an indication of the social role. If viewers recognize equivalents of their own seeing in Brakhage's films, they may become increasingly open to ways of seeing that do not conform to the social conventions respected by the 'tutored' eye and that are not incessantly reinforced by conventional techniques of image making."[3]

The sort of defense that Wees mounted for Brakhage specifically was earlier given general formulation and theoretical intensity by Jean-François Lyotard in his essay on experimental cinema, "Acinema," originally published in the early 1970s. Here, in a short text typical of its left avant-garde milieu, Lyotard weighed the potential politics of avant-garde filmmaking by appealing to the avant-garde work's transgression of normative limits. Narrative and, more generally, representational film, the argument went, require conventions and norms of movement, sensory amplitude, and relation between images. Therefore, direction is as much an ensemble of exclusionary acts as a creative, constructive process. Yet, since cinema, in particular, is so closely associated with the movement of the body, with bodies in space, and the perceptual-affective capacities of bodies, these exclusions are also immediately libidinal and political.

In an analogical chain running from the image to the social body, Lyotard argued that "The film is the organic body of cinematographic movements . . . just as politics is that of the partial social organs. This is why direction, a technique of exclusions and effacements, a political activity *par excellence*, and political activity, which is direction *par excellence*, are the religion of the modern irreligion, the ecclesiastic of the secular."[4] He went on to identify two polarized means by which this normalized movement can be undone cinematically: extreme immobilization and the mobilization of the support (both of which are amply exemplified in Brakhage's films). Although casting his discussion in the terminology of a poststructuralist Freudianism, Lyotard's advocacy of experimental cinema rests on a version of avant-garde exemplarity: The sensuous intensity of the work unleashes "excessive" and "perverse" libidinal charges in the spectator, which makes the experience of the avant-garde work a kind of training ground or laboratory of liberation from the wider field of social repressions and norms.

Wees, in his critical appreciation of Brakhage, and Lyotard, in his more general consideration of experimental cinema, help focus our attention on a crucial, often-overlooked, mechanism by which avant-garde works such as Brakhage's could be granted political significance in their situational moment and context. Moreover, we should not underestimate the degree to which the reception of avant-garde artistic works of the 1960s and 1970s was itself "theory-laden" for their particular audiences. In other words, the ground for such works being taken as politically effective by students, artists, cultural intellectuals, and other constituencies was prepared precisely by the political modernist criticism and theory that argued persuasively that they *should* be taken as such.[5] Yet, from our quite different theoretical and political context, it must be observed that, in their political defenses of experimental cinema, neither Wees nor Lyotard stepped outside this period's ideology of the avant-garde to examine its conditions and limits.

In taking precisely this further critical step, David James's sensitive probing of Brakhage's aesthetico-political predicaments recalled the sinuous aporias of Theodor Adorno's analyses of modernist art. As James wrote, for example, of Brakhage's most explicitly "politically themed" film, *23rd Psalm Branch*:

While *23rd Psalm Branch* embodies the inability of Brakhage's Romantic aestheticism to transcend privatized individual consciousness and engage history, it offers itself as a cautery for the horror of contemporary political life by presenting itself as the site of aesthetic values, public espousal of which would lead to the regeneration of the public realm. Nowhere is Brakhage's visual articulation more exact and exacting. In the Western tradition, the comprehensive term for these values is beauty, and it is appropriate finally to consider one of Brakhage's most beautiful films and an event in his life which dramatically illustrates the crippling conditions under which that beauty could be secured and the price he would pay to secure it. The whole event has the tension of an allegory.[6]

Bringing in resonance Brakhage's economic marginality with his weak margin of cultural resistance, his aestheticist pathos with the transgressive sensuality that pathos unleashes, James thus disclosed the fragile constellations of beauty that flash up in the films, allegorizing a utopian world and lamenting its damage. The stars *are* beautiful, if endangered, and Brakhage's work helps us to hold this dangerously free beauty briefly in mind. Yet, for all its aesthetic success, the film's sequential closure strains political credibility: Who could really believe that it is the children with sparklers (the final image of *23rd Psalm Branch*) and not the bursting of bombs that get the final say?

Romantic Occasionalism

> *All the accidents of our life are the materials from which we can make whatever we want.*—Novalis[7]

> *I am stating my given ability, prize of all above pursuing, to transform the light sculptured shapes of an almost blackened room to the rainbow hued patterns of light without any scientific paraphernalia.*—Brakhage[8]

Since the trope of romantic politics or, from more sympathetic critics, political romanticism, predominates in those criticisms of Brakhage that are not simply technical or formalist commentaries, it is worth giving some conceptual explication of what this conjunction of romanticism and politics might mean. The 1919 (revised 1925) essay of the Catholic jurist Carl Schmidt on "political romanticism," still one of the most searing indictments and insightful critiques of romantic thought, offers a useful set of tools for this task. Schmidt's thought revolved around two basic themes: the defense of *norms*, laws, and definitions, within legal, religious, and moral orders; and the concept of the *political*, as a sphere of decisive action, of decision, to constitute those norms and orders when they are absent or in crisis. His aversion to the romantics was accordingly twofold. They failed to accept the necessity and legitimacy of constituted, conventional, codified orders. At the same time, however, they fled from the consequences of political action and decision that an authentic revolutionary opposition to a *particular* set of norms might entail.

This paradoxical coupling of pseudoradical rejection and political passivism is for Schmidt the basic structure of political romanticism. In turn, it explains another characteristic aspect of romanticism: that extraordinary productivity to which it gave impulse in the arts, as well as the corollary hypertrophy of the *aesthetic* among the publicists and thinkers of the movement. The arts, as a fictive domain in which causal consequence may be suspended, served as a veritable haven for the romantic attitude. What underlies the whole romantic politico-aesthetic ensemble, however, is that which Schmidt characterized as its subjectivistic "occasionalism": the romantic subject's denial of a necessary order of causality and his taking of any object, event, or feeling as the "occasion" for a surprising, undetermined effect. As the Novalis passage quoted in the epigraph of this section indicates, for the romantic subject any accidental material can become the occasion of any outcome at all. The mediating link is the subject's inventive fancy, which allows all spheres of his life, "artistic" or not, to be cut to the measure of aesthetic consciousness.

Schmidt's description of the particular dimensions of this occasionalism could almost have been written with particular works of Brakhage's opus in mind, for example, *The Text of Light*, in which the patterning of light he accidentally caught glinting off an ashtray became the occasion of an extraordinary exploration of that object's ability to generate a wide range of optical effects. Schmidt, referring specifically to Novalis, wrote that any instant may become for him an occasional point for transformation and crystallization of forms:

A circle can be wrapped around it as the center. It can also be the point at which the tangent of infinity is contiguous with the circle of the finite. It is also, however, the point of departure for a line into the infinite that can extend in any direction. Thus every event is transformed into a fantastic and dreamlike ambiguity, and every object can become anything. . . . Instead of mystical forces, the emanations are geometric lines. The world is resolved into figures[.][9]

"Figures" is the operative word here, the romantic's resolution of the world into aesthetic patterns or poetic tropes, at the expense of identifiable, exchangeable, manipulable objects:

For a productivity of this sort . . . correctly considered, we can no longer speak of an object. . . . Surrender to this romantic productivity involves the conscious renunciation of an adequate relationship to the visible, external world.[10]

Though of course Brakhage would say that the whole question of an "adequate" relationship to the visible, external world is precisely what is at issue in his art, even an intransigent such as he had to admit that there is a difference between driving on the freeway and "an eye so lost in space that fall feels ascensional."[11] In the everyday world, it matters whether you are going up or down, moving forward in your freeway lane or traveling in reverse. The eye has to help us figure these things out, or we are soon in big trouble. Only in the special framework of the artwork or in an aesthetic life approximating the experiences of art can such modes of vertiginous vision be admitted; in everyday life, they could be literally fatal.

Even more important for Schmidt, however, than the figural extravagance and aestheticist specialization of such a romantic outlook is its implications for the structure of time, tradition, and history. Since any instant can be the temporal vessel of an occasion, there is no necessary link of one moment to the next. Hence, the occasionalist attitude implies an emptying out of the temporal infrastructure of tradition and historical thinking. In a familiar modernist argument for the "defamiliarization" of perception through formal innovation, Brakhage presents his techniques for occasional vision as a breaking free of language- and habit-engrained patterns. Yet, as he recognized already at the time of *Metaphors on Vision*, these procedures also hold crucial implications for *memory*, which appears to Brakhage more an aesthetic shackle rather than a historical faculty: "Willful attention, forced beyond the natural capacity for mental absorption, produces a willy-nilliness less memory-dominated than when one is unegoed."[12] Occasionalist vision shatters time, to quote Brakhage's 1967 script, "The Stars are Beautiful," into "the broken fragments of the mirror that reflects reality,"[13] turning that reality into prismatic flashes and sudden depths of a crystal world rotating before an amazed eye.

Brakhage's programmatic statements often explicitly embrace the romantic ideology that Schmidt calls occasionalist. Nevertheless, I believe his work cannot be reduced to this ideology. His procedures and materials have further tacit dimensions that exceed their explicit intention in their original context. In the next two sections, I chart two aspects of the works that in my view move beyond the orbit of romantic occasionalism. The first of these is Brakhage's implicit rethinking of consciousness and sensibility as what Deleuze would call a "plane of immanence," a neutral and impersonal medium in which events register themselves as pure modifications of the medium itself. I believe that Brakhage's consistent interest in psychophysical phenomena and his attempts to find "equivalents" for them in the material medium of film represent an attempt to move beyond the subjectivistic fancy that Schmidt saw in romantic occasionalism into a vitalistic apprehension of life itself as a self-modifying medium of formative events: life as immanent difference, autodeviation, productive *error*. Coexisting with this aesthetic vitalism, however, is an even more radical move in the direction of a desubjectified state of immanence: Brakhage's artistic appropriation of death, not simply as an omnipresent theme of his work, but as the very condition of its possibility. Taken together, I want to suggest, these adumbrate a different artistic politics no longer centered on the romantic problematic of the subject but rather focusing on the immanent domains of life and death, and emerging out of the unexpected occasions, they present a "biopolitical" art, to use Michel Foucault's suggestive term.

Immanence I: Spiritual Automata

> *Their bare and lovely bodies sweep, in round*
> *of viscera, of legs*
> *of turned-out hips and glance, bound*
> *each to other, nested eggs*
> *of elements in trace.*
>
> —CHARLES OLSON, "The Moebius Strip"[14]

The concept of immanence, which I am using to understand the ways in which Brakhage moved beyond subjectivistic occasionalism, had an important representative in the poet Charles Olson, whom Brakhage read and visited with profit.[15] Above all, in his essay on Melville, "Equal, That Is, to the Real Itself," Olson concerned himself with a vision of an immanence in which space, bodies, and movements might appear as different aspectual descriptions of a single, continuous topography of change. Within this all-encompassing topography, passion and action, cause and effect would have to be seen not as fundamental oppositions, but rather as modal states of a single warping, dissolving, reforming material field. Olson thus spoke of an "inertial structure of the world" as a material thing "which not only exerts effects upon matter but in turn suffers such effects."[16]

Our bodies exist as aspects of that field—and here Olson anticipated the more systematic conceptual frameworks of Gilles Deleuze—as mobile loci amid degrees of inertia, relative speeds, accelerations and decelerations. It is our grammatical categories and language, including the whole grammar of pronouns and personal identifications, that reify the folds and differences in this univocal Being into discrete objects, entities, types. Yet for Olson, the art of poetry, despite its being embedded in the discontinuous structures of language, provides an important clue to ways in which this concept of immanence might be "applied" to various spheres of thought and life to effect a sea change in our social existence. The key for him is the notion of metric, which poetry shares with mathematics and with other arts:

> The metrical structure of the world is so intimately connected to the inertial structure that the metrical field (art is measure) will of necessity become flexible (what we are finding out these days in painting writing and music) the moment the inertial field itself is flexible. ("Equal," 52)

To put it more abstractly, qualitative relations between things, seen from the perspective of a univocal immanence, resolve into metrical relations between "events": the intervals that divide and connect vectors of deviations, differences from the background of inertia.

In his later philosophy, from *Anti-Oedipus* to his last book *What Is Philosophy?*, Deleuze developed under the term *plane of immanence* this very conception of an inertial field that registers events as modifications, "actualizations"—foldings, warpings, movements—of and within itself. As for Olson, Deleuze's intention was to destabilize the notions of background and figure, object and context. In fact, for Deleuze it is not even relative fixity, but *chaotic movement* that gives the plane of immanence the character that Olson called "inertial":

> The plane of immanence is like a section of chaos and acts like a sieve. In fact, chaos is characterized less by the absence of determinations than by the infinite speed with which they take shape and vanish. This is not a movement from one determination to the other, but, on the contrary, the impossibility of a connection between them.[17]

The plane of immanence is the nonmeasurable limit, a space of pure virtuality, against which any metrics becomes possible. In both Olson's and Deleuze's theoretical writings, the "stillness" of objects or backgrounds is a special state of generalized motion and can only be perspectively described. In other words, slowness, speed, or stillness can only be spoken of relative to another observation point in the system that is also in a state of motion. Variable metrics, correlations of relative intervals in time and space, rhythms, thus replace the idea of absolute measure or a view of a stable whole.

Immanence defines a space no longer split into subject and object but rather distributed into zones of order and disorder, patterns coming together and coming apart in ever-new configurations. It thus corresponds, as the historian of science Michel Serres suggested, to the world conceived in terms of thermodynamics and information theory. Redescribing the world of subjects and objects as an immanent continuum of matter becoming ordered or chaotic over time, Serres wrote that, from the point of view of thermodynamics,

> Each term of the traditional subject-object dichotomy is split by something like a geographical divide...: noise, disorder, and chaos on one side; complexity, arrangement, and distribution on the other. Nothing distinguishes me ontologically from a crystal, a plant, an animal, or the order of the world; we are drifting toward the noise and the black depths of the universe....Knowledge is at most the reversal of drifting, that strange conversion of time, always paid for by additional drift.... Virtually stable turbulence within the flow. To be or to know from now on will be translated by: see the islands, rare or fortunate, the work of chance or necessity.[18]

How does this conception of immanence, developed in their respective disciplines by Olson, Deleuze, and Serres, relate to Brakhage's filmic work? Probably the most direct way that we can imagine the plane of immanence and the events that take place upon it—as modifications of it—is to think of one of Brakhage's late hand-painted films. In many cases, these are presented as allegorical journeys through spiritual spaces (e.g., *The Dante Quartet*); as virtual movements in which observer and observed indiscernibly blend (*Black Ice*); as representations of inner states such as hypnogogic vision (*Night-music*), pure affect (*Rage Net*), or Freudian cathexis (*Glaze of Cathexis*). Regardless of their allegorical motivations, however, these films have in common that they define the space of their occurrence in the same, immanent way. Each seems to take place in an indefinite space and is a complex combination and sequencing of different genres of abstract motion: unfolding, contraction, expansion, smearing, scintillation, breccelation, crystallization, and random agitation, just to enumerate a few. We cannot begin, amid such complex, multidimensional movement, to stabilize visually a containing space or flat background against which "figures" emerge. The dimension and boundaries of the space seem to be continually warping, continually re-forming with new parameters. And yet, the motion is not chaotic either. As the result of the duration of some types of movement, or their relative slowness with respect to changes going on elsewhere in the image, or through color and shade contrasts, or by other means, distinct patterns and types and vectors do emerge temporarily, creating internal structure for the film and differentiating it from other of Brakhage's hand-painted work. We can think of the plane of immanence as the horizon of chaos, which is the limit of discernible figuration, as the mobile background that *does not appear*, but *so that* the forming and collapsing patterns of Brakhage's hand-painted films *can* be perceived and even treated as allusive signs of narratives, psychological events, or affects.

Of course, the characteristics of this wholly immanent space of the late hand-painted work had been intimated much earlier in Brakhage's oeuvre, even in films that retain a much higher degree of photographic reference to external objects, movements, and locations. To take one example from an earlier film, in *The Dead*, Brakhage often brings together several different sources and directions of motion in a single complex. For example, in any given sequence, we see: the movement of a boat up or down a river, the flow of the river itself, the movement of people or vehicles on the shore, the movements of the camera or of its operator, and the apparent intervallic movement (or stasis) caused by superimposition of multiple versions of any one type of movement. David James singled out Brakhage's use of multiple superimposition as a means of challenging the centering of vision in a monocular perspective; he drew the analogy to the decentered field and indiscernible surface/depth and figure/ground relations in abstract expressionist painting.[19] Through his range of interventions into the film-stock itself and in the printing process, Brakhage had thus already begun to immanentize cinematic space and relativize movements in it to the plane of projection itself, the chaotic, infinitely mobile plane of white light against which the film strip occasions its patterned events.

Elsewhere, James gave an encapsulated formulation of Brakhage's pursuit of total immanence (which I would argue he ultimately accomplished in the hand-painted films). "Brakhage's project," James wrote:

> Is...to return to continuity what film history, in its reproduction of Western ontology, has distinguished as three separate realms: the phenomenal world; the optical apparatuses, both mechanical and biological; and the work of the brain—memory, imagination, 'close-eye vision,' hypnagogic and eidetic imagery, and dream. In the integration of these realms, the dualisms that sustain almost all other uses of film—the dualisms of subject and object, of physiological and psychological, of perception and creation, and of vision and its instruments—are subsumed in a single gestalt.[20]

This is excellently put, and I believe it accurately describes the ideal toward which Brakhage's whole opus strives, through restless attempts with a vast number of techniques, film works, and invented genres. I do, however, then question James's and other critics' continuing use—albeit authorized by Brakhage himself—of the notion of "first-person vision" or "first-person cinema," which implies both a superseded philosophy of consciousness and a traditional rhetorical logic of figuration that Brakhage's practice of immanence confounds. At the same time, however, it is clear that what tempts critics toward use of this terminology is the need to capture a sense that the oscillating signature "by Brakhage" nevertheless marks a singular point in the continuum into which he draws us—a distinct individual, *a life*, if not a "person" or an "I" in the sense of a subject that is transcendent to the material plane of life as such.

In the second volume of his study of cinema, *The Time-Image*, Deleuze introduced a neologistic term to suggest a way of characterizing this kind of nonpersonal individuation, the emergence of a singular "style" of thought and being precisely insofar as the boundaries between the human and technology, living and nonliving, become indiscernible. Deleuze called this hybrid individual the *spiritual automaton*. Automaton signifies that the fusion of organic and nonorganic matter, human and technology, involves a surrender of many of the illusions of human free will and a greater appreciation of the possibilities opened to the human by its assimilation to the nonhuman realm, ranging from physical and chemical phenomena to animal life to computing and robotics. The term automaton also—in keeping with Brakhage's interest in the psychophysical—focuses new attention on the "machinic" complexity of the human body and its perceptual organs, a complexity that has been reduced by denying the body's intricately assembled, yet largely automatistic character in the name of humanistic ideals. But, the modifier spiritual indicates that what is at issue here is ultimately a variety of *thought* that such assemblages of elements occasion. Deleuze summed up this dual aspect of the spiritual automata as follows:

> The automaton has always had two coexistent, complementary senses, even when they were in conflict. On the one hand, the great spiritual automaton indicates the highest exercise of thought, the way in which thought thinks itself in the fantastic effort of autonomy.... But... the automaton is also the psychological automaton who no longer depends on the outside because he is autonomous but because he is dispossessed of his own thought.[21]

The space of immanence—for example, that space defined by a Brakhage hand-painted film—is a thinking and experiencing that is going on, not in the head of a subject, whether artist or spectator, but precisely as an outside occasion, in the temporary, continuous, techno-imagistic-vital space in which both he and we commingle. This "thought of the outside" can be experienced as an exhilarating richness, an ecstatic passing beyond the boundaries of one's sensory and intellectual limits into a space of surprise and wonder: "The stars are optical nerve endings of the eye which the universe is."[22] But, it is also a loss of self, a sacrifice, a frightening evacuation of the romantic subject of creativity. The actual practice of art, then, for Brakhage, involved dangerous contact with forces that threatened the sovereignty of the romantic subject within: a communication with the material continuum, with the animal and vegetative world, with the inorganic life of chemicals and crystals and light. It is an exemplary occasion that the artist offers his audience: a way into the continuum of material life, with its turbulence, its unexpected intensities, and its risks. The problem, however, may be that once inside this continuum, there may be no respite, no way back out. And, as Brakhage already very early recognized, it may be only the dead who are so thoroughly freed from their natural limits as to move freely in the domain of immanence.

Insofar as he discovered an immanent occasionalism no longer reducible to a traditional subject, Brakhage took a crucial step beyond the subjectivistic occasionalism that Schmidt denounced in romanticism. True, objects or events indeed served Brakhage as occasions for filmic "effects." Yet, he did not spin out webs of poetic or romantic figures from subjective play with these occasions, but rather surrendered himself over to material events that only retrospectively can be taken as analogous, "equivalent," to something subjective. In other words, the "effect" or artistic "event" is the outcome not of some inaccessible mental happening in the head of the artist or spectator, but rather a singular interaction of the artist's and spectator's body with the chemistry of film, the physics of light, the machinery of filmmaking and projection, and the social context of reception. This surrender of the self, however, has a limit, and Brakhage did not fail to take his work knowingly to its border and prospect what might lie beyond. That limit is a total immanence beyond consciousness or bodily limitation: Its figure is the evacuation of figure, the literality of the body at the brink of obliteration, Death.

Immanence II: Death

> For philosophers are beings who have passed
> through a death, who are born from it, and go
> towards another death, perhaps the same one.
> —Gilles Deleuze[23]

Brakhage's fascination with death is well known. It is a central theme in several of his greatest films, from such early works as *Sirius Remembered,*

The Dead, and *Anticipation of the Night,* through *Mothlight, The Act of Seeing With One's Own Eyes,* and *23rd Psalm Branch,* to later works such as *The Dante Quartet* and *The Dark Tower.* What is perhaps less appreciated is the degree to which death was not simply an issue for Brakhage, but an imagined point of identification, a positive pursuit that was unrealizable in life, but approachable in art. In his often-quoted 1963 conversation with P. Adams Sitney published in *Metaphors on Vision,* Brakhage spoke of his suicidal urges in making *Anticipation of the Night:* "That was in one sense to be my last film: I had seen myself, cast before where I was as a human being, as leading to inevitable suicide. Certainly by the age of 26 I was getting too old to still be alive and fulfilling the myth of myself. *Anticipation of the Night* was the vehicle out."[24] Despite his self-deprecating irony, I suggest that Brakhage's phrase "vehicle out" does not simply mean that he escaped the necessity of committing suicide by making art. Rather, *Anticipation of the Night* was a landmark for him in an "art of dying"[25]: a "way out" of his life as he had lived it up to that point, as well as an escape from self-inflicted death. *Anticipation* defined a path into death, a way of moving toward the dead's total freedom from limitation, from a suffering body, from personal history, from the terrible myth of the self. Henceforth, for Brakhage film was a way of being posthumous long before the man himself died.

Brakhage spoke in analogous terms of his film *The Dead. The Dead,* he claimed, served a therapeutic function by confronting the imprisoning potential of the "symbol," which he suggested is related complexly to both unfulfilled wishes ("anticipation") and to monuments or tombs (memory). The personified figure of unfulfilled anticipation in the film is Brakhage's fellow filmmaker Kenneth Anger: "All the rest of the people in *The Dead—* are dead. They're the walking dead; but he was a living dead. So he became my double in a sense—my 'stand-in,' you might say."[26] He went on to conclude that *"The Dead* became my first work in which things that might very easily be taken as symbols were so photographed as to destroy all their symbolic potential. The action of making *The Dead* kept me alive" (*Metaphors on Vision*). By setting up a parallel ghost world in the transparency of light, Brakhage could have his death and live on, too.

Brakhage's thoughts on death reached an acme of complexity in a reference to the philosopher Ludwig Wittgenstein, who defined death as a limit of the knowable world and therefore consigned to metaphor any possible speech about death. In his 1963 conversation with Sitney, Brakhage quoted a passage from Wittgenstein's *Tractatus Logico-Philosophicus* (a work, significantly, begun during combat in World War I by the often suicidally inclined philosopher). Brakhage referred the passage to his own anticipation and fear of death from asthma:

> I was again faced with death as a concept; not watching death as physical decay, or dealing with the pain of death of a loved one, but with the concept of death as something that man casts into the future by asking, "What is death like?" And the limitation of finding the images for a concept of death only in life itself is a terrible torture, i.e., Wittgenstein's *Tractatus Logico-Philosophicus* 6.4311 "Death is not an event of life. Death is not lived through. If by eternity is understood not endless temporal duration but timelessness, then he lives eternally who lives in the present. Our life is endless the way that our visual field is without limit." (*Metaphors on Vision*)

As understood by Brakhage, Wittgenstein's observations have two important implications. First, the past and the future are threatening dimensions, spaces of death arrayed against the punctual life of the present. And, second, the present must be grasped in an instantaneous vision of *fact*, of "what is the case." Figurality, metaphor, or the images of memory testify, instead, to the admixture of death with that present-tense life: Figuration marks the mind's grasp for what is gone or its fear of what is to come.[27] Thus, the poetics of desymbolization—of "disfiguration" of the threatening symbol—to which Brakhage alluded in his discussion of *The Dead* follow coherently from this attempt to release the grip of death, in its guise of the past and future, on the eye's vision of the present. Taking Wittgenstein to the letter, through reiterated acts of disfiguring vision, Brakhage sought to give to life the endlessness of the visual field.

Nowhere can these acts of disfiguration be seen more literally than in Brakhage's notorious autopsy film, *The Act of Seeing With One's Own Eyes* (1971), which follows a Pittsburgh pathologist's systematic cutting away of the very foundation of the human figure, the skin and tissue that lend it contour, to reveal the viscera and bones that lie beneath. Nowhere, moreover, does the aporetic nature of Brakhage's striving for the eternal present reveal itself more clearly. True to his conception of exorcising the fear of death by confining it to a visible present, Brakhage is quoted as having said

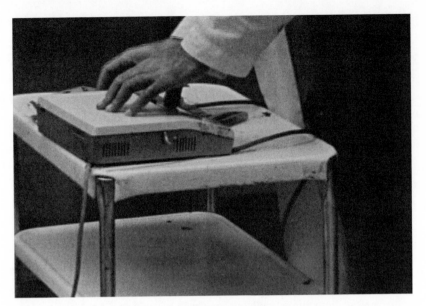

Stan Brakhage, *The Act of Seeing With One's Own Eyes.*

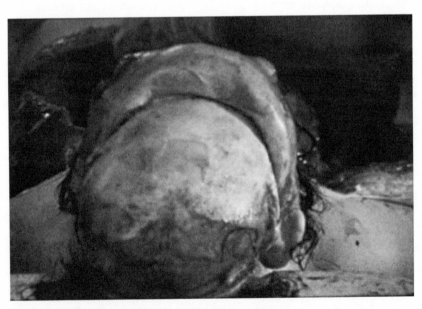

Stan Brakhage, *The Act of Seeing With One's Own Eyes.*

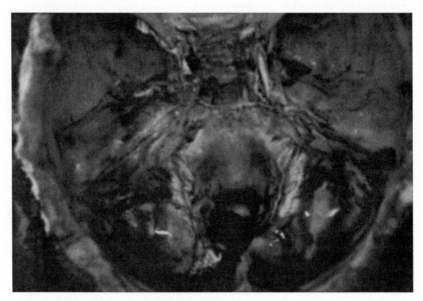

Stan Brakhage, *The Act of Seeing With One's Own Eyes.*

at a screening of his film that, "It was nothing to be afraid of, it was only about light hitting objects and bouncing back and seeing it with your own eyes."[28] Yet this "apathia" in the face of death as *result* (the corpse) comes at the cost of identifying with death as a *force*, either as entropic repetition or active destruction of order, figure, and pattern. With the final scene of the film, in which the pathologist finishes recording his notes and surrenders the scene to the lone reel-to-reel tape recorder, which may repeatedly turn and recite its traces in a limitless present mechanically detached from any living and dying body, Brakhage signaled his position as the unmoved, unaffected recorder of the facts of light bouncing off of objects.

Despite the interesting fact that in making this film Brakhage was "required not to show any identifiable faces,"[29] two of the most striking images of this powerful film nevertheless involve the most intensely "figural" zone of the whole body, the face. In one scene, we see the scalp being cut away from the skull, then peeled back and dropped, like a caul, over the face of the corpse. No more effective exemplification of an active disfiguration can be imagined than this literal "loss of face," and Brakhage wholly identified his own gaze with the instruments of this dissection.[30] In another scene, however, at a later point in the autopsy, in which not only the scalp has been peeled back, but also the skull cap has been sawed through and the brain removed, Brakhage's camera moves in to contemplate the result. What it discovers in this acephalic vacancy is a cosmos of matter, an inhuman beauty, absolutely without intentions: the symmetries and arabesques of the skull without the brain, yet full of color, of pattern, of complex nuance. In short, beyond the border of disfiguration, a new world of intentionless figure emerges, as if the ascesis of the "deadened" eye were in the end repaid by a new, unexpected wealth of figural order.

The most authentic political ambiguity of Brakhage's work, however, comes to light when we recognize that not only in the images of *The Act of Seeing With One's Own Eyes*, are the social circumstances, the lives and deaths, of the visible "objects" effaced by design. Brakhage also subjected the historical images of fascism, war, and concentration camps in *23rd Psalm Branch* to an analogous "disfiguring" treatment. What would it mean to achieve a state of mind in which one could see the images of mass death in Auschwitz or Treblinka as just "light bouncing off objects"? Or the incinerating flash of an atomic bomb as just one more occasion for the ultimate visual rush? Its achievement would mark a point of indiscernability between a final release from the traumas of mid-twentieth century history and the repression that would allow this trauma to return in new, unrecognizable forms of the same (like, say, the Vietnam War). But, it should be noted, Brakhage only effaced these images; he did not erase them. Like Alain Resnais, whom Deleuze discussed in relation to the passage through the imagination of mass death in Auschwitz and Hiroshima, Brakhage's film points to the inescapable admixtures of repetition and forgetting, anguish and abstraction, that characterize contemporary modes of memory. As Deleuze wrote, in Renais's films, "Memory is clearly no longer the faculty of having recollections; it is the membrane which . . . makes sheets of past and layers of reality correspond."[31] Seen from this perspective, Brakhage's film is not just *about* the politics of memory of history in light of the history of the present; it is an exemplification of that memory itself, in all its political ambiguity.

We might say in conclusion that at key moments Brakhage's work may indeed be "occasionalist," but that it is not—or no longer—subjectivist, hence also not—or no longer—"romantic." It stands at the juncture of two phases of radical desubjectification that are not just aesthetic strategies of an individual artist, but epochal characteristics of our biopolitical present: absorption into the immanence of universal life and assimilation to death. Brakhage's work unfolds in the dimension of impersonal occasions, through a psychophysical passion that no longer requires a *subject* of seeing or emotion, but just seeing and affect as such. Rather than romantic self-assertion, it is a pure expenditure, an exemplary art of dying, an impersonal vital persistence in the perpetual extinction of self. If political romanticism still means anything in such a case, then it is surely something not encompassed by Carl Schmidt's critique. Brakhage—like his biopolitical *frère*, Samuel Beckett—projected a future politics that still awaits its proper description.

NOTES

1. A. L. Rees, *A History of Experimental Film and Video* (London: British Film Institute, 1999).

2. See, however, Brakhage's letter of 11 March 1962 to P. Adams Sitney, excerpted in Stan Brakhage, *Metaphors on Vision*, 2d ed., ed. P. Adams Sitney (New York: Film Culture, 1963, 1976), unpaginated: "Cage has laid down the greatest aesthetic net of this century. Only those who honestly encounter it . . . and manage to survive (i.e., go beyond it) will be the artists of our contemporary present." And cf. Brakhage's punning evocation of Cage in "Margin Alien," in which, following a quotation from Cage's *Silence*, he speaks of his attempts "to avoid John's Cage, per chance, these last several years." Stan Brakhage, "Margin Alien," in *Essential Brakhage: Selected Writings on Filmmaking* (Kingston, NY: Documentext, 2001), 67.

3. William C. Wees, *Light Moving in Time: Studies in the Visual Aesthetics of Avant-Garde Film* (Berkeley and Los Angeles: University of California Press, 1992), 80.

4. Jean-François Lyotard, "Acinema," in *The Lyotard Reader*, ed. Andrew Benjamin (Oxford, UK: Basil Blackwell, 1989), 176.

5. For a more extensive discussion of this relation between avant-garde art and theories, see my essay "Avant-Garde and Theory: A Misunderstood Relation," *Poetics Today*, 20, 4 (1999), 549–79.

6. David E. James, *Allegories of Cinema: American Film in the Sixties* (Princeton, NJ: Princeton University Press, 1989), 54–55.

7. Novalis, quoted by Carl Schmidt, *Political Romanticism*, trans. Guy Oakes (Cambridge, MA: MIT Press, 1986), 83.

8. Brakhage, "My Eye," in *Essential Brakhage*, 31.

9. Schmidt, *Political Romanticism*, 76.

10. Schmidt, *Political Romanticism*, 84.

11. My reference to driving on the freeway is to his 1974 remarks published as "The Seen" in *Essential Brakhage*, 165. My reference to "an eye so lost" is to his essay "My Eye," *Essential Brakhage*, 26. Notably, in his notorious attack on 1960s minimalist art as "theatrical" in "Art and Objecthood," Michael Fried chose as a central exhibit an aberrant freeway drive described by the sculptor and painter Tony Smith. In a published text, Smith recounted his experience of driving blind across a stretch of unfinished New Jersey Turnpike at night.

Fried used this example to point to how minimalist sculptors worked directly to aestheticize experiences of real space and events rather than focusing on the *causal* ground of aesthetic feelings, the objectified forms and structures of the artwork. For example, he wrote: "But what was Smith's experience on the turnpike? Or to put the question another way, if the turnpikes, airstrips, and drill ground are not works of art, what are they?—What, indeed, if not empty, or 'abandoned' *situations?*" Following Lessing, Fried calls this invitation of effects "theatrical"; he meant essentially what Schmidt meant by the term "occasionalist." See Michael Fried, "Art and Objecthood," originally in *Artforum*, 5 (1967), 12–23, reprinted in *Art and Objecthood: Essays and Reviews* (Chicago: University of Chicago Press, 1998), 148–72.

12. "My Eye," in *Essential Brakhage*, 34.

13. "The Stars Are Beautiful," in *Essential Brakhage*, 137.

14. Charles Olson, "The Moebius Strip," in *Selected Writings*, ed. Robert Creeley (New York: New Direction Press, 1966), 163.

15. See, for example, the account of a free-wheeling conversation and visit with Olson in the final pages of *Metaphors on Vision*.

16. Charles Olson, "Equal, That Is, to the Real Itself," in *Selected Writings*, 52.

17. Gilles Deleuze and Félix Guattari, *What Is Philosophy?* trans. Hugh Tomlinson and Graham Burchell (New York: Columbia University Press, 1994), 42.

18. Michel Serres, "The Origin of Language: Biology, Information Theory, and Thermodynamics," in *Hermes: Literature, Science, Philosophy*, eds. Josué V. Harari and David F. Bell (Baltimore, MD: Johns Hopkins University Press, 1982), 83.

19. James, *Allegories of Cinema*, 47.

20. James, *Allegories of Cinema*, 43.

21. Gilles Deleuze, *Cinema 2: The Time-Image*, trans. Hugh Tomlinson and Robert Galeta (Minneapolis: University of Minnesota Press, 1989), 263.

22. Brakhage, "The Stars Are Beautiful," in *Essential Brakhage*, 134.

23. Deleuze, *Cinema 2: The Time-Image*, 208.

24. Brakhage, *Metaphors on Vision*, unpaginated.

25. For a rich theoretical treatment of this notion, see Michel De Certeau, "The Arts of Dying: Celibatory Machines," in *Heterologies: Discourse on the Other*, trans. Brian Massumi (Minneapolis: University of Minnesota, 1986), 156–67.

26. *Metaphors on Vision*, unpaginated.

27. For an insightful consideration of this temporal structure in modernist poetics, see Paul De Man, "Literary History and Literary Modernity," in *Blindness and Insight: Essays in the Rhetoric of Contemporary Criticism*, 2d ed. (London: Routledge, 1983), 142–65. De Man's exposition of modernist temporality offers an important critical perspective on Brakhage's quest to actualize the present shorn of pretentions and retentions: "All these experiences of immediacy . . . strive to combine the openness and freedom of a present severed from all other temporal dimensions, the weight of the past as well as the concern with a future, with a sense of totality and completeness that could not be achieved if a more extended awareness of time were not also involved" (157).

28. Brakhage, "The Seen," in *Essential Brakhage*, 156.

29. Fred Camper, noted to "The Act of Seeing With One's Own Eyes," in *By Brakhage: An Anthology*, DVD (Criterion Collection, 2003).

30. Compare Deleuze's commentary on Francis Bacon: "Bacon...pursues a very peculiar project as a portrait painter: *to dismantle the face*, to rediscover the head or make it emerge from beneath the face." Gilles Deleuze, *Francis Bacon: The Logic of Sensation*, trans. Daniel W. Smith (London: Continuum, 2003), 20–21.

31. Deleuze, *Cinema 2: The Time-Image*, 207.

Notes on Sincerity and Irony

Lingering IMAGES

Jane playing with her dog at twenty—jumping in intermittent slow motion, sensuous youth and animal power—in body, embodied: a fleshy exuberance, animal ferocity and loving memory. A kind of home movie "call me savage" moment that appears throughout the first third of Brakhage's *Sincerity: Reel No. 2* (1978). In its insistence on the sensuous ground of earth and gravity—Jane lands on her back at one point, the dog mounting her as she playfully bats him away, demonstrating a very *mater*-like material energy—the film makes compact with Brakhage's allegiance to the cinematic body, to a truth of the world that cinema allows us to enter. His *Sincerity* is presumably emotional, but it is also the "sincerity" of the (celluloid) images to which his title refers, to their ability "to hold water" or "grow straight." Brakhage writes of his intent:

This the first completed reel of work-in-progress, draws on autobiographical energies and images which reflect the first 20 years of my living. I have three definitions of the word "sincerity" to sustain my working along these lines of thought with this autobiographical material: (1) Ezra

Pound's marvelous mistranslation of a Chinese ideogram—"Sincerity—the sun's lance coming to rest on the precise spot verbally" . . . (of which I would change, for my purposes, the last word to "visually"), (2) Robert Creeley's trace-of-the-word for me on the back of a Buffalo restaurant menu— "Sym—keros . . . same—growth (ceres) create of the same growth," and (3) Hollis Frampton's track-of-it to the "the Greek," viz.—"a glazed pot" (i.e., one which will hold water)."[1]

In contrast, the young girl in *Murder Psalm* (1981) jumps back as the ball hits the bird fountain, splashing water. Her young friends laugh, her face is haunted, the speckled ball's surface crumbles, and under the piece is a pulsating montage: the American West represented through an over-exposed wagon wheel and the letters for "mother" (advertising for Mother's Day sales?) on a store window. Here is trauma, commercialism, a history of cruelty and territorial expansion, with female epileptic (to boot) to haunt the telling. Brakhage wields these dissonant materials with surety into a powerful condemnation of national destiny, rewriting American myth, redescribing our "motherland" under the gaze of washed-out national fathers superimposed within the montage.

These two films set up a provocative dialectic in Brakhage's work, between the re-edited home movie and the re-worked found footage, between familial content and public reference, between lyric improvisation and what seems strongly a project with a set (however wide) of differentiated "found" material— between "same growth" and hybridity, between holding water and falling apart. Not insignificantly, both are compilation films: the first composed of a wide palette of black-and-white and color stocks, as Brakhage noted, "2000 feet of home-movies, out-takes"[2] and footage shot by others, Bruce Baillie and Larry Jordan among them, the latter utilizing footage shot from the television screen and clips from medical/educational films mixed with his own work. Brakhage's editing dynamics appear somewhat different in these respective works, as do his tone and overall meaning and intentions. An investigation into his art seeking its parameters of public and private, personal and social—analyzed through re-spective filters of irony and sincerity—could provide fruitful indices in which to locate the work.

There is a heroic sincerity in Brakhage that I distrust, a reliance on unitary consciousness, purity, and wholeness, that takes me away from his work. I would posit a more useful way to look at his films, both his camera work and montage, is as a series of "re-descriptions," the word Richard

Rorty used in *Contingency, Irony and Solidarity*. For Rorty, ironists are always aware "that the terms in which they describe themselves are subject to change, always aware of the contingency and fragility of their final vocabularies and thus of their selves."[3] And, "The ironist is . . . a historicist."[4]

A Little Personal History

I first saw Brakhage's film work in college, sophomore year: *Dog Star Man* shown along with Len Lye's *Trade Tattoo* and Arthur Lipsett's *Very Nice, Very Nice.*[5] For me as a college student, the Brakhage film was the least favorite. For one thing, there was no humor; for another, what did I to have to do with a bearded great man with a dog in the snow trying to climb a slope? Surely I was struck with the mythological dimensions in the effort, but put off simultaneously by the maleness, the overwhelming narcissism, or should I say, solipsism, of the work. This aspect, in particular, made a negative impression in contrast to the critical, and light and deep irony of Lipsett's and Lye's work, their ironic worldliness, if you will.

I grew up through the 1960s and 1970s, and a social polity was deeply embedded in my sense of media, coming as I did out of documentary film, having worked with the cooperative group Newsreel and later Young Film-makers, then located on Rivington Street in a dilapidated Lower East Side environment. My sense of art-making was political, influenced by history and by philosophy; indeed, my move to experimental forms came out of this sense that nothing radical would be stated, no matter how radical the content, unless you *changed the form*. Even as I realized art does not directly change the world, I felt art asks the questions the world needs to hear. The poets I met in San Francisco mid-1970s agreed: Politics, or a sociality, runs through aesthetics *and* the body, motors it with or without our acknowledgment. These poets were reading Marx and Benjamin, Brecht and Sartre, reviving aesthetics of political form in their own work, a community activated with print and a series of Talks and Poet's Theatre. One poet at that time spoke critically of Brakhage's films, likening his work to the New York School Poets, seeing both as involved in an insistent first-person pronoun. To some, Brakhage was an internalized romantic, and for all his material experimentation, the solipsism of the work, its self-regard, and its near-religiosity derailed their detailed interest.

I understood this response; it paralleled my own youthful reading of *Dog Star Man*. Perhaps if I had encountered *Art of Vision* (1961–65), the deconstructed version of *Dog Star Man*, I would have felt differently. I didn't see this film until the 1980s, co-hosting a screening with dinner for the epic event of this four-and-a-half-hour movie.[6] Here, Brakhage takes apart the original film into its A, B, C, and D rolls. The re-description attains something more than the original. There is more to see—literally—since in *Dog Star Man* the superimposed parts white out the total; there is also the mathematics of the project—to re-examine "all the suites of which it is composed."[7] *Art of Vision* breaks down the single language of expressive filmmaking into multiple strands of constitutive combinatrics, opening up the structure or *techne* of filmmaking to the viewer. The audience re-recognizes parts from the original film to enrich the experience of viewing this new duration. The whole creates an organized unspooling, a textured dismemberment in which the melodrama of *Dog Star Man* is subordinated to the apparatus in ways that become visually ecstatic and mentally satisfying.

By the late 1970s, on the West Coast, accompanying colleagues and friends regularly to Carmen Vigil's house for screenings, homemade wine, and just-picked mushrooms, I came to fully appreciate Brakhage. Whether we were watching the latest film, or an earlier piece selected from Canyon's archive, sitting with knowing audiences composed of Susan and Carmen Vigil, and alternately of Nick Dorsky, Warren Sonbert, Jerry Hiler, Henry Hills, David Gerstein, Gary Adkins, and others, we became devotees. After a night of screening, walking out of the Vigils' house, faced with its site at the end of the block, bordering a surprisingly empty arm of marshy land in southwestern San Francisco, full of open space (then) and night stars (still) with headlights in the distance and pavement at our feet, I would re-recognize a world of presence, lit by internal rhyme, ordinary day/rock/glance made splendid as Brakhage had caressed it on screen. The world, from parking garage to houseplant, children's toy to face, leaf to light, to infamous ashtray became through his attention, aglow, lighting space and mind. At best, Brakhage's work is rigorous and complex as well as beautiful, taking you closer to world, not away from or out of it, but magnified, evanescent. Holds life still. Or, imagines that you can, you can "have" it. For the moment.

Non-Heroism and World

Is this sincerity? Have I not fallen into a heroic posture myself? A lyric *I*? Seduced into Brakhage's illusionistic unity, mirrored in my own (memoried) prose? My instinct is to reject the ingestion of the world into a single person or into the assumed unity of the Brakhage family. Even as I agree that, yes, all art is personally motivated, I am not convinced as is Brakhage that

> the only thing that we really share: That each person is unique and lonely and then working out of that uniqueness and that loneliness or insides of the self comes something along the line of feeling, shaping form that does seem to be meaningful to others who are also equally alone and unique."[8]

This seems paradigmatically romantic—out-of-date, non-communal, and strangely conservative, isolated and isolating. Perhaps true for Brakhage, but less true for an urban community of artists who are socially engaged, in discussion with peers. Phil Solomon once described Brakhage as "gregariously solipsistic." This was said fondly in the context of Stan's Sunday night shows in Boulder, where he shared from his fantastic library of films and from his profound understanding of the making of the works and the circumstances around the particular artist's life. Surely, Brakhage's talent and generosity were apparent; he was a pyramid with the center unto himself. When the world forced itself upon him, when he looked beyond his domestic fictions, beyond the window, as it were, as he did in *The Act of Seeing With One's Own Eyes* (1971), the results were profound.

A brain pulled from its casing and you can't look away. The act leaves one breathless. As Frampton writes, the autopsy room in which *The Act of Seeing With One's Own Eyes* occurs is "one of the forbidden, terrific locations of our culture" "a room full of appalling particular intimacies, the last ditch of individuation."[9] Brakhage said once that he needed a week to adjust to the smell. He is our witness, our stand-in in an unspeakable mirroring act. You are confronted with history in skin and fragments of clothes, imagining crimes, the horror of death by fire (at least one body charred), the overwhelming transitory nature of life. Brakhage's fleetness meets its subject matter here: his camerawork harvesting glimpses, shocking derangements, straight looking and askance. His sincerity is constructed in his flight toward and from death.

Yet, irony is here as well: in the "act" itself, the live searching out the dead. Both coroner and filmmaker participate in this gathering of knowledge distanced from human grief: as scientists of knowledge. They become our lens and the event's parenthesis (our prosthesis?), establishing a dissonant grammar inside the film. The colors of live gloved fingers and dead ones are distinct; early on, Brakhage noted this difference, and his notation has viewers shifting in our seats, in our identifications with the dead, with coroner or camera (corpse is us or us to be). The coroner's report at end becomes a textual (technical) punctuation: the blood-stained lab coat over street shoes, the green Dictaphone, poignant and toy-like (as all outdated technology becomes when we look back at the frail metal that hopes to cross "immeasurable" distance). The closure these (imagined) words intend, and yet their incompleteness before our sense of being alive, the routine or roteness in the coroner's body posture as he "reports," recording facts about the body as its parts are wheeled away. The body parts can be read here as a profound metaphor for montage, for Eisenstein's "cadres," that is: parts that mean nothing without context. Organs without syntax. The workers— always black—play a part, cleaning the room. The live bodies speak devastatingly of the disinterested distance created through science, even as Brakhage's hand shakes, of what is left out, ignored, the subtle but present racism in allotment of jobs, asking who cleans up after us?[10] These are indices, "tones" in a film largely of the body, requiring the audience to confront "the act of seeing" blood, ends and the fragility of life. We are face-to-face, and it is grotesque, factual.

Have we fallen into the world of Bakhtin and his Rabelaisian grotesques? In his late notes, Bakhtin writes of "The culture of multi-tony. The sphere of serious tone. Irony as a form of silence. Irony (and laughter) as means for transcending a situation, rising above it."[11] Brakhage is rarely funny; when he's not wise, he's more often magisterial, ponderous, but he has a gift for re-framing reality. In naming his fourth work in the autobiographical series *Duplicity: Reel 1 (1978)*, he suggests a re-description for his own project. "Duplicity" signals a doubling—reminding us of irony's function—though with what we might describe as a more *low-down* tone.

At this point in his life, Brakhage was traveling and lecturing frequently away from home, publicly promoting his portrait of the nuclear family even as he was distant from it.[12] You feel a subtle sense of alienation in the speed and darkness of the piece, a loss of innocence in the camera work, a faint distrust of camera midst the weave. This work is not all "same growth," but bent. Jane has aged, rides a donkey, looking both roughly attired peasant and strangely crowned Madonna. There is elision here, but it is not the idyll of *Sincerity 2* and newfound love, but rather a dialogue with intention, dysfunction, and reality: a dialogue that negotiates the past, an ellipsis that is both a central matter of autobiography (how selective our creation of self becomes) and a larger ontological issue of film (how images are "captured" in celluloid, how film language is an act of articulation after-the-fact, a selection of the real). *Duplicity*, neither ironic nor insincere exactly, implies a covert reading, one that negotiates memory. The shot of Jane comforting the crying child toward the end of the film becomes paradigmatic: you don't know the cause, the camera is intrusive. Herein Brakhage acknowledges the contingency of celluloid to tell the truth, yet he has not yet let go of his mythos. He acknowledges the craft(y) nature of the artist, but re-inscribes his sincerity in the process of recognizing his "duplicity" and declaring it so (!). Brakhage has re-imagined personal history, prescribed what will constitute *his* history, and internalized its elisions.[13]

Montage as Re-siting

However I would like to suggest however much Brakhage can't live in the gap, his work does. That is, his best work has the potential to be not all-whole, but to move complicatedly through material and ideas. That the varied multi-planed thoughts engendered in this work break from the il-lusion of a unitary voice, do not limit themselves to surface meaning or allegory or narrative, but weave complex destabilizing fields. Perhaps montage itself is an ironic gesture, a re-situating of parts, a taking-out-of-context, a constant re-framing? As such, montage becomes constant mo-tion, a repositioning, and a constant unequalizing: things substituted for things, variation *is* motion. If this suggests rootlessness, it also suggests more affirmatively, change or what Charles Bernstein describes as a rejec-tion of "any fixed meaning that can be assigned and that persists out of context—a perpetual motion machine that never stops pinging and ponging off the walls, ceilings, floors. So returns to . . . let's say "the absolute," maybe the ineffable—everywhere said, nowhere stated."[14] Movement, substitution, relativity—as worldview.

The metaphysician in Rorty's analysis responds to "that sort of talk by calling it 'relativistic' meaning negative and insisting that what matters is not what language is being used but what is true."[15] Rorty posits a differ-ent universe in which the true is not attainable, a universe rather of ironic re-description that through its multiplicities, its de-stabilizations provides solidarity with the mass of mankind.

> Such a turn would be emblematic of our having given up the attempt to hold all the sides of our life in a single vision, to describe them with a single vocabulary. It would amount to recognition of... the "contingency of language."[16]

Or in terms of film, the contingency of image, which Brakhage's montage enacts so distinctly: through his speed, omniverousness of subject, precision of composition, its very repetition as he constructs and reconstructs new ideas out of an alphabet of favored sources. Brakhage's montage, I maintain, is a complex of re-descriptions, transitory attentions, improvisations, re-thinking, re-telling, re-framing world.

Bakhtin again: "The problem of silence. Irony as a special kind of substitute for silence."[17] If irony is a special kind of substitute for silence, for when we cannot speak (think of the anecdotal story-telling so highly developed and utilized by citizens under Soviet rule), then—is silence a kind of irony? A search or retreat or re-positioning where fact (or subject or object) is distorted so that to speak clearly would be a lie or dangerous, when the social language (of film or speech) is corrupted by economic and political forces, so that another, an under-language is called into being. One could read Brakhage's silence in this way: as anti-Hollywood grammar, wherein avant-garde film restores primacy of image over language, poetry against mainstream narrative convention. Here, I am not reading his silence as pure, but rather as a reaction against, a protest.

Amid his prolific work, there are lots of Brakhages—difficult to contain or describe, and to his credit, he trusts where he goes: The investigation can start somewhere and go somewhere else. The films are not created to fulfill a form. Thus, his fierce argument with a priori structures that we read about in the debates with Malcolm LeGrice of 1977.[18] Working this way, through "feeling" and intuition, Brakhage created masterpieces, and on occasion, interesting failures where one can enter and locate his process.

Withal, his *Sincerity 1* (1973): the beginning of his autobiographical series which has its moments—all Brakhage films have their moments—yet seems loose and untaut to me. It opens beautifully, alternating still photos with live action pullaways, focused on hands and eyes, startling us as he intercuts these photos with world. There is in these intercuts a paradigm for the autobiographical series as a whole and perhaps for film itself: this weave between past and present, between the captured and breathing, between world and celluloid. In the Dartmouth sequence in the middle of the work, Brakhage returned to his college days, and the obscure agonies he suffered are apparent in the repetition of takes and exaggerated re-enactments we in the audience suffer. For me, the value here lies in the opportunity to examine his camera work: where the lens returns to a glowing doorframe, back down the hallway, posting across the wall, swinging into the light—his fascination with windows obvious, the praxis of his repetition (obsession) revealed.[19] He used all or nearly all of the shooting (so it seems) to make the work, and sometimes I wish he rejected more: the pieces go on and on, no structure, just repetition and duration. The lyricism leaks, the self-absorption redundant, indulgent at times. I prefer the tighter works, the work with less to work with (perhaps)—thus the creative findings are more startling, more thrilling, more defined. One isn't in a hallway of shadows trailing through the solipsism of the great heroic eye.

Though perhaps it is the "sacredness" to which Brakhage is committed that causes me discomfort, more than the indulgences, since there is in the latter the power of revealing himself, of not making the "perfect" film(s). Rather it is the "mother" that is the "church" that he scrawls onto his *Marilyn's Window* (1988) that becomes difficult to swallow. Too much magisterial pronouncement, no matter how sincere. Here, the self-educated paradigmatic romantic insistent on personal vision is more apparent than the visionary upending expectations. In time, he himself becomes genre.

Yet, so creative a force is Brakhage that he locates his own forgeries. Writing about *Duplicity: Reel #2* (1978) he noted how "the mind 'dupes' remembered experience into some semblance of, say, composed surety rather than imbalanced accuracy."[20] At best, Brakhage's work lives in this imbalanced accuracy, rejecting symmetry, foregrounding "re-descriptions" of world, offering us multiple surfaces and re-definitions, processing light and speed, radiance and intelligence.

> More important, it [a disbelief in final language] would regard the realization of utopias, and the envisaging of still further utopias, as an endless process—an endless, proliferating realization of Freedom, rather than a convergence toward an already existing Truth.[21]

I started writing this as a memory piece: what I like most of Brakhage's multitudinous works, and why these and not others? Not surprisingly, I like the more tightly edited works and gravitate toward the hybrids—*Murder Psalm* and *Sincerity 2*—as well as films that look at the world beyond the window: *The Act of Seeing With One's Own Eyes* or *Window Water Baby Moving.* The last title might seem surprising in this context, yet I would maintain the domestic lyricism of the opening intercut between tub, light, and body is unnerved, undone as it were, with the film moving into the operating room to include Jane's pain and blood, and Brakhage himself, flushed, ecstatic, strangely *outside* the picture, pushing in. The contradictions within the piece are measures of its power. As an artist, I look to what I can use, and Brakhage's celebration of the nuclear family, his position as labored romantic, his personalism, are less useful to me than his creative syntax, his precise and idiosyncratic rhythms, his ability to engender both perfect and imperfect works. Let his films be the non-closure.

Lingering IMAGES

He was born, he suffered, he died (1974) matches brevity to the summative quality of the title (from Conrad's presumptive koan-like novel). The ordinary (even hyper-ordinary) images of basketball lines on gym floor and scratched black leader play off against the weight of the narrative. The lines mime chalkboards of physicists, quivering, temporary, speculative. The quixotic visual comparison contributes to the film's ironic power: testament to the immense fragility of description to inscribe a life, and Brakhage's repeated attempts to do so.

NOTES

1. *Filmmakers Cooperative Catalogue No. 7* (New York: Filmmakers Cooperative, 1989), 50.
2. Ibid.
3. Richard Rorty, *Contingency, Irony and Solidarity* (Cambridge, UK: Cambridge University Press, 1989), 73.
4. Ibid., 74
5. In retrospect, I suggest that these three filmmakers are touchstones of what my film work becomes: the sound-image relations of Lipsett in conjunction with Lye's musical humor and Brakhage's inestimable wideness of what constitutes a subject for filmmaking.
6. Co-hosted with Henry Hills at the famous *Rafik's* on Broadway and 12th Street. Rafik was an immigrant Palestinian who loved experimental film. His loft had been host to innumerable

screenings since the 1970s, in the incarnation as *OP Screen*. Later in the 1980s, he was selling film supplies in the front room and renting out editing suites on other floors, but around 1981–83 when we were curating, he showed movies in the back room: sometimes group shows, sometimes single artists, off-and-on-host to the likes of Jack Smith, George Kuchar, Jim Jarmusch, Betty Gordon, Nick Zedd, Ela Troyano, Hills, and myself. Nearly everyone making movies downtown passed through.

7. *Filmmakers Cooperative Catalogue*, 43.

8. *Stan Brakhage and Malcolm LeGrice Debate, Cinema News*, 3 and 4 (San Anselmo, CA: Foundation for Art in Cinema, 1978), 4.

9. *Filmmakers Cooperative Catalogue*, 48.

10. Reminding me of the division between scientists and workers and what they study in Wiseman's *Primate*, in which at times it seems the humans with their endless note taking amid corridors of cages are jailed while the apes watch and wonder.

11. M. M. Bakhtin, "From Notes Made in 1970–71," in *Speech Genres and Other Late Essays*, trans. Vern W. McGee, ed. Caryl Emerson and Michael Holquist (Austin: University of Texas Press, 1986), 134.

12. Discussed in a phone conversation with P. Adams Sitney, 30 October 2003. Sitney's notes and comments on the autobiographical films were invaluable.

13. Saul Levine in a recent conversation pointed out that in *Tortured Dust* (1984) Brakhage brought self-critique into public space, broadcasting the failure of his personal mythology and the nuclear family. The kids in the film look as if it's a "drag" to be filmed, and the plastic sheeting behind which B. needs to live materializes the distance between real and ideal.

14. Charles Bernstein, "Characterization," in *Content's Dream* (Los Angeles: Sun and Moon Press, 1986), 462.

15. Rorty, 75.

16. Ibid., xvi.

17. Bakhtin, 148.

18. *Stan Brakhage and Malcolm LeGrice Debate*, 4.

19. Seeing Brakhage's final work-in-progess (2003) at the 41st New York Film Festival, "Views From the Avant-garde," was interesting in this regard, having just seen the same set of objects/shots/views (standing lamp, gated window, doorway with light beyond) edited in his last completed work, *Stan's Window* (2003). One compares his topography and attention, sees the "round" of them.

20. *Filmmakers Catalogue*, 56.

21. Rorty, xvi.

PAUL ARTHUR

Becoming Dark with Excess

of Light

The Vancouver Island Films

And when she sang, the sea
Whatever self it had, became the self
That was her song, for she was the maker.
—WALLACE STEVENS, "The Idea of Order at Key West"

1.

The allegorical rendering of landscape, a practice of central importance to the visual and literary cultures of this continent, appears as but a sporadic, surprisingly weak impulse across the sixty-year history of American avant-garde film. Although traces of a more concerted recruitment of landscape imagery may be identified with specific periods and by geographic locations,[1] among the movement's major figures only Stan Brakhage, whose career simultaneously provides the rule as well as the exception to nearly every tendency in experimental cinema, made the depiction of natural perspectives an imperative, enduringly personal concern. If a *tradition* of avant-garde landscapes could be assembled from disparate manifestations, Brakhage would be its unchallenged avatar. While the grounds, as it were, of his commitment are formed by matters of personal circumstance or artistic influence—including the legacy of romantic poetics—the terms of the broader movement's desultory relationship to landscape are predominantly material and social. As commentators following Walter Benjamin have suggested, the epistemology of cinema discovers a distinctly social optic on the terrain of modern urbanism.[2] Ironically, despite individual mobility afforded by artisanal patterns of production, the avant-garde has remained tethered to urban resources and institutional networks of support. It is not simply that the imprint of what Louis Wirth famously called an "urban way of life" is reified in the structures and iconography of numerous avant-garde styles[3]; mundane activities of funding and equipment access, of arranging screenings and publicity, underwrite conditions of possibility for the avant-garde generally, even in projects undertaken far from the thrum of industrial cities. That is, the singular manner in which avant-garde filmmakers administer, or at minimum engage with, every stage of cinematic realization, from funding to circulation, virtually ensures the presence of urban society as symbolic discourse, the inevitability of "machines in the garden."[4]

The deployment of nature in Structural films of the 1970s complicates any attempt at sketching a coherent landscape tradition. Fueled in part by reaction to the radical subjectivity of earlier psychodramatic and lyrical styles, the Structural mode imposed predetermined, rationalized schema for ordering relations between shots (or sequential units) as a strategy by which to blunt the intercession of poetic imagination, in particular the exfoliation of metaphor and quasi-musical articulations.[5] In an effort to bypass iconographic categories "overdetermined" by ideologies of personal or cathected vision, a number of films harnessed supposedly neutral signifiers to fixed-frame, often long-take, tableau compositions. The wholesale evacuation of human figures, along with recurring references to temporal cycles, created an opening for an antisubjectivist approach to landscape, an approach ironically mobilizing motifs such as streams and waterfalls closely identified with nineteenth century romantic poetry and painting.

Frequently, rural vistas serve in Structural films as backdrops against which viewer recognition of material or ontological properties of cinema becomes amplified. For instance, in Larry Gottheim's *Horizons* (1973), a series of lengthy shots of distant hills alternately solicits and suppresses film's illusion of depth. In similar fashion, Joyce Wieland's *La Raison Avant la Passion* (1969) enlists traveling shots of a variegated landscape to call attention to, among other issues, the perceptual transformation of still frame into moving image. Michael Snow's *The Central Region* (1971) explores a host of illusionistic effects through the gyrations of nonlinear camera movements across an isolated mountain scene. Other filmmakers utilizing pastoral imagery as a prop of modernist reflexivity include James Benning, Louis Hock, Paul Sharits, Hollis Frampton, Martha Haslanger, David Rimmer, Al Razutis, and Richard Kerr.[6]

What is of course absent from Structural film's representation of natural settings is the possibility of an integral connection between affective qualities and an empathic artistic consciousness. Cast in adamant neutrality, sites are stripped of tonal, psychological, or metaphysical resonances; they are presented as simply generic "mountains" or "fields" with shapes or movements that summon tropic connections solely with the cinematic apparatus. In this guise, landscape emerges as an implicit rebuke to native traditions, such as the Hudson River School of painting, as well as to the underpinnings of European romanticism. No intimations of the sublime emanate from these films, and there is nothing remotely redemptive in the imaging of nature as foil to technology. Brakhage, a persistent advocate for the power of subjective imagination in confrontation with the visible world, was vehement in his opposition to the Structural ethos, deeming it "absolutely preclusive of what to me are the most valuable parts of the process of creativity."[7] Clearly, for Brakhage the treatment of *any* profilmic scene as mere pretext for the operation of "nonintuitive," demonstrative meaning would have been anathema; that a group of the most celebrated Structural projects adopted landscape as a privileged class of images proved especially roiling.

Brakhage's massive engagement with the expressivity of landscape began in the late 1950s, while living with his family in an isolated cabin in the foothills of the Colorado Rockies. *Sirius Remembered* (1959) is typical of this lyrical period, an overlapping rhythmic orchestration of parallel movements and sensory impressions of a neighboring woods—envisioned from a dog's perspective—with images of his dead, decaying pet taken over several seasons. Reimagining the topography of rural surroundings as spontaneous first-person seer—or as relayed through a secondary embodiment (his wife Jane, his children, or domestic animals)—achieves a summary statement in the mythic density of *Dog Star Man* (1961–64). A formally simpler, less-turbulent focus on landscape resurfaces in the 8 mm. *Songs* (1964–69), perhaps most strikingly in the Cezanne-inspired *My Mountain Song 27* (1969), and this line of development continues in such works as *The Wold Shadow* (1972) and *Desert* (1976). In the latter films, Brakhage is less reliant on gestural camera movement and montage juxtapositions; instead, he discovers points of contact between external and inner bodily rhythms suggestive of a merging of the consciousness of self and nature.

The previous account is deficient insofar as it fails to acknowledge the filmmaker's long-standing fascination with water, evident in the filming of

lakes and rivers but revolving primarily around Brakhage's affinity for the
sea's infinite variety. As Guy Davenport remarks, "Water is one of Brakhage's verbs."[8] For a person born in landlocked Kansas, it is telling that
ocean imagery has rippled through every stage and thematic category of his
monumental output. For instance, *Songs 3, 7, 8,* and *22* are, in slightly
different ways, devoted to the rhyming of land-based shapes with waves,
streams, or the underwater movements of sea creatures. In each case, the
play of light on or through a liquid surface generates additional metaphoric
associations as formal elements are fused or shown as interpenetrating.
Creation (1979) plumbs the mysteries of iceberg-laden waters off the Alaska
coast in a manner that reanimates as it personalizes a series of paintings by
Frederick Edwin Church.[9] *Made Manifest* (1980) underscores the intimate
exchange of light—or fire—and water, these two elements constituting the
ontological bedrock of Brakhage's meditations on nature. Together, they
would seem to emblematize what the filmmaker has referred to as "moving
visual thinking," the ambient disposition of consciousness itself.

During the last decade of his life, Brakhage worked almost exclusively on
short films in which nonrepresentational images were painted, scratched, and
otherwise inscribed directly onto 16- or 35 mm. film stock. His only large-
scale photographic project in that span is the remarkable set of seascapes
known as the "Vancouver Island films": *A Child's Garden and the Serious Sea*
(1991), *The Mammals of Victoria* (1994), and *The God of Day Had Gone Down
Upon Him* (2000).[10] With a total running time of over two hours, the series is
perhaps Brakhage's most extensive study of a single location, the childhood
environs of his second wife, Marilyn Jull, in Victoria, British Columbia. He
has said that they were conceived as an imaginary biography of different stages
of Marilyn's life as refracted through "the weave of sea and light and seen," in
which the first part corresponds to her early childhood, the second to adolescence, and the third to a purported "mid-aged crisis."[11]

As is almost always the case with Brakhage's assumption of a tutelary
perspective, the passage limned in the three films has as much to do with the
filmmaker's own imagined states of development as those of his wife. Due to
the manner in which they were shot and edited, these works are exceptionally
difficult to describe, bearing a stronger relation with the all-over, loosely differentiated mode of Brakhage's painted films—what he called "the most concrete pieces of my making, because they come most directly from my synapses
and my thinking"[12]—than to the thick autobiographical condensations of

multipart projects like *Scenes From Under Childhood* (1967–70). Somber and technically austere, the Vancouver Island films can be understood as "late" works in the same sense as certain Beethoven string quartets or Rembrandt self-portraits. They are valedictory, embracing ideas or images from earlier films in a spirit of prudent mastery while pushing outward toward a palpable horizon of mortality.

Having already committed to celluloid an inquiry called *The Text of Light* (1974), the films under consideration could merit the subtitle "The Text of Light on Water." In virtually every passage, the interplay of these twin elements evokes a common physical identity as simultaneously un-broken wave and stream of particulate matter. That is, just as light is shown as constantly atomized into tiny beads or moving points, the liquid surface absorbing and reflecting light is presented not only in unceasing undulation but also as it harbors constellations of solid vegetable or animal matter. In the history of cinema, the ocean has never before been cloaked in as many colors, textures, rhythms, moods, or material states—opaque in one shot, a transparent medium of teeming subsurface life in the next shot. Building an extensive network of repetition and variation around a central motif, Brakhage annotated the familiar paradox of the ocean as always one thing and many things, every thing, the "hidden generator of it all."[13]

Two conceits can be distilled from the handling of water as continually moving light-struck surface. The ocean is an analogue for the filmstrip, or vice versa, due to its combination of continuous flow and discrete internal parts (frames), a smooth skin that ingathers, resists, and recomposes emanations of light. All three Vancouver films are punctuated by irregular clusters of in-camera fades, a technique allowing successive images of the sea and its "contents" to accumulate into passages of formal or iconographic connection only to recede into momentary darkness—the fades, mimicking cresting waves, last from a second or two to twenty seconds—that in turn prompts our awareness of the blank screen and interrupted light of movie projection. To be sure, this reading sounds suspiciously similar to the play of landscape images in Structural films, but there is a marked difference. For Brakhage, the material facts of cinema serve primarily as a membrane joining external reality with subjective consciousness, an extension of the body's apperceptive mechanisms as filtered by the contours of memory and imagination.

In a separate register, as the profilmic movement of the sea is accentuated, at times counterbalanced, by insistent sweeps of handheld camera movement,

Brakhage summons a primordial recognition of external rhythms answered by the inner tides of the human body, with both camera and editing voicing the ebb and flow of corporeal cycles. The effect approximates what Brakhage dubbed "moving visual thinking," the ocean—or rather, the terms of its visualization—held as isomorphic with thought itself, not in a Freudian sense of unconscious process but something closer to the surging of electrical energies within the body,[14] the "nerve system's most hidden sparking innards."[15] In this sense, the sea is a mirror, its flickering reflections and immeasurable depth an apt metaphor for the endless spiral of self-scrutiny. In yet another search for origins ballasting material reference with metaphysical impulse, the Vancouver Island films invoke the infinite and uncontrollable through the limitations of cinematic space and time, figuring eternity in a cascade of immediate impressions. They are, finally, dramas of personal isolation unveiled in formal strategies of integration and macrocosmic oneness.

2.

What makes these films so hard to describe, either separately or as a continuous series, is in part a function of their resistance to the barest trappings of linear time. It is not that they lack iconographic range or clarity (although some sequences are visually indistinct); rather, the twin spectatorial tasks of ordering successive moments into coherent patterns and anticipating what might come next are, to a significant degree, confounded.[16] The feeling of being held in a perpetual present, of assimilating images without recourse to their place within larger orders of meaning, is at the core of Brakhage's oceanic design. There are few pictorial horizon lines, muted contrasts between seasons, and but a handful of sequences in which the viewer is afforded a stable vantage from which to regard the ceaseless motion of the sea. To be sure, there are ample instances of successive rhyming of shots as well as wider inter- and intrafilmic associations. Moreover, the repertoire of techniques employed in rendering aqueous states is relatively straightforward: zooms and nonlinear camera movements of several types, contrasting color film stocks, different camera speeds, gradations of exposure and focal setting, several different lenses, and occasional hand-formed mattes. Transitions between adjacent shots tend to be fluid, matched on speed or direction of movement, often softened by intervening black frames;

hence, there few instances of montage collision or metric exchanges between clusters of images.

All three contain residues of a tenuous, almost-spectral human presence in which figures are depicted either in silhouette, at the margins of the frame, or rendered insubstantial by anamorphic lens distortion, the intrusion of flares, extreme close-ups, and so on. All three feature land-based vegetation, from bright flower gardens to dim overhead views of a forest. Dogs, waterfowl, and other birds make fleeting appearances. Several types of boats, buildings perched on a distant shoreline, hands, the exterior of a house, a tacky amusement park are motifs that bridge at least two of the films. The point of this rough inventory is to suggest that, when viewed in order, it is possible to establish common threads without ever intuiting an overall thematic trajectory or progressive formal development. Nonetheless, *A Child's Garden and the Serious Sea* can be said to exude a relatively warm, summery tone, while *The God of Day Had Gone Down Upon Him* has an appropriately autumnal disposition. In terms of duration and mood, at thirty-five minutes *The Mammals of Victoria* has the air of a jittery fugue nestled between two longer, more impacted symphonic meditations. Viewed end to end, the films display a remarkable unity of purpose, although each segment maintains singular stylistic or thematic elements.

Of the three, *A Child's Garden* reaps the boldest metaphoric convergence of land and water and sky, the master trope of Garden signaling transformations of flowers or flotsam into star maps via deeply occluded exposures or, reciprocally, the animation of a nighttime sky by swish-pans such that heavenly bodies seem elongated into shimmering stalks. From the perspective of Brakhage's imaginary child, beams of light on water can be made to coincide with the rollicking dance of backyard foliage. The mood here is playful, at times exuberant, beginning with a frisking whale with a churning motion that is recapitulated by a set of subsequent camera movements mimicking waves, not only an image of enchantment but also a faint memory of the birth trauma. As Marjorie Keller reminds us, "At almost every juncture . . . [Brakhage] calls upon childhood to represent an aspect of film theory, perception, artistic creation, universal history, or autobiography."[17] *A Child's Garden* encourages the gradual dissolution of boundaries between personal and universal frameworks of knowledge.

There are few hints of encroaching civilization in the first half: An overturned lawn chair and the outlines of a shed barely hold their own against the tactile articulations of colored light.[18] It is as if the ocean, in its reflections of sky and containment of the land—manifest in shots of floating leaves, plant life, and driftwood—creates an all-encompassing framework for addressing the external world. Its sovereignty is acknowledged not only through camera movement and editing, but also in devices such as visible moisture on the lens, focus pulls that slide like waves, and layered superimpositions that mime the mercurial shifting of images on the surface of water.

In the second half of *A Child's Garden*, Brakhage introduces scenes taken at a nearby amusement park: a painted fairy castle, the rigging of a pirate ship (Victoria was once a retreat for buccaneers), an outsized clock sporting hectic figurines, a miniature golf family in white shorts, and, tellingly, a "dancing" fountain. Despite the slightly ominous inflection given to "leisure-time" shots by angle or choice of lens, they seem imbued with the false promise of artificially controlled nature (just as shots of a blue-tinged TV screen in *Mammals* briefly substitutes for the ocean in adolescent consciousness). Objects seen through a prismatic lens splinter color into striated bands and turn volumetric shapes into thin, unsteady sheets. These disruptive ghosts of a man-made, commercial realm are presented as less solid, less mobile than the harmonious community of whale, starfish, swaying seaweed, flowers, and other pastoral manifestations. Whatever is harvested from the landscape is briefly illuminated, as in a text, then returned just as quickly to an omnipresent, tidal order of shoreline and sea plunging toward darkness. In the midst of this generalized round of hide-and-seek, a group of allegorical images hovers near the end of the film that deflates our reckoning of childhood enchantment. First, two tiny figures in a rowboat, an adult and child, appear suspended in a glittering swell. Their fragility and, in context, their existential insignificance augur the inevitable undoing of all self-willed Gardens. Stretched over several shots, an even less-sanguine image of a scavenging crow casts an implicit shadow over the filmmaker's avid appropriation of the watery world.

Throughout the series, Brakhage cultivates the impression of a primeval environment over which water exerts near-total dominion, in which human products and activities are reduced to the periphery, and even vibrant earthbound matter longs for contact with the sea. If the sea, as mirror of a perfect consciousness, contains every possible physical shape and material state, the films' implicit inadequacy as reanimator of the natural world diverges from appropriative certainties apparent in works such as *My Mountain* or, indeed, in the projection of Brakhage's creative ego onto the filmmaker's wife, children, friends, pets, household insects, and so on. In these late films, he is content to install visually fragile human/animal traces that function as signs of a diminished, evanescent self.

The Mammals of Victoria is simultaneously the most "inhabited" and agitated piece in the series. Tokens of human activity in the form of blond hair seen through a yellow filter, a blue hand emanating from a TV screen, hazy swimmers, an arcing slow-motion volleyball scanned against a brilliant blue sky, and, particularly, a boy stumbling into the surf shot from behind a ragged sand castle spike the film with an air of dramatic expectancy largely missing from other sections. This impression is abetted by a gradual visual trajectory in which obscure shapes—such as the rephotographed hand— become clearer and more resolved with each iteration.

In addition, Brakhage recruited a wider range of materials, including shots of flames (rhymed at different junctures with hair and with the outline of the sand castle) and short clips of hand-painted images. Camera movements pile up with jarring intensity, and there is a heightened attention to tactile or manual images. A typical pattern of sharp cuts segues fire, lapping water, and painted globs of bright color. Correspondences involving color, shape, and rhythm link shots that nonetheless maintain an isolable, "nameable" aspect at odds with the largely muffled transitions in the rest of the series. Perhaps the moments of dissonance courted in *Mammals* have something to do with an imagined anxiety of adolescence. A couple in distant silhouette emerges from the gleaming surf, one of the few shots figuring a voluntary passage from sea to land. In the film's final moments, a traveling shot of light blasting through an opening in a tree line tenders a provisional marker for closure that deflects, although it fails to cancel, the doleful implications of the crumbling sand castle. Regardless, it is that brief figment of a disintegrating symbol of habitat, of home gouged by waves, that anchors the film's overall tone and meaning. Try as he might to see his wife's biography stamped in her immediate landscape, the sea remains memory's enemy, a blank slate upon which nothing can finally be written.

Films built around, or concluding in, prolonged contemplation of the ocean form a provocative strand of avant-garde achievement belied by an otherwise desultory engagement with landscape. From Bruce Baillie's mythic voyage aboard a fishing boat in *To Parsifal* (1963), to the ambiguous still photo at the end of Snow's *Wavelength* (1967), to Ken Jacobs's molten optical cataclysm in *Bitemporal Vision: The Sea* (1994), the collision of water and moving image has been an impetus for landmark gestures of self-recognition and/or abnegation. In *The God of Day Had Gone Down Upon Him*, Brakhage attempted to chart the limits, exhaust the possibilities of what can be shown of the sea in cinema.[19] The title was drawn from Dickens's *David Copperfield*, and in a talk following a public screening, he characterized the film as imbued with "a certitude of death felt in the bones" made manifest in "a fading of the light" and, one might add, in the absolute impermanence of his subject.[20]

In contrast to *A Child's Garden*, the color scheme for *God of Day* is bracketed by a rich palette of browns, grays, and blues—supplemented by autumnal threads enhanced by red and yellow filters, images linked formally to camera roll flares and metaphorically to fall foliage. There are a substantial number of nocturnal views of sky and sea, although the image flow is punctuated by fewer fades. A shot may reveal the water's surface as clogged with enough green vegetation to constitute an undulating garden, while a succeeding shot conjures it as dark and thick as tar; in this work, legible distinctions between liquid and solid and air are all but nullified. The amusement park returns via a blurry horse's head whirling past the camera on a carousel ride, a shot with ominous associations that are extended by a seal's dark head surfacing above the waterline like the skull on a pirate ship flag and, secondarily, by crab shells and bleached driftwood that resemble bones scattered on the tide. When coupled with other human/animal images, the reappearance of the eroded sand castle along with its hazy double, a factory floating on an unseen shore—instances of what the filmmaker calls "frets of Symbol"—summon the inescapable conclusion that, as life forms, we are simply bits of flotsam already receding back into the eternal embrace of the sea.

Midway through *God of Day*, shots of storm-whipped, violent waves signal an emotive change from unsettled foreboding to a calmer tone of resignation. Toward the end, a series of brighter, somewhat saturated shapes—leafy trees, flowers in bloom, a kite's twirling tail—combine with silhouettes of a dog frolicking in the surf, a string of floating geese, and a pair of anamorphically stretched kayakers, to reestablish a domain of hopeful, if ultimately illusory, struggle enacted against the pulsing axiom of water. To a greater extent than in earlier films, physical implications of land are virtually absent, with ocean vistas proceeding not from a landlubber's security of

Stan Brakhage, *The God of Day Had Gone Down Upon Him.*

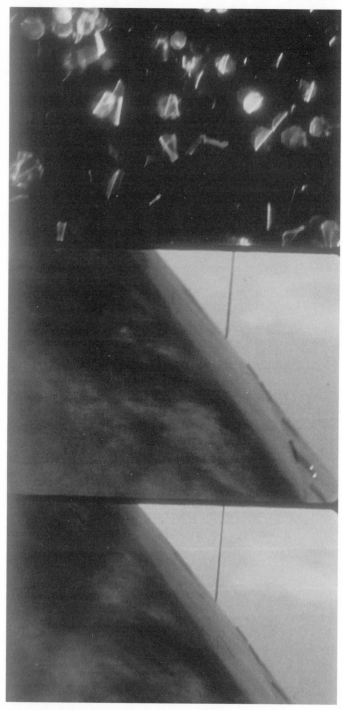

Stan Brakhage, *The God of Day Had Gone Down Upon Him.*

firm shoreline but from inside a borderless, teeming magnitude. Impossibly, *God of Day* is like a vision of sea as the sea might see itself if it had eyes and a sentience capable of grasping its own complex inner process. A supreme fiction then, an "Anticipation of the Sea," poised near the end of a long history of supreme fictions, the *idea* of water fusing with a visual sensibility bent not on appropriating or subduing the threat of personal extinction but, at last, taking shelter in the ocean's relentless eschatological pull.

3.

Across the body of his copious writings, Brakhage often spoke of tensions and reciprocities between film and other art forms, especially poetry, music, and painting. Despite his well-known repudiation of the tyranny of language in the perception of image—"Imagine an eye . . . which does not respond to the name of everything"[21]—the titles or themes of at least a dozen films derive from literary sources, while an additional group of scratched or painted films offer lyrical permutations on orthographic figures.[22] Something similar can be said of Brakhage's relationship to painting.[23] Philosophical inquiries around what is specific to a given medium and what might be shared with, or impacted by, the particularities of "sister arts" constitute a storied tradition in Western aesthetics. For Brakhage, an historical nodal point in that line of investigation was undoubtedly nineteenth century debates in romanticism over the attributes of poetic language in relation to those of pictorial image, an issue that drew the concerted attention of Wordsworth, Coleridge, and Shelley, among others.[24] As P. Adams Sitney has argued, Brakhage's practice is steeped in the discourse of romanticism, in its desire to recover and re-present an original response to nature through the intercession of subjective consciousness.[25]

There is no indication that he was thinking about, much less paying homage to, any artist of the romantic period during the genesis of the first three Vancouver Island films. Nonetheless, it is instructive to consider various parallels between Brakhage's threnodic multipart contemplation of the ocean and J.M.W. Turner's extraordinary seascapes, a lifelong motif that deepened during the 1830s, near the end of his career.[26] As Lawrence Gowing observed, "Perhaps the whole essence of Turner's last works might be gathered from the compound, infinite meanings that he gave to water."[27] A major figure in the internecine dialogue on the value of literature for visual artists, Turner used lines from his own poetry in the titles of many canvases and declared that good painters could not function "without some aid from Poesy."[28] He was an astonishingly prolific artist who worked in nearly every genre and pictorial medium. As is the case with Brakhage's monumental output, the volume of Turner's work—roughly 500 paintings and over 90,000 watercolors, sketches, and engravings—is far from incidental; it is integral to the ambition of transforming prospects of his art through personal struggle.[29]

Turner was celebrated, as well as critically scorned, for breaking reigning academic standards of composition and coloration. Regarding his seascapes, contemporary critics complained that water in certain pictures resembled "veins in a marble slab," "soapsuds," "whitewash," and other supposedly invidious substances.[30] The strategy of blurring or fusing the categorical distinctions between separate elements led Turner to paint reflections of fire on water or foreground the meeting of wind-whipped waves and lowering clouds, in short, to represent nature in a manner of indissoluble wholeness.[31] In "Sunset, Returning From Torcello" (1835), "Rough Sea With Wreckage" (1830), "Yacht Approaching the Coast" (1840–45), and "Shade and Darkness—the Evening of the Deluge" (1843), the idea of a maritime sublime is pursued by reducing traces of objects or human activities to fragile, almost insignificant, outlines while swamping visual boundaries separating ships' hulls or sails from the surrounding atmosphere of clouds and sea.

Turner delivered academy lectures on the pictorial vagaries of watery reflections; his last words were reportedly "The Sun is God,"[32] and he was consumed with depicting the interdependency of color and light, with celebrating the "unearthly majesty of light."[33] As Kenneth Clark put it, he elevated the function of light such that "his pictures not only represented light, but were symbolical of its nature."[34] In late paintings, according to Gowing, the mixture of light and water registers not only as subject, but also as the very medium and metaphoric embodiment of an epistemological framework.[35] Nature prompted Turner to create visual ciphers for the creative mind interacting with external appearance. As early as 1816, romantic sympathizer William Hazlitt chided Turner's tendency toward "abstraction" as follows:

> The artist delights to go back to the first chaos of the world, or to that
> state of things, when the waters were separated from the dry land, and
> light from darkness, but as yet no living thing nor tree bearing fruit was

seen on the face of the earth. All is without form and void. Someone said of his landscapes that they were *portraits of nothing and very like*.[36]

Revising Hazlitt's comment in the wake of abstract expressionism's transmutation of the landscape format—an initiative for which Turner was frequently invoked as precedent—Gowing suggested that Turner's vision "offers, perhaps, pictures of everything rather than of nothing . . . eventually no single touch of paint corresponded to any specific object; the equivalence was between the whole configuration and the total subject." The implication of that equivalence is a "return to a primal flux which denies the separate identity of things.[37]

If this is not quite the impression created in the Vancouver Island films, it does capture something of the experience instilled by Brakhage's obliteration of conventional spatial coordinates and pictorial scale, his undermining of temporal sequence and iconographic hierarchy—features consistent with the hand-painted ventures. Michael McClure averred in an interview with Steve Anker that Brakhage's refusal of scale is critical to his mature aesthetic: "Microscopically and monumentally are beside the point if there isn't any sense of scale. And if there isn't any sense of scale, if there's no proportion, if there is sizelessness, we're free in it."[38]

The filmmaker himself adds credence to McClure's idea in a 1995 essay, "Having Declared a Belief in God," written during the making of the Vancouver series. Here, Brakhage ponders the felt need, as well as the impossibility, of Western artists to represent a concept of deity through tropes entailing infinite variety: "The inverse of this imagined variability of one's diminished self, would most reasonably be a macrocosm in which one's self-shape didn't exist at all, coexistent with an imagined BEING, larger and ever larger, multiply amorphous shape-shaping of oneself." His reference to "deity" draws us close to the fixation in nineteenth century romanticism on the sublime, in which natural vistas are made to function as signifiers transcending the possibility of subjective containment through art.[39] What traditional approaches to God lack, according to Brakhage, is a recognition of "moving at-oneness," and he goes to on to propose that "the ultimate sense of deity as all-pervasive and encompassing peace and protectiveness . . . is [still] a feeling of movement, of being so much at-one with the intricacy of cosmic rhythms, with felt radiant particle/waves . . . in cancellation of chaos and stasis at one once forever."[40]

Beset by serious illness and immersed in the editing of *God of Day*, Brakhage's thoughts on representing the infinite and the eternal reaffirm the Vancouver films' eschatological impetus. Turner addressed the sea in a poem as "Thou dreadful and tumultuous home of Death."[41] Brakhage recorded the sea *as* home, as his ultimately accepting projection of wife Marilyn's life cycle, and in that double synapse of otherness produced one of cinema's profoundest meditations on mortality, death as an emptying and dispersion of self. The final word is best given to John Ruskin, Turner's early champion, who spoke across the ages when he proclaimed: "Here and there, once in a couple of centuries, one man will rise past clearness and become dark with excess of light."[42]

NOTES

1. What I mean is that, predictably, heightened levels of interest in landscape correspond at times to wider cultural currents, as the emphasis on nature in countercultural music, poetry, and cinema of the late sixties suggests. Similarly, the landscape impulse in avant-garde film is occasionally linked to the makers' domestic or vocational experience of rural settings.

2. In "The Work of Art in the Age of Mechanical Reproduction," for instance, Benjamin remarked that: "The film corresponds to profound changes in the apperceptive apparatus—changes that are experienced on an individual scale by the man in the street in big-city traffic, on a historical scale by every present-day citizen"; *Illuminations*, ed. Hannah Arendt, trans. Harry Zohn (New York: Schocken Books, 1969), 250.

3. See Wirth's seminal 1938 essay, "Urbanism as a Way of Life" (written around the same time as Benjamin's "The Work of Art in the Age of Mechanical Reproduction"), in *The City Reader*, ed. Richard T. LeGates and Frederic Stout (New York: Routledge, 1996), 189–98.

4. Other writers have attributed to landscape an idealized function within avant-garde history, but I see little evidence to support this claim. Jan-Christopher Horak, in "The First American Film Avant-Garde, 1919–1945," asserted that a key difference between experimental movements is that: "A particularly American romanticism, which manifests itself in a longing for (wo)man's reunification with nature, informs the early American avant-garde's visualization of the natural environment and the urban sprawl," in *Lovers of Cinema*, ed. Jan-Christopher Horak (Madison: University of Wisconsin Press, 1995), 30. On the surface, Scott MacDonald's recent book, *The Garden in the Machine: A Field Guide to Independent Films About Place* (Berkeley: University of California Press, 2001), affirms the importance of landscape, yet, oddly, despite some intriguing analysis of landscape films by Larry Gottheim and others, he devoted relatively little space to filmic "gardening." Indeed, of the roughly 200 avant-garde titles listed in his filmography, fewer than thirty—excluding works by Brakhage—can reasonably be classified as "landscape" films. Nor does landscape merit a separate niche in P. Adams Sitney's morphology, *Visionary Film: The American Avant-Garde, 1943–2000*, 3d ed. (New York: Oxford University Press, 2002). On the other

hand, the avant-garde has been a minor beneficiary of a recent spurt in urbanist film studies; see, for example, David E. James, "Toward a Geo-Cinematic Hermeneutics: Representations of Los Angeles in Non-Industrial Cinema—*Killer of Sheep* and *Water and Power*," *Wide Angle*, 20, 3 (July 1998), 23–53. I map a range of approaches to urban subjects and filmic protocols in "The Redemption of the City" in *A Line of Sight: American Avant-Garde Film, Since 1965* (Minneapolis: University of Minnesota Press, 2005).

5. For the clearest analysis of this style, see Sitney, *Visionary Film*, 347–70.

6. Bart Testa asserted that the Canadian branch of avant-garde film can be distinguished from its American counterpart in both the frequency and thematic thrust of its mobilization of landscape: "The history of the Canadian nation is the story of exploration into a frontier that did not appear like a garden, did not offer itself as a meeting-place of nature and culture as it seemed to in the United States"; *Landscape in the Image* (Toronto: Art Gallery of Ontario, 1989), 1. Testa made a fairly persuasive argument—it is perhaps no accident that five of the aforementioned makers of Structural films are Canadian—but at times must bend the discourse in certain films, especially the work of Jack Chambers, to fit the rubric of landscape.

7. "Brakhage Uncensored," *The Cinemanews*, 78-6, 79-1 (1979), 15. In this transcription of comments made following a 1977 screening at Millennium Film Workshop in New York, Brakhage went on to stipulate "that process [of creativity] wherein the maker is called upon to work with what he or she doesn't know at every frame's existence, whether it shall be or whether it shall not be, not as a choice of anything that can be taught academically, but as an act of absolute urgency in what, for me, is a kind of trance state involving that work."

8. "Brakhage's Songs," reprinted in *Chicago Review*, 47, 4 and 48, 1 (Winter 2001, Spring 2002), 160.

9. P. Adams Sitney offered a scintillating interpretation of this film in "Tales of the Tribes," *Chicago Review*, 47, 4 and 48, 1 (Winter 2001, Spring 2002), 98–103.

10. In a videotaped interview conducted on Vancouver Island by Pip Chodorov just two months before his death, Brakhage introduced one of his final, entirely hand-painted, films, *Panels for the Walls of Heaven* (2003), as the fourth part of the Vancouver Island films. He said that he had begun to feel that the series should not end on a note of despair and was determined to create a more exalted conclusion. I have been able to see this work only once and, frankly, have yet to fully comprehend its relationship to the earlier films. Brakhage often conceived of large-scale projects as encompassing four parts—*Dog Star Man* is the obvious example—corresponding roughly to the natural unities of seasons, elements, and so on. Thus, it is in some sense logical for him to have made the late addition of *Panels*. At nearly thirty minutes, it is among his longest nonphotographed films, and it consists predominantly of multibanded vertical striations of color against dark backgrounds, interrupted occasionally by short bursts of brighter, single-frame blobs and shards of color. Brakhage implied that it fosters an "upward" perspective, and in passages of flowing strands the movement is vaguely reminiscent of water in the three earlier sections. I regret that, for now, there is little more I can say about the significance of this film.

11. The quotation is taken from Brakhage's program notes, dated 1 March 2000, for a screening of *God of Day* at Millennium Film Workshop. Brakhage discussed the genesis of the Vancouver series in "*Chicago Review* Article," *Chicago Review*, 47, 4 and 48, 1 (Winter 2001, Spring 2002), 39–41.

12. Stan Brakhage and Ronald Johnson, "Another Way of Looking at the Universe...," *Chicago Review*, 47, 4 and 48, 1 (Winter 2001, Spring 2002), 33.

13. Program notes for *God of Day*.

14. On the idea of "visual moving thinking," see Bruce Elder, "On Brakhage," in *Stan Brakhage: A Retrospective 1977–1995* (New York: Museum of Modern Art, 1995), unpaginated.

15. Brakhage, "*Chicago Review* Article," 38.

16. Fred Camper, while acknowledging the difficulty in "narrativizing" the development of these films, provided an overview of important themes in "Brakhage's Contradictions," *Chicago Review*, 47, 4 and 48, 1 (Winter 2001, Spring 2002), 78–87.

17. *The Untutored Eye: Childhood in the Films of Cocteau, Cornell, and Brakhage* (Rutherford, NJ: Fairleigh Dickinson University Press, 1986), 179.

18. As Brakhage put it in program notes to *The God of Day*, "These nameable objects (sometimes at first quite enigmatic) are the frets of Symbol; but always the symbolic content is swept back into the weave of sea and light and seen."

19. The title phrase warrants some further elucidation. It occurs fairly early in the novel in a chapter titled, "I Begin Life on My Own Account, and Don't Like It," that reports on young Copperfield's grinding routine at Murdstone and Grinby and his felicitous acquaintanceship with Mr. Micawber (*David Copperfield* [New York: Bantam Books, 1981]). Indeed, the passage in question occurs as Micawber reaches the nadir of his financial difficulties, coinciding with his arrest and imprisonment: "He told me, as he went out of the house, that the God of day had gone down upon him—and I really thought his heart was broken and mine too" (152). The chapter's opening lines rehearse a keen ache of childhood abandonment: "I know enough of the world now, to have almost lost the capacity of being much surprised by anything; but it is a matter of some surprise to me, even now, that I can have been so easily thrown away at such an early age" (142). It is well known that Brakhage had a difficult, orphaned childhood, and it is possible that the "midlife crisis" inscribed in this film includes a recent reckoning with the filmmaker's earliest memories. Interestingly, *David Copperfield* is an extremely watery novel, even for Dickens; there are a multitude of maritime tropes and scenes at or near the sea. One pivotal chapter, "Tempest," contains stunningly detailed descriptions of a storm at sea, utilizing a color palette and barrage of violent movements that might have been a source of inspiration for Brakhage's treatment of the sea.

20. The screening took place at Bard College on 28 March 2000.

21. Stan Brakhage, *Metaphors on Vision* (New York: Film Culture, 1963), nonpaginated.

22. Among the works buttressed by literary connections are *Fire of Waters* (1965), from a phrase by Robert Kelly; *Made Manifest* (1980), from the Bible; and *Tortured Dust* (1984), dedicated to novelist Marguerite Young. *Egyptian Series* (1983) and one of his final completed films, *Chinese Series* (2003), were inspired by visual patterns in language.

23. Among works that Brakhage explicitly cited are *The Garden of Earthly Delights* (1981), after Bosch and Emil Nolde, and *Panels for the Walls of Heaven*, inspired by Pavel Tchelitchew's paintings on the theme of purgatory. The remarkable *Dante Quartet* (1987) pays tribute both to the poet and to Robert Rauschenberg's series of lithographs corresponding to individual cantos in *The Divine Comedy*.

24. James A. W. Heffernan provided a thoughtful summary of romantic artists' ideas about the collision of poetry and painting in efforts to render the natural world: *The Re-Creation of Landscape* (Hanover, NH: University Press of New England, 1984), esp. 16–53.

25. *Visionary Film*, esp. 155–88.
26. In a 1993 interview, the filmmaker reported, "When I was living in New York in the 1950s and 1960s, I became an avid gallery-goer. I discovered Turner, who is probably still the most pervasive influence on me because of his representations of light." "Brakhage at Sixty," *www.smoc.net/mymindseye/naples/brakhage.*
27. *Turner: Imagination and Reality* (New York: The Museum of Modern Art, 1966), 51.
28. Cited in *The Re-Creation of Landscape*, 39.
29. See Jack Lindsey, *Turner: The Man and His Art* (New York: Franklin Watts, 1985), 154.
30. See Gowing, *Turner*, 10; also Luke Hermann, *Turner* (Boston: Phaidon Press, 1975), 50.
31. See Heffernan, *Re-Creation of Landscape*, 222–224; also James Hamilton, *Turner: The Late Seascapes* (New Haven, CT: Yale University Press and Sterling and Francine Clark Art Institute, 2003), 65, 121.
32. Heffernan, ibid., 157.
33. Gowing, *Turner*, 7.
34. *Landscape Into Art* (Boston: Beacon Press, 1961), 97.
35. *Turner*, 51.
36. Quoted in Lindsay, *Turner*, 89.
37. Ibid., 16.
38. Michael McClure and Steve Anker, "Realm Buster: Stan Brakhage," *Chicago Review*, 47, 4 and 48, 1 (Winter 2001, Spring 2002), 174.
39. Heffernan provided a rewardingly clear discussion of the dynamics of the sublime in relation to romantic culture in general and to Turner specifically: *The Re-Creation of Landscape*, 125–33. For our purposes, it is worth noting that Wordsworth believed that the price paid for imaginative participation in sublime landscapes was the surrender of determinate categories, wherein the inability to comprehend allowed the creative imagination access to "unknown modes of being" (130).
40. Stan Brakhage, "Having Declared a Belief in God…," *Chicago Review*, 47, 4 and 48, 1 (Winter 2001, Spring 2002), 53–54.
41. Gowing, *Turner*, 52.
42. Ibid., 53.

PHIL SOLOMON

As I Am Writing This Today

A s I am writing this today, crisp dead leaves are strewn about in the late afternoon wind, as fall breaks back to winter . . . Stan Brakhage has left our town—crossed over the river, so to speak, to "another country"—to bring Marilyn and the boys home, to her source . . . the Island of Victoria, with its charmed gardens and surrounding waters so vividly depicted in Stan's *Child's Garden* . . . down from the mountains, at long last, to the *Serious Sea*, to begin yet another chapter in his ongoing book of family, his extraordinary venture of life. Leaving the west behind in rear view, heading north. . . . In the wake of his absence, Boulder now begins to look more like the *Pleasantville* it has always really been after all, a little drained of color, a little more bland, commonplace—and utterly predictable. It has bid goodbye to its First Citizen of Light and the brilliant, enchanted aura that emanated from his indomitable and irrepressible creative spirit, which enveloped us for so many years, like a protective dome over the town, making it a safe haven for the open-hearted reception of light in all its manifestations, for the ever-changing circles of friends and students who for years gathered around his hearth, and for giving safe harbor for weary travelers who came from long distances, beckoned by the twinkling lights in the distant mountains . . . the shimmering aurora that is his art, that, for half a century, has moved us so inexplicably, so truly, madly, deeply . . .

Everything now seems somehow smaller. Life here is now . . . plain.

Ours is not an age that has much use for the notion of mastery in the arts or reveres the uncanny uniqueness of singular genius. We march toward some aesthetic techno-democratic fantasy of the "interactive," Here Comes Everybody (and their Web sites . . .). Being an artist is "up for grabs" or maybe just beside the point. And the humility, patience, and quietude of spirit required to really give yourself completely over to a work of another, in the dark, seems no longer possible, or even desirable. Art as a contemplation of form, as a morphological semblance of human feeling, seems to have been taken to its end game sometime in the last century, as works of ephemeral formal beauty have been superseded by concerns mostly outside the frame, unambiguous socio/cultural essays, the winks and nods of endless loops of meta-ironies, meaningless flash, etc. The immaturity and disposable nature of our culture have taken over much of the visual arts, where the "received and noted," the instant "get it" pleasures of the one-liner still reign supreme in museum galleries. We have no time in our schedule for jeweled, ineffable mysteries, no time to negotiate the raptures of the ambiguously inevitable, the beauties of "otherwise unexplained fires" . . . So what are we to say about an artist such as Stan Brakhage that can be of any use to anyone, in these, the end of days of an art form that is on the verge of extinction and has been long ago abandoned by any critical culture? Paraphrasing what Alfred Kazin wrote about James Joyce, "Alone among the artists of our time, he has assumed the overpowering importance of his soul and written as if the world were well lost for art."

There is simply no precedent in film history for what Stan Brakhage has done, continues to do, and I suspect we won't truly understand the nature and importance of his monumental achievement for some time. It has been, and continues to be, a lifelong project of unfailing faith, discipline, and devotion, a tireless and heroic quest for *a sincerity of vision in light on film* that can now stand alongside any body of work in the history of the arts. He has moved, forever, the course of "moving picture visual thinking" into unchartered realms of luminous perception, and the very light we are given to see with has changed, seems to me, because we have. He has said in recent years (and devoted a series to the notion) that, "Art is the truth, the whole truth, and nothing but the truth." The final part of the oath is (deeply) implied...

His aim is, and has always has been, true...it has always been about the work at hand. He's as excited about whatever he is currently working on as he was about his very first film, some fifty years ago. Whenever I would see him in the hallways of the university, or at a booth in one of the many restaurants where he would do his hand-painting while knocking down a root beer float, he would always grab a roll from his pocket and unravel a few feet for me to look at against the ceiling light—"Phil, look at this!" Creativity is simply the most natural way of being for him, woven into the fabric of his daily life, the most normal thing to do. Our collaborations were a natural extension of the flow of energy from our friendship and our work, our conversations. We hung out and jammed, then searched for buried treasures with flashlights in the dark, learned how to cue each other with zany metaphors, wordless sounds, by dancing in our chairs—and managed, somehow, to realize an integrity of making something new that was not either of us, but was in fact both of us.... These works are labors of love, spun from a generosity of spirit and friendship, for which I am forever grateful. While working on *Seasons*..., I mentioned to him that I was having some trouble with the summer section, that I needed more material, more sun; the very next day, a baggie showed up in my mailbox, containing a loop of brilliant, beaming yellow carvings into leader, with a piece of tape over the bag that said "summer...for Phil."

Thank you, Stan, for giving me a season in one day...

He has honored his gift by always, *always* heeding the call, so to speak, and mostly by *paying attention*, as we say—and he has, against all odds, taken good care of his enormous legacy all these years as an act of un-breakable faith in us, in our luminous communion into the future, which is, finally, our great gift from him. He has said on more than one occasion, "All I ever wanted to do was leave a snail's trail in the moonlight..."

The trail is there, glistening, glistening. The rest is up to us.

November 16, 2002

Boulder. Colorado

Contributors

Paul Arthur is a professor of English and Film Studies at Montclair State University. He is the author of *A Line of Sight: American Avant-Garde Film Since 1965* and is a regular contributor to *Film Comment* and *Cineaste* magazines.

Bruce Baillie describes his relationship to Stan Brakhage as that of "friend and comrade in and out of Purgatory."

Filmmaker and writer **Abigail Child** has made more than thirty films and published four books of poetry. She has two projects forthcoming: *Cake and Steak*, an experimental sound film on suburbia, gender, and assimilation; and *This is Called Moving: A Critical Poetics of Film* from University of Alabama Press, in their Modern and Contemporary Poetics series.

Craig Dworkin is author of *Reading the Illegible* (Northwestern University Press, 2003) and the editor of the collected poems of Vito Acconci (M.I.T. Press, 2005); he curates the digital archive Eclipse (www.princeton .edu/eclipse).

R. Bruce Elder is a filmmaker whose work has been the subject of numerous retrospectives in Canada, the United States, and Europe. He is the author of (among other books) *The Films of Stan Brakhage in the American Tradition of Ezra Pound, Gertrude Stein and Charles Olson*

(Waterloo, Ontario, Canada: Wilfrid Laurier University Press, 1998), and is now collaborating with members of Ryerson University's Electrical Engineering Department in research on applying machine intelligence to image processing for film and video.

Nicky Hamlyn is a filmmaker and writer. He teaches in Video Media Arts at Kent Institute of Art and Design in Maidstone, England. His book *Film Art Phenomena* was published in 2003.

David E. James teaches at the University of Southern California. His most recent book is *Power Misses: Essays Across (Un)Popular Culture* (New York: Verso, 1996).

Jonas Mekas is a poet and filmmaker and the artistic director of Anthology Film Archives.

Tyrus Miller is Associate Professor of Literature at University of California at Santa Cruz and the Director of the University of California Budapest Study Center for 2001–2004. He is the author of *Late Modernism: Politics, Fiction, and the Arts Between the World Wars* (Berkeley: University of California Press, 1999) and a recent study of postwar avant-garde aesthetics and politics.

Carolee Schneemann is a multidisciplinary artist who has transformed the very definition of art, especially regarding discourse on perception, the body, and sexuality. Her video and installation works have been widely shown in the United States and Europe. *More Than Meat Joy: Complete Performance Work and Selected Writing* was published by McPherson and Company in 1979 and reprinted in 1997; in 2002, the MIT Press published *Imaging Her Erotics—Essays, Interviews, Projects*.

P. Adams Sitney is Professor of Visual Art in the Council of the Humanities at Princeton University. He is the author of *Visionary Film, Modernist Montage,* and *Vital Crises in Italian Cinema,* and the editor of Brakhage's *Metaphors on Vision, The Film Culture Reader, The Avant-Garde Film, The Essential Cinema,* and Maurice Blanchot's *The Gaze of Orpheus.*

Phil Solomon is a filmmaker and a Professor of Film Studies at the University of Colorado at Boulder, where he has been teaching filmmaking and critical studies since 1991. He collaborated with colleague and friend, Stan Brakhage, on *Elementary Phrases* (1994), *Concrescence* (1996), and *Seasons* (2002). Phil Solomon is currently finishing two works-in-progress that were started with Brakhage entitled *Congenial Meninges (Fred and Ginger)* and *Alternating Currents.* He is also working on a book of edited transcriptions of Brakhage's weekly salons entitled *A Snail's Trail in the Moonlight: Conversations with Brakhage*. Phil Solomon delivered a eulogy for his friend in Victoria, British Columbia, on 14 March 2003 (http://www.fredcamper.com/Brakhage/Funeral.html).

Chick Strand is a filmmaker.

James Tenney is a composer, pianist, conductor, and theorist, currently teaching at the California Institute of the Arts, where he holds the Roy E. Disney Family Chair in Musical Composition. A long-time friend of and collaborator with Stan Brakhage, who made two films based on preexisting pieces of Tenney's music, *Christ Mass Sex Dance* and (. . .) or *ellipses*. Tenney also composed the music for Jim Shedden's documentary film, *Brakhage* (1998).

Willie Varela is a moving image artist, photographer, programmer, and installation artist. For the past thirty-two years, Varela has worked in film and video and has exhibited nationally, including two Whitney Biennials and a midcareer retrospective at the Whitney Museum of American Art in the spring of 1994. Varela currently is an Assistant Professor of Film Studies in the Department of Theatre Arts and Film at the University of Texas at El Paso.

Index